Education at SAGE

SAGE is a leading international publisher of journals, books, and electronic media for academic, educational, and professional markets.

Our education publishing includes:

- accessible and comprehensive texts for aspiring education professionals and practitioners looking to further their careers through continuing professional development

- inspirational advice and guidance for the classroom

- authoritative state of the art reference from the leading authors in the field

Find out more at: **www.sagepub.co.uk/education**

Children's Rights in Practice

Edited by Phil Jones and
Gary Walker

Los Angeles | London | New Delhi
Singapore | Washington DC

Editorial arrangement, Chapter 15 and all other materials
© Phil Jones and Gary Walker 2011
Chapters 1, 2, 4 © Phil Jones
Chapters 3, 5 © Gary Walker
Chapter 6 © Mike Wragg
Chapter 7 © Carol Potter and Chris Whittaker
Chapter 8 © Caroline Bligh
Chapter 9 © Jon Tan
Chapter 10 © Avril Brock and Jean Conteh
Chapter 11 © Diane Lowcock and Ruth Cross
Chapter 12 © Tracey Race and Alison Bennett
Chapter 13 © Phil Jones and Alan Smith
Chapter 14 © Daniel Marshall and Terry Thomas

First published 2011

SAGE Publications Ltd
1 Oliver's Yard
55 City Road
London EC1Y 1SP

SAGE Publications Inc.
2455 Teller Road
Thousand Oaks, California 91320

SAGE Publications India Pvt Ltd
B 1/I 1 Mohan Cooperative Industrial Area
Mathura Road
New Delhi 110 044

SAGE Publications Asia-Pacific Pte Ltd
33 Pekin Street #02-01
Far East Square
Singapore 048763

Library of Congress Control Number: 2010936355

British Library Cataloguing in Publication data

A catalogue record for this book is available from the British Library

ISBN 978-1-84920-379-1
ISBN 978-1-84920-380-7 (pbk)

Typeset by C&M Digitals (P) Ltd, Chennai, India
Printed in Great Britain by CPI Antony Rowe, Chippenham, Wiltshire
Printed on paper from sustainable resources

MIX
Paper from
responsible sources
FSC   FSC® C013604

With Love to Jonathan Glover
P.J.

To Mum and Dad, who taught me rights from wrong
G.W.

'*Children's Rights in Practice* is a highly accessible text, which will be useful for students on a range of courses and for professionals where the focus is on working with children and young people. The book's strength lies in examining children's rights from a range of professional perspectives and across a wide age-span. The review activities at the end of each chapter are excellent and encourage the reader to reflect in detail on their practice in the light of some of the ideas introduced – the activities will be valuable for students and professionals alike.'

Deborah Albon is a Senior Lecturer in Early Childhood Studies at London Metropolitan University

'This is a very informative book that gives a realistic and thought-provoking insight into legislation and its interpretation in practice. The importance of the child at the centre of policy design comes through loud and clear, and the writers include examples of children from a broad range of perspectives and countries.'

Denise Chadwick, Senior Lecturer in Early Years, University of Huddersfield

Contents

About the Editors and Contributors

The editors

Phil Jones

Dr Phil Jones, Director of Research and Reader, Faculty of Education, Social Sciences and Law, Leeds University, has researched areas relating to children and young people, inclusion, the arts and therapy for a number of years. His books have been translated into Chinese, Korean and Greek, and include *Rethinking Childhood* (2009, Continuum), *The Arts Therapies* (2005, Routledge) and *Drama as Therapy* (2008, Routledge); edited books include *Childhood: Services and Provision for Children* (with Moss, Tomlinson and Welch, 2007, Pearson). He is also Series Editor of Continuum's 'New Childhoods', a research-driven initiative looking at different aspects of children's lives.

Gary Walker

Gary Walker is a Principal Lecturer in Childhood and Early Years at Leeds Metropolitan University. He has worked in a variety of social care settings with and for children and families for over twenty years. This includes day and residential settings, and as a child protection social worker. He has been child protection education coordinator and children in care education coordinator for a large education authority. He has extensive experience of teaching and training adults in social care issues. Specialist interest areas remain child development, child protection and social work, and children in care. Publications include *Working Together for Children* (2008, Continuum), as well as chapters for edited volumes covering safeguarding and looked-after children.

The contributors

Alison Bennett

Alison Bennett joined the Social Work team in the Faculty of Health at Leeds Metropolitan University in 2003. Prior to this, she worked in children and family social work in the statutory and voluntary sector, mainly in Yorkshire. She has responsibility for teaching Children and Family Social Work and has specific interests in participation, child protection and domestic violence.

Caroline Bligh

Caroline was a state registered nurse prior to starting her teaching career at a multilingual school in south-east London. Having taught throughout the key stages in primary schools for several years, she developed an active interest in bilingualism in the early years. Following completion of her Masters in Education (Bilingualism in Education) at the University of Birmingham, she began teaching as an associate lecturer for the Open University on their professional early years courses, and in 2007 started teaching at Leeds Metropolitan University where she is now a Senior Lecturer teaching across Early Childhood and Primary Education. Caroline is in her final year of doctoral study with the Open University, where she is focusing her current research on an ethnographic study into the 'silent period' in a young bilingual learner from a sociocultural perspective. She presented a paper on her research at the Ethnography and Education conference at St Hilda's College, University of Oxford, in 2009, and at New College, Oxford, in September 2010.

Avril Brock

Dr Avril Brock is a Principal Lecturer in the Carnegie Faculty of Sport and Education at Leeds Metropolitan University. She lectures in Childhood and Early Years Education and is the Award Leader for the MA Childhood Studies and MA Early Years. Before moving into higher education, Avril was a Deputy Head, Primary and Early Years teacher. She has edited and written several books on bilingualism, early language development and play, including *Communication, Language and Literacy from Birth to Five* (with Rankin, 2008, Sage) and *Perspectives on Play* (with Dodds, Jarvis and Olusoga (eds), 2008, Pearson).

Jean Conteh

Dr Jean Conteh, Senior Lecturer, Faculty of Education, Social Sciences and Law, Leeds University, worked as a primary teacher and teacher educator in different countries for many years, including Sierra Leone, Ghana, Nigeria, Pakistan, Bulgaria and Poland, and has spent almost 20 years as a teacher and then a language tutor on PGCE Primary, BA QTS and MA courses in West Yorkshire. She has published several books, chapters and articles including *Multilingual Learning Stories in Britain* (with Martin and Robertson (eds), 2007, Trentham), *Promoting Learning for Bilingual Pupils 3–11* (ed., 2006, Sage) and *On Writing Educational Ethnographies* (with Gregory, Kearney and Mor-Sommerfeld, 2005, Trentham).

Ruth Cross

Ruth Cross is a Senior Lecturer in Health Promotion – Public Health at Leeds Metropolitan University. She is a nurse by profession with ten years nursing experience in acute and emergency medicine and HIV/AIDS. She has a BSc in Psychology, an MSc in Health Education and Health Promotion and a Post-Graduate Certificate in Higher Education. In addition to teaching on the UK MSc Public Health – Health Promotion course and transnational MSc courses in the Gambia and Zambia, she teaches on a range of undergraduate and postgraduate allied health professional and health-related courses, including Nursing. Ruth is an active member of the Centre for Health

Promotion Research, her recent research projects including attitudes to smoking in public places, evaluation of Sure Start programmes and parent/child interaction around road safety.

Diane Lowcock

Diane is a Senior Lecturer in Public Health – Health Promotion and has taught young people's health promotion for several years. In her previous role as a public health specialist she worked in the field of sexual health promotion. The work involved training practitioners to facilitate sexual health advice and education and encouraging children and young people to participate in decision-making processes about their health. Diane has considerable experience working alongside young people, teachers, healthcare practitioners and parents to promote sexual health.

Daniel Marshall

Daniel Marshall is a Doctoral Research Student at the Institute of Criminology, University of Cambridge. His thesis focuses on implementation issues of Criminal Justice Intervention Programmes with young people and, the experiences of those young people; he has also worked on the Criminology, Law and Sociology courses at Leeds Metropolitan University and University of York. Daniel graduated from the University of Teesside in 2006 with a BSc in Criminology and Psychology. In addition, he received the Dick Richardson Memorial Award for best student dissertation. Daniel spent the following year studying for an MA in Criminological Research at the University of Leeds. His dissertation focused on The Changing Characteristics of First Time Entrants to the Youth Justice System between 2002/03 and 2006/07, working with Leeds Youth Offending Service. Daniel has also spent five years working as a Special Constable with Durham Constabulary.

Carol Potter

Carol Potter is Senior Lecturer in Childhood and Early Years at Leeds Metropolitan University. She has worked with disabled children in both residential and educational settings for a number of years, teaching children with autism and learning disabilities over a seven-year period. She has taught several courses relating to disability in higher education, and has conducted funded research in the area of communication enabling environments for children with severe autism and little or no speech. Publications include: *Enabling Communication in Children with Autism* (with Whittaker, 2001, Jessica Kingsley).

Tracey Race

Tracey Race joined the Social Work team in the Faculty of Health at Leeds Metropolitan University in 2004. Prior to that, she spent nearly 20 years working in various social work posts in the Yorkshire region, mainly working with children and families. This included working for Leeds Social Services and, within the voluntary sector, for Family Services Units, Barnardo's and the NSPCC. She has particular interests in child protection, partnership working and children's rights, and has published work on the subjects of family support and participation. She is involved in a research project with the NSPCC exploring the views of parents and carers who have had contact with child protection agencies. Tracey is currently the Course Leader for the MA in Social Work, and her teaching focuses on work with children, young people and families.

Alan Smith

Alan Smith is a Principal Lecturer and Head of Youth Work and Community Development at Leeds Metropolitan University. As a qualified Youth and Community Worker, Alan had many years experience working with young offenders, and for the last 16 years he has been teaching and managing youth and community work courses in London, Lancaster and Leeds. Alan has played a key role in the professional association for lecturers in youth and community work as a member of the DfES Transforming Youth Work National Advisory Group, The LLUK Occupational Standards Reference Group, The NYA Workforce Development Group and the HEA Integrated Children's Services in Higher Education Project. Alan was awarded a Teaching Fellowship in 2007 for his work around Inter-Professional Education and *Every Child Matters*; his research and publications have focused on Connexions and the Casework Relationship, Quality and Standards in Youth Work, and Inter-Professional Education and *Every Child Matters*.

Jon Tan

Dr Jon Tan is a Senior Lecturer and Research Coordinator in the field of Education at Leeds Metropolitan University. Graduating from the University of York with a DPhil in Social Policy, his work draws from a range of disciplines including social welfare, education and critical social theory. His current research in the area of professional learning and critical reflective pedagogies interconnects work with both practitioners in urban educational contexts and with undergraduate and postgraduate students of teacher education. In recent years, in collaboration with co-author Christine Allan, he has conducted research focusing on student teachers' experiences of school practice placements in international settings.

Terry Thomas

Terry Thomas is Professor of Criminal Justice Studies, School of Social Sciences, Leeds Metropolitan University. A former local authority social worker and team leader, he is currently engaged in research in the areas of youth offending, anti-social behaviour and sexual offending. He is author of the books *The Police and Social Workers* (1994, Arena), *Privacy and Social*

Services (1995, Arena), *Sex Crime: Sex Offending and Society* (2005, Willan) and *Criminal Records: A Database for the Criminal Justice System and Beyond* (2007, Palgrave Macmillan). He is also a regular contributor to the journals *Childright* and *Youth and Policy*.

Chris Whittaker

Chris Whittaker is currently Honorary Research Fellow at Manchester Metropolitan University and teaches on the Open University Master's in Education. He has been involved in the education of children with complex learning disabilities, including autism, as a teacher, lecturer and researcher for forty years. He led a full-time teacher training course in the area of Special Education, and is a former Vice President of the Down's Syndrome Association. He has undertaken wide-ranging research in the field of disability, specialising in the needs of non-verbal children with complex learning disabilities. Publications include *Enabling Communication in Children with Autism* (with Potter, 2001, Jessica Kingsley).

Mike Wragg

Prior to being appointed Senior Lecturer in Playwork at Leeds Metropolitan University, Mike Wragg held the post of head of play services for Stoke-on-Trent City Council. Within this role, and previously that of play development officer with Bradford Metropolitan District Council, Mike was involved in the development and implementation of play policy and strategy at a local and national level. Mike sits on a number of playwork committees and is a regular contributor to the national and international playwork conference scene. He has authored several articles and chapters, most recently in the book *Foundations of Playwork* (with Brown and Taylor, 2008, Open University Press) and the *International Encyclopaedia of Play in Today's Society* (2009, Sage).

Preface

Children's Rights in Practice aims to provide the reader with insights into the interactions between broad perspectives, such as the United Nations Convention on the Rights of the Child (UNCRC), and children's lives as experienced in different areas of services and provision. The first part of the book offers an introduction to relevant conventions and legislation, creating directions for the reader to follow into the chapters in Part 2. It offers insight into the practical implications of child rights as well as critiques and debates. The second part addresses specific areas of practice. We have aimed to cover a broad range of services, from early years to youth work, from health to youth justice. We invited contributors to give a critical account, and an analysis, which would combine general perspectives with particular issues which highlighted or exemplified an aspect of rights in relation to their area. All chapters contain activities to invite the reader to reflect on the implications of the content for practice.

Each chapter contains references to guide readers across the book, and Part 3 consists of a substantial development of this idea – taking key themes from across the book and offering structured activities to help the reader develop their understanding and awareness of the interrelationship between chapters, disciplines and services. The UNCRC sees childhood as the period up to the age of 17. This book acknowledges this, but also reflects the authors' uses of the term child or young person as referring to this period: hence both terms are used, depending on individual author's usage.

Phil Jones
Faculty of Education, Social Sciences and Law, Leeds University

Gary Walker
Carnegie Faculty, Leeds Metropolitan University

Part 1

Children's Rights in Practice: an Overview of Key Themes and Debates

1

What Are Children's Rights? Contemporary Developments and Debates

Phil Jones

Chapter Overview

This chapter will introduce the broad context for children's rights, drawing on areas of recent research and enquiry that illustrate current developments, debates and tensions. This will include looking at the need for rights and the effects of a rights perspective on different areas of children's lives. It will also look at some of the tensions which have emerged concerning children's rights. The idea of child rights has developed from the convergence of different pressures for change. This chapter introduces the different ways this is happening, giving brief examples of the kinds of policies that are emerging and showing how changes in long-held attitudes and practices relate to child rights. The United Nations Convention on the Rights of the Child (UNCRC) is the touchstone for work being developed in many countries. Key articles from the UNCRC and other sources such as the European Convention on Human Rights (ECHR) will be outlined and linked to the sections of this book which consider their implications for different areas of work. Criticisms of the UNCRC and challenges to its implementation are also explored. After over two decades of living with the UNCRC there is a wealth of experiences of the practical application of the Convention in different areas of children's lives. This section introduces examples that link child rights to their lived experiences.

Rights and responsibilities

In day-to-day contact adults in working situations relate to children in many different roles and contexts. This book examines and supports such relationships in relation to child rights. One way of looking at these concerns how we engage with areas such as policy or practice in terms of 'rights' and how these affect working with children. There are many definitions of rights, normally drawing on broad conventions or legislation such as the United Nations Convention on the Rights of the Child (UNCRC), the European Convention on Human Rights (ECHR) and the UK's Human Rights Act 1990 (HRA) but developed for different audiences. The UK Government, in a publication aimed at young people, used the following broad definition:

> Q. What is a Right?
> A. This is something you should always be able to do, to have, to know, to say or to be protected from.
>
> Q. What is a Responsibility?
> A. This is something you should do for other people, for society or for the environment.

(Ministry of Justice, 2009: 5)

Here child rights are connected to the responsibilities children are seen to have (see Chapter 3 for more details on this perspective). Another definition sees this connection differently. It sees rights developing from 'long-established moral and legal traditions' and situates child rights and responsibilities within the idea of a *contract*:

> The core concept of a right is that of an agreement or 'social contract' which is established between the person(s) who holds a right (often referred to as a 'rights-holder') and the person(s) or institutions(s) which then have obligations and responsibilities in relation to the realisation of that right (often referred to as the 'duty Bearer') (Save the Children, 2005: 14).

An example from Franklin helps illustrate a practical implication of the relationship between rights, responsibility and this *contract*: 'Children have a right to education but they can only exercise that right if government locally and nationally assumes responsibility for its provision' (Franklin, 2002: 27).

Such rights and responsibilities for children, and related 'contracts' for their definition and implementation, are linked to different conventions, acts and laws. The following sections explore the ways child rights are currently defined and implemented.

What are child rights?

The Participation Works organisation foregrounds the way children and young people's rights relate to the ECHR and the UK's HRA, which commit all public organisations to follow the rights in the ECHR. These include early years provision, play work, schools, children's services, health, youth and social services, the police and youth courts. Examples of the ways the HRA relates to children and young people are explained by Participation Works as including:

> **Article 5** – If you are arrested or charged with committing an offence, you should be promptly told the reasons why. You should be given information in a language and way that you understand …
>
> **Article 6** – You have the right to fair trial. This means you should be able to follow what is going on in court, and you should have a lawyer to help you and question people giving evidence against you. You have the right to an interpreter …
>
> **Article 8** – This is your right to respect for private and family life. This right covers many different matters relating to your own choices and decision making, and whether others can interfere with these … It also protects your relationships with your family, and is relevant when decisions are being made about who you should live with …
>
> **Article 9** – This is your right to freedom of thought, conscience and religion. This is relevant to the choices you make for yourself about what you believe and if you follow a religion or not.
>
> **Article 10** – This is your right to freedom of expression. This includes what you wear, as well as giving and receiving ideas and information …
>
> **Article 11** – This is your right to peaceful assembly and association – being on a public protest for example, or being able to form and join groups, such as school councils, trade unions and political parties …
>
> (Participation Works, 2009)

The United Nations Convention on the Rights of the Child was adopted by the United Nations in 1989. Child, within the UNCRC, is defined as an individual aged 17 or under. Within the convention children have a set of *economic, social, cultural, civil* and *political* rights. The rights guaranteed by the Convention are afforded to all children without exception. The UNCRC is defined as an agreement between countries and consists of a number of articles. Specific governments need to ratify such a convention. This means that they agree to obey the articles set out in that convention. Ratification UK ratified the Convention in December 1991: by doing this the UK government has incorporated the UNCRC into its national legal framework and confirmed that the government should make sure that every child has all the rights outlined in the treaty. Most world governments ratified the Convention in full, but the UK government would not do this and entered specific reservations about some of the articles. Some of these, such as the 'UK Reservations' on Articles 10 and 37, were lifted in October 2008. The United Nations' Committee for the Rights of the Child reviews specific countries' responses and issues periodic reviews.

A number of authors have indicated that different areas of rights will be foregrounded, or understood and acted on differently, depending on the political, social and economic contexts of different societies. So, for example, in some situations child rights in relation to child labour or poverty will be at the fore of attention for change, whereas in other societies issues concerning change in relation to children's participation in decisions about the services they access may be given priority. How action develops is usually arrived at through pressure and debate involving children and young people, lobbying groups, workers or government. As this book will show, this process is one that involves powerful forces that work both for positive change in children and young people's lives, and those that act to preserve or increase ways of working, or seeing children, that have a negative impact on their lives. The ratification of the UNCRC includes over 40 specific rights for children in the UK. These are prioritised and summarised in different ways. The following material introduces different ways of approaching the idea and practice of child rights.

One much-used approach, for example, sees the UNCRC as concerning three broad areas: provision, protection and participation. Some organisations, such as Save the Children, approach the UNCRC by describing the rights enshrined in the convention as falling into four broad categories:

- the right to survive;
- the right to be safe;
- the right to belong;
- the right to develop.

Unicef foregrounds what it calls the *four core principles of the Convention* and locates these in some of the specific articles of the UNCRC:

- non-discrimination, or universality (Article 2);
- best interests of the child (Article 3);
- right to life, survival and development (Article 6);
- respect for the views of the child (Article 12).

Unicef and the 'four core principles' of the UNCRC

Non-discrimination is reflected in articles such as Article 2 which states that signatories 'shall respect and ensure the rights set forth in the present Convention to each child within their jurisdiction without discrimination of any kind, irrespective of the child's or his or her parent's or legal guardian's race, colour, sex, language, religion, political or other opinion, national, ethnic or social origin, property, disability, birth or other status' (Unicef, 2009: 9). Unicef foregrounds the special relevance to the situation of children living with disability and to undocumented migrants, and emphasises the article's statement that children must also be protected from discrimination that is based on the beliefs of their parents, other family members or legal guardians. Other practical considerations considered within this book include the ways in which children are made aware of their rights in relation to non-discrimination (see pages 110–16), when tensions occur between the rights of children and those of parents in areas such as sexuality and gender (see page 18, see also pages 143–4) and where the UK government discriminates against children, for example in relation to those who are asylum seekers or refugees (see page 23, see also page 33).

The best interests of the child are presented in Article 3 which states that, 'in all actions concerning children, whether undertaken by public or private social welfare institutions, courts of law, administrative authorities or legislative bodies, the best interests of the child shall be a primary consideration'. Such articles and the concept of 'best interests' relate to the legal protection of children and to evidence-based care of children. Unicef particularly notes that this principle requires governments and other agencies involved in provision, legislation, policies and programmes 'to review *any* of their actions for the impact on children' (Unicef, 2009: 9, author's emphasis). Other practical considerations for children include how to work with the concept of best interests in relation to areas such as youth justice (see page 195), or in complex dynamics such as family break-up or in child protection cases (see pages 60–1, see also page 166) or challenges to practice which purports to be in a child's best interests but is actually reflecting adult desires and agendas (see page 19, see also pages 212–13).

The right to life, survival and development can be seen in Article 6 where the Convention says that 'every child has the inherent right to life' and that states parties 'shall ensure to the maximum extent possible the survival and development of the child'. Unicef notes that these rights are connected to the enjoyment of the 'highest attainable standard' of provision in areas such as health services and to an 'adequate standard' of living (Unicef, 2009: 9). Practical considerations for children include: issues with regard to child protection (see pages 165–6) and health promotion (see page 141) and issues concerning poverty (see page 65) and in relation to care (see page 144).

Respect for the views of the child concerns children's right to have their views heard and respected. Article 12 of the UNCRC says that states 'shall assure to the child who is capable of forming his or her own views the right to express those views freely in all matters affecting the child, the views of the child being given due weight in accordance with the age and maturity of the child' (Unicef, 2009: 9). Practical considerations for children include the ways organisations working with children enable and empower them to participate in areas such as decisions about their own lives (see page 84), the design and implementation of services (see pages 181–2) and how differences in areas such as age (see page 190), understanding and communication (see pages 47–8) are worked with.

Drawing on the UNCRC and the ECHR, the UK government has highlighted the following rights as key:

- the right to life, survival and development;
- children's right to have their views respected, and to have their best interests considered at all times;

- children's right to a name and nationality, freedom of expression, and access to information concerning them;
- the right to live in a family environment or alternative care, and to have contact with both parents wherever possible;
- health and welfare rights, including rights for disabled children, the right to health and health care, and social security;
- the right to education, leisure, culture and the arts;
- special protection for refugee children, children in the juvenile justice system, children deprived of their liberty and children suffering economic, sexual or other forms of exploitation.

(UK government: basics – see http://www.direct.gov.uk/en/parents/parentsrights)

Children's Rights As Voted For By Children

In a recent exercise over 1,800 UK children were given details of child rights from the UNCRC and the HRA and asked to vote for them from their own point of view as children. This offers yet another perspective on the meaning and significance of rights. The five most prioritised were:

1 To be protected from abuse (HRA)
2 To have an education (UNCRC)
3 To be helped to keep alive and well (HRA)
4 Not to be discriminated against because of my race, colour, sex, disability, language or beliefs (HRA)
5 Not to be treated or punished in a way that is cruel or meant to make me feel bad about myself (UNCRC)

(Ofsted, 2010)

Child rights in children's lives

The relationship of rights to children's lives can be seen in terms of different areas or domains: from the playground to the classroom, from home to youth courts. A child's relationship to their family, for example, can be seen within a framework of rights and the relationship between child, family and state:

> The family is in the middle of these relationships and is meant to be supporting the child as an individual while ensuring they develop positive relationships as part of the family and as part of society. However, each family will have a set of beliefs and values that influence their expectations of the child and their relationships. These may not be in keeping with either the principles of the UNCRC or with the expectations of state policies (Jones and Welch, 2010: 136).

The focus of this book is on the domain of services and provision for children and the ways that a framework of rights connects to our work with children. Looked at from the perspectives outlined in this chapter, aspects of the ways we relate to children are governed and influenced by written policies and procedures, largely created by groups of adults. These shift and change in time, reflecting developments and preoccupations in broad societal attitudes and concerns, political influences such as those from changing government policies as well as the ways any specific organisation is managed and handles the services for children provided by the individuals who work within it. Child rights can be seen as part of this 'landscape' and the following section examines them from this perspective.

One of the areas of rights this book will examine in terms of practical work with children concerns the rights to protection, provision and participation, for example. On a macro level over recent years UK government initiatives such as 'Quality Protects' and 'Connexions' link participation rights to the *involvement* of young people. On paper, and often in practice, many councils are committed to including young people in decision-making in relation to policy priorities. On a small scale, specific providers of local services for children have increasingly reflected the ideas and practice of child participation in their individual policies and practices. Table 2.1 in Chapter 2 samples areas of the UNCRC, while Examples 1.1 and 1.2 below offer illustrations of the specific ways that children and adults can work with child rights to try to apply the broad statements to their everyday relationships and work.

EXAMPLE 1.1 Local Services and Child Rights: A Children and Young People's Active Involvement Service

Telford and Wrekin Council have a Children and Young People's Active Involvement Service. Their work includes developing and supporting children and young people's participation groups, and looking at the specific involvement of groups such as disabled children and young people or looked-after children and care leavers. The initiative has been created to 'offer advice, information and support on actively involving children and young people … helping children and young people to be actively involved in: play and fun activities; making changes; learning about their rights and responsibilities; expressing their opinions; giving their views; making decisions' (http://www.telford. gov.uk/ Education+learning/Support+for+young+people). They support service providers in developing awareness of how to reflect child

(Continued)

(Continued)

rights in their structures and practice, and in identifying participatory methods and techniques that workers can use themselves
with groups of children and young people. This has included
work on specific arenas of children's lives, for example on safeguarding and corporate parenting, and on the production of a
report with children on 'How children and young people living in
residential care can participate fully in inspection processes'.
Another area of action has concerned involving children and
young people in the recruitment and selection of staff. This initiative has produced a 'Good Practice Guide' and a training programme has been developed which has encouraged more posts
to have a children and young people's panel of interviewers working alongside the adult panel.

EXAMPLE 1.2   Local Services and Child Rights: A School and Day Nursery Rights Policy

Specific service providers have begun to reflect rights in their individual policies. The following example is an illustration from a
Montessori School and Day Nursery in Leeds, where they have created a 'Children's Rights Policy' (revised 23 January 2009) that cites
the UNCRC as a source:

> All children that are capable of forming their own views are
> encouraged to express those views freely in all matters affect-
> ing the child and the views of the child are given due weight
> in accordance with the age and maturity of the child.

> All children are given the right to freedom of expression; this
> right includes the freedom to seek and receive information and
> ideas, either orally or in print, in the form of art, or through any
> other media of the child's choice. (http://www.leedsmontessori.
> co.uk/downloads/policy-pdfs/childrens-rights.pdf)

Other aspects of the ways we create working relationships are not laid
down on paper or dealt with by local government units in this way, but
are equally visible. These consist of less easily defined influences, but
include:

- cultural attitudes about children and adults' relationships with children;
- children's responses to us as adults and in the roles we have as
  professionals;

- children's responses to each other and how this influences the way relationships form;
- the contexts that surround and affect the relationship – this can be looked at in terms of areas such as age, class, poverty, gender, race, disability and sexuality or in relation to forces such as disempowerment and empowerment or exclusion and inclusion;
- our memories and responses to our memories of our own childhoods and child – adult relationships.

These are not fixed, but are part of ongoing negotiations between children and adults. They operate at wide societal levels, can contain differences and tensions at local or community level and are also lived with and changed in the interactions between individuals and within specific settings and groups. Sinclair's (2004) description of the ways these changes are occurring sees them as a result of new, and developing, ideas from a number of different perspectives. These are identified by her as:

- *pressure* from children and young people, researchers, policy-makers, practitioners working with children;
- *new paradigms* within the social sciences that have increased our understanding of the child as a competent social actor, seeing their capacity to be commentators in their own lives and to be involved in decision-making;
- the *children's rights agenda*.

The following material gives more details of each of these as a way of helping to show how child rights as an area of concern has emerged and is emerging.

Pressure

The kind of pressure talked about by Sinclair are reflected on a large scale by legislation such as the UNCRC and the ECHR. On more localised levels, it is shown by the work of charities and groups, or by adults and children, in specific services such as schools or centres. This book will include both perspectives, offering material containing details of key broad legislation and of national organisations, but will also provide examples of specific local initiatives, research and ideas to show how adults and children are developing the ideas and practices of rights within their daily lives together. An illustration of this is that, in the consultation referred to earlier (Ofsted, 2010), the children reflected rights that were already recognised in the UNCRC and the UK's development of the Human Rights Act in 1998, but added two that were not in the conventions or legislation. The report concludes that:

> Any future Act, Bill or Charter of Rights and Responsibilities also needs to take note that the children added in this top 10 two new rights that had come from our other consultations with children:
>
> - the right not to be bullied, and
> - the right to keep in touch with parents, grandparents, brothers and sisters.
>
> (Ofsted, 2010: 31)

This is an example of the ways in which children's perceptions are developing society's understanding and approach to rights.

New Paradigms

The idea of childhood as a construction is relevant to our examination of the practice of child rights. Moss and Petrie (2002) have summarised this approach as arguing that, though childhood is a biological fact, the way it is understood and lived varies considerably. This variety is created through interactions between people, and through the kinds of images of children that inform the ways we act and interact. There is never only one version of what a child is: different professions, disciplines and communities create particular versions of what children are, or can be, shaped by politics, history and culture. I have summarised this emerging way of looking at children as being typified as a set of specific images of a child and children, and to be associated with the advocacy of certain kinds of relationships and processes. Two of the key elements of this are reflected in the approach to children and adults within this book – that children are:

- agents in their own lives;
- able to contribute and participate in decision-making.

(Jones, 2009: 29)

The child rights agenda

It has been over two decades since the UNCRC and, during this time, the responses in different countries and societies have seen the development of what can be called a 'rights agenda'. Twenty years after the UNCRC, for example, the UN Committee on the Rights of the Child criticised the UK government's failure to implement the Convention in many areas of children's lives. It mentioned, in particular, the need to recognise the rights for some of the most vulnerable children in conflict with the law and subject to immigration control. A report from the Children's Rights Alliance for England summarised the situation in the following way.

> The UK Government has taken some significant steps to uphold children's rights, including the introduction of the first Cabinet Minister and Department for Children, Schools and Families, but more must be done ...

> The UNCRC sets out the rights that all children need to thrive. Existing legal mechanisms to hold the Government and public authorities to account for protecting all children are under-used, largely due to lack of awareness among the public, including children, lawyers, the courts and decision-makers. Making the UNCRC part of UK law would make the Convention justiciable in the UK courts (Children's Rights Alliance for England, 2010: 7).

Over the years, general patterns have emerged in the way the UNCRC is being practically realised – this can be called an *agenda* for change. This book will look at the move from the original Convention to the notion of a child rights agenda and to the way specific action in workplaces is occurring: exploring the ways policy and practice connect in changing children's lives and the way adults work with them.

It can seem an enormous journey from statements made by the United Nations or the European Union to life between a specific child and worker in an individual school, clinic or court. Experience in many countries and in many communities is showing that real changes are being made that affect children and adults in positive ways. Other pictures are also emerging, though. There can be tensions between the agenda set by broad statements of rights and the specific experience of individuals, or groups, in everyday life. This book will not ignore the actual complexities of creating time, space and opportunities to work in a daily way that is informed by rights. It will draw on ideas, practical work and research that can usefully see both how ideas can be realised, but which also give examples of ways of positively engaging with the tensions, frustrations and variety of situations that test and develop the ideas of rights in everyday practice.

On a national level government organisations use the UNCRC to frame the way they form initiatives. An example of this, from *Righting the Wrongs: The Reality of Children's Rights in Wales,* says that:

> The development of a children's rights perspective throughout governmental structures is best achieved by designing strategies to implement the guiding principles of the Convention, non-discrimination (Article 2), best interests (Article 3), survival and development (Article 6) and participation (Article 12). The Guiding Principles are the backbone to the Convention and instrumental to achieving all of the other rights. (Croke, 2006: 2)

Children in Scotland parallel this in noting that the three UNCRC Articles most often cited in child policy work in Scotland are:

> *Article 2*: that all UNCRC rights apply to *all* children without discrimination;
> *Article 3*: that the best interests of children must be a *primary* consideration;
> *Article 12*: that children's views must be taken into account in decision-making.
>
> (http://www.childreninscotland.org.uk/html/poly_righ.htm)

However, the Articles reflect a much wider set of concerns than these three, and all are relevant to different aspects of working with children, covering a range of areas of children's lives: social, economic, civic, political, cultural and participation rights. The next chapter offers a summary of selected, key elements of the UNCRC to help orientate the discussions in this book.

Summary

This chapter has described how the idea of child rights has emerged, identifying the ways in which different pressures for change continue to develop the way rights are legislated for and understood. It has given brief examples of the kinds of policies that are emerging and has shown how changes in long-held attitudes and practices are a consequence of the child rights agenda. The chapter introduced areas key to child rights including the United Nations Convention on the Rights of the Child (UNCRC), the European Convention on Human Rights (ECHR), and the UK's Human Rights Act 1996 (HRA). Examples that link child rights to their lived experiences were used to illustrate the ways in which the practical application of legislation affects children and those working with them.

Question 1.1   How has a rights perspective emerged in relation to children?

Review Activity

Refer to the examples of the Children and Young People's Active Involvement Service and the Leeds Montessori School and Day Nursery.

1 Think of how the setting you work in or a service provider such as a school or health centre might engage with the areas described in the Children and Young People's Active Involvement Service.
2 Look at the extract from the Leeds Montessori School and Day Nursery and the full policy online (http://www.leedsmontessori. co.uk/downloads/policy-pdfs/childrens-rights.pdf), or find another example of a local service provider's rights policy.

Either:

(a) If your setting does not have such a specific policy, do you think it could be useful? How would you adapt a policy so as to fit the specific context of the setting?

Or:

(b) Adapt a policy such as that of the Leeds Montessori School and Day Nursery for another setting such as an early years setting or a youth club.

Question 1.2   What are child rights?

Review Activity

Refer to examples of child rights given in this chapter that you consider are relevant to children in a specific service or in the service within which you work:

1 Create a poster that would enable children to understand the meaning of the rights and the implications for them in their lives and experience of the setting they are in (for example, a day nursery or law court).

2 Develop this further by devising a practical activity that you could use in supporting children to understand the poster and how to act on the information it contains.

3 Try to think of alternatives to the poster and activity to engage with factors such as working with children of different ages or with children with learning disabilities.

Question 1.3   How are the ideas of child rights being reflected in practice?

Review Activity

The chapter refers to Children in Scotland's statement that the Article 12 of the UNCRC is one of the most frequently cited in child policy work:

Article 12 – The right to express his or her views freely and these must be given 'due weight' depending on his or her age and maturity. (Unicef, 2009: 9)

Example 1.1 talks about Telford and Wrekin Council interpreting rights to include 'helping children and young people to be actively involved' in a number of specific processes. Consider the following three areas they mention:

- learning about their rights and responsibilities;
- expressing their opinions and giving their views;
- making decisions.

Either:

1 How might you develop active involvement with children in your work setting?

Or:

2 Consider aspects of daily life in an early years setting, a school setting or a youth work setting, and how each of the three areas mentioned by Telford and Wrekin council could be developed.

Example might include:

(a) How might children and adults be helped to connect the processes involved in the daily life of a setting as relating to child rights?

(b) How could children be given more opportunities to express opinions and views and:

(i)   be helped to understand the potential effect or impact of their views on their daily life in the setting;

(ii) be engaged in dialogue with adults about their ideas and their implications; and

(iii) see their opinions and views acted on in ways that give their perceptions equal weight with those of adults?

Further Reading

Children's Rights Alliance for England (2010) *Children's Rights Part of UK Law.*
    Available from: http://www.crae.org.uk/protecting/uk-law.html.
A useful and clear summary of the situation regarding child rights in the UK,
both in terms of progress and barriers. The Children's Rights Alliance for England
website (http://www.crae.org.uk) is a useful source for information, initiatives
and a child-centred position on current and future developments in the area of
child rights.

Ofsted (2010) *Children on Rights and Responsibilities: A Report of Children's Views
    by the Children's Rights Director for England.* Manchester: Ofsted.
This is an examination of children and young people's perspectives on their
rights. It provides an interesting parallel to formulations of rights created by
adults, and offers alternative perceptions of child rights, as well as giving rich
detail of the meanings given by children and young people to existing rights and
responsibilities.

Unicef (1989) *Summary of the UNCRC Made for Children.* Available at: http://
    www.unicef.org.uk (Accessed 21 February 2009).
A good source for a basic overview of the articles in the UNCRC in a format that
is useful and clearly accessible for children.

Welch, S. (2008) 'Childhood rights and responsibilities', in P. Jones, D. Moss,
    P. Tomlinson and S. Welch (eds), *Childhood: Services and Provision for
    Children.* London: Pearson.
A thorough, succinct overview of the development of child rights, a review of
the different types of rights, along with a useful consideration of the relationship
between rights and needs and who is responsible for ensuring child rights.

2

Child Rights and Their Practical Application: Definitions, Questions and Practice

Phil Jones

Chapter Overview

This chapter offers details of the ways rights can be seen in relation to practice with children and young people. Key parts of the United Nations Convention on the Rights of the Child (UNCRC) are summarised and developed to help form questions about how to work with children. The questions are then connected to areas of discussion and examples of practice contained within this book. This chapter will include brief summaries of key articles of the UNCRC, and will introduce how they can be seen as connected to practical work. Rights can be seen as developing and active, having different potentials in a variety contexts. The chapter will explore how different articles of an international convention can be useful in developing questions related to working with children in specific areas such as early years, play, education, social work, health or youth services. The chapter will create connections between specific details in the UNCRC and provide questions about practice and examples concerning different areas of practice with children contained in this book. It aims to help readers link the UNCRC to different practical applications and to assist them to see where different rights are dealt with in the various chapters of Parts 1 and 2.

Child rights: fact and process

Child rights are both a *fact* and a *process*. As the previous chapter showed, child rights have been established through the UNCRC, the European Convention on Human Rights (ECHR) and the UK's Human Rights Act 1998 (HRA). The UNCRC is *ratified* by governments and practitioners can see its impact in law and on policy, but rights are also *evolving* – they are in process. This evolution is occurring as the rights move from international conventions and national governments to the daily experiences of children and those who live and work with them. As a process, rights are being tested and developed as they meet challenges to the ideas and practices they represent or provide new opportunities to be understood in different ways as they interact with shifts and changes in society. An example of the ways in which ideas are tested is the challenge that some have offered to the notion that 'rights' as a concept is too connected to a Western emphasis on individualism and that they undermine, or are less relevant to, cultures, communities or societies that are framed by communitarian values which emphasise interdependence. An example of the new opportunities to reflect changes in society are those offered by the need to address more effectively the recognition of the rights of lesbian, gay and transgender children and young people. This is an area that reflects tensions in education, for instance, between policies concerning equity and those that enable faith schools that are Catholic, for example, to exempt themselves from UK policies that recognise the rights to equal treatment for those who are lesbian, gay and transgender. Beadle reports on an aspect of this area as follows:

> If the human rights of gay and lesbian children in our schools are ... ignored, then the rights of transgendered children are not even recognised as existing ... in a large, British secondary school, as many as 10 or so kids could be transgender ... Whereas gay, lesbian and bisexual children may come to a realised understanding of their difference post-puberty, transgendered children often come to this awareness before they are eight years of age ... In Doncaster last year, 10-year-old Cameron McWilliams, who had been asking permission to wear makeup and girls' underwear, hanged himself (Beadle, 2009: 6).

Beadle quotes Kennedy, a former primary school teacher who is transgender and has conducted research into the experience of children, asserting that there is 'no effective recognition' of the problems that transgendered children face: 'Most of them are aware they are transgendered for most, if not all, of their time in school. Most leave as soon as they can because in the school system, which demands that they show respect and tolerance for other minority groups, they are not tolerated themselves by others' (Beadle, 2009: 6). Beadle indicates the need to develop the UK's response to this area of rights: 'How, then, are schools to deal with this issue? Should there be compulsory gender studies as part of the citizenship curriculum?' (Beadle, 2009: 6).

This is an example of the ways in which new questions, tensions, challenges and needs continue to emerge as part of a dynamic relationship between service provision, child rights, children and the communities and society they live within.

The previous chapter looked broadly at conventions such as the UNCRC and the ECHR; this chapter focuses in more detail upon the UNCRC as the source of much impetus for action and change in the daily lives of children. The approach is to avoid seeing the UNCRC as a series of statements set in stone, but to engage with it as a way of offering questions and inviting responses. A selection of UNCRC articles which recur within the consideration of practice in this book are summarised: each article is seen as a way of asking active questions about how we work with children. The questions are then linked to sections of this book where the issues they raise are examined by the different authors, looking from early years to youth work, from child protection to youth justice. Table 2.1 gives an overview of the UNCRC by means of a selection of key articles from the Convention, and then links them to different areas of practice with children from the chapters this book.

Criticism of the UNCRC and implications for practice

The relationship between the UNCRC and the UK's response contains many positive examples of policies and resulting practice which, as Table 2.1 indicates, this book will detail. Criticism of the UNCRC and the UK's response to it, however, has identified ambiguities, tensions and omissions. These include the UNCRC's lack of enforceability unless it is incorporated though national law; the lack of promotion of children's participation through political rights; that definitions – such as that of the child's 'best interests' – may be made by adults rather than involving children's own ideas and agency; and that it does not pay adequate attention to the ways in which forces such as poverty and structural inequalities within society and families affect children. The recent UK Children's Commissioners' Report to the UN Committee on the Rights of the Child (2008) reveals that child rights, in policy and practice, are still very much a work in progress. It noted in 2008, for example, that for Northern Ireland:

> Currently, there is no protection in constitutional terms for children's rights in Northern Ireland. The UNCRC is not enshrined in domestic legislation. There is an opportunity for this to change, with the introduction of a Bill of Rights for Northern Ireland. The Commissioner wishes to see as a minimum, the full principles and provisions of the UNCRC incorporated into law through the Bill of Rights in Northern Ireland. (2008: 6)

And in England:

> The UNCRC has not been fully brought into legislative and policy processes in England. (2008: 5)

Table 2.1 Samples of the UNCRC and their relationship to practice with children

UNCRC and practice with children

Article 1 states that the Convention applies to everyone aged 17 or under. Article 2 says that all the rights in the Convention apply to all children and young people without any discrimination. Unicef has commented on these rights in a way that indicates that both adults and children have responsibilities in relation to the Articles:

If every child, regardless of their sex, ethnic origin, social status, language, age, nationality or religion has these rights, then they also have a responsibility to respect each other in a humane way. (UNCRC – see: http://www.unicef.org.uk)

UNCRC Article	Questions related to practice and the UNCRC Article	A sample of sections from this book which concern the article and questions
Article 3 Adults should always try to do what is best for children and young people.	How to effectively understand and act on 'what is best' for children and young people?	*Article into practice:* Working with best interests of the child in social work – pages 163–6.
	How can children be most effectively involved in decisions about what is best for them?	*Article into practice:* Best interests, youth work values and practice – pages 175–6.
		Article into practice: Best interests in education – pages 110–11.
		Article into practice: Dealing with tensions between best interests of the child and conflicts with other interests such as those of the family or state:
		• for youth justice – pages 194–5; • for child welfare and safeguarding – pages 60–1; • regarding power dynamics in health – pages 156–7; • challenging adult practices that do not serve children's interests in different service areas – pages 37–9.
Article 4 Governments must do all they can to make sure children's and young people's human rights are upheld.	How to support children's rights most effectively within the structures and practice of provision for children?	*Article into practice:* Encouraging the interaction between children, national and local government or in national guidelines for practitioners – pages 116–17.
	How to respond to international and national legislation and policies in everyday practice?	*Article into practice:* Government policy, rights and specific areas of practice – pages 39–42.
		Article into practice: Examples of, and challenges to, government action in relation to rights – pages 183–5.

Table 2.1 (Continued)

UNCRC Article	Questions related to practice and the UNCRC Article	A sample of sections from this book which concern the article and questions
Article 9 If a court is thinking about who a child should live with, everyone affected by the decision should have the chance to be heard, including the child. Every child has the right to keep in regular contact with both parents, so long as this is the best thing for the young person.	How best to involve children in decision-making in complex family situations? How to work with the relationship between issues such as safeguarding and a child's wishes? How to understand and act on concepts such as 'best interests'?	*Article into practice:* In relation to social care and welfare practice – pages 89–91. *Article into practice:* In relation to safeguarding children – pages 61–2. *Article into practice:* In relation to youth justice issues concerning children and their family – pages 190–8.
Articles 12, 13, 14 and 17 *Article 12:* The right to express his or her views freely and these must be given 'due weight' depending on his or her age and maturity. *Article 13:* The right to freedom of expression, including the right to all kinds of information and ideas. *Article 14:* The right to freedom of thought, conscience and religion. *Article 17:* The right to information and protection from harmful information and materials.	How to create structures and ways of working with children that maximise their capacity to develop and communicate their views? How to work with the complex factors that interact in forming each individual child's capacity to understand and respond to situations? How to work with areas that potentially conflict with each other, such as the right to information and the right to protection from harmful information and materials? How to engage with the concept of 'due weight' within work in a meaningful and practical way?	*Article into practice:* Play as a right and play work and play spaces in relation to freedom of expression for children – pages 76–8. *Article into practice:* Participation and decision-making in policy and in practice contexts – pages 201–5. *Article into practice:* Working with difference in expression and capacity to make decisions in areas such as communication and disability – pages 89–91. *Article into practice:* Informing and involving young people in their rights – pages 180–3. *Article into practice:* Encountering tensions between children and their families in relation to freedoms of thought, conscience and religion – pages 179–80.

(Continued)

Table 2.1 (Continued)

UNCRC Article	Questions related to practice and the UNCRC Article	A sample of sections from this book which concern the article and questions
Article 18 Parents must always do what is best for children and young people and governments should help them.	How to practically create structures and ways of working that manage the tensions and relationships between different perspectives on 'what is best' for a child or acting in 'the best interests' of a child? How to work with dynamics between workers, family members and children in relation to understanding, identifying and acting on the 'best interests' of a child?	*Article into practice*: Engaging with dynamics or tensions concerning rights and responsibilities between children and their families in areas such as health or safeguarding – pages 143–8, 155–7. *Article into practice*: Working practices that support families and children in rights-related areas such as decision-making or safeguarding – pages 60–1. *Article into practice*: The potentials and tensions of interagency practice in relation to identifying and working with parents concerning what is 'best' for children – pages 58–63.
Articles 19, 20, 34, 35, and 39 (included out of sequence as they are thematically linked) *Article 19*: The right to protection from all forms of violence, abuse, neglect and mistreatment. *Article 20*: The right to special protection and help when separated from parents. *Article 34*: The right to protection from sexual exploitation (including prostitution) and sexual abuse. *Article 35*: The right to protection from being taken away, sold or trafficked. *Article 39*: Governments must give good support to children and young people who have been hurt, abused or exploited.	How to create structures, practices and relationships that manage and resource the relationship between policies and practice in relation to protection and safeguarding? How to manage contradictions in children's lives – for example, in squaring these articles with the UK government's persistent refusal to respond to the UNCRC committee's ongoing criticism of the lack of a ban on smacking children.	*Article into practice*: Policy and practice relating to safeguarding, protection and welfare of children – pages 32–42. *Article into practice*: The contradictory attitudes of adults regarding children and protection – how this impacts on practice with children – pages 62–6. *Article into practice*: Tensions between areas such as state paternalism, rights and intervention – pages 62–6. *Article into practice*: Children, young people and knowledge about areas relating to sexuality, safeguarding and protection – pages 143–5. *Article into practice*: Violence against children within services – young people in the youth justice system – pages 188–98.

Table 2.1 (Continued)

UNCRC Article	Questions related to practice and the UNCRC Article	A sample of sections from this book which concern the article and questions
Article 22 The right to protection and humanitarian help for children and young people who are refugees, or who are trying to be accepted as refugees.	How to engage with the UK governments' refusal to respond meaningfully to the UNCRC's criticism of their violation of the rights of children who are seeking refuge and asylum?	*Article into practice:* Issues concerning provision, protection and participation and children who are asylum seekers or refugees – pages 6–7.
Article 23 The right to a full life and to active participation in the community for disabled children and young people.	How best to realise the concept of 'active participation' in all levels of provision for disabled children young people?	*Article into practice:* Rights and practices concerning children as experts in their own lives – pages 125–6. *Article into practice:* Issues in practice concerning rights to provision and participation – pages 202–9. *Article into practice:* Rights in relation to practices of advocacy, self-advocacy, communication and decision-making – pages 89–91. *Article into practice:* Work in relation to young people representing themselves in service user groups – pages 179–82.
Article 24 The right to the best possible health and health services.	How best to provide services that address the demands and needs of children? How to redress the history of health services for children being primarily based on adult services and perceptions?	*Article into practice:* Rights and health in different contexts such as education and youth work – pages 140–62. *Article into practice:* Rights and practices concerning physical health – pages 141–3. *Article into practice:* Rights and practices concerning emotional and mental health – pages 150–3. *Article into practice:* Children's voice and perspectives within health and health promotion – pages 148–57.

(Continued)

Table 2.1 (Continued)

UNCRC Article	Questions related to practice and the UNCRC Article	A sample of sections from this book which concern the article and questions
Article 26 and 27 *Article 26:* The right to have enough money. *Article 27:* The right to a standard of living that helps them develop fully.	How to reflect an engagement with the social divisions of society, for example, of inequality and poverty in the way services and provision are framed and delivered?	*Article into practice:* The ways in which rights and their relationship to social divisions in society feature within practice and children and young people – pages 32–42. *Article into practice:* Education, rights and social equity – pages 116–19. *Article into practice:* Working with the impact of poverty on children's lives – pages 35–8. *Article into practice:* Challenges to the idea that practice with children is a way of social control rather than engaging with inequality – pages 195–8.
Article 31 The right to rest, play and leisure.	How best to deliver play and leisure services in a way that reflects children's ideas? How to involve play in different arenas of children's lives?	*Article into practice:* Child rights and play work practice – pages 71–3. *Article into practice:* Young people's rights and leisure – pages 176–9. *Article into practice:* Challenging adult-centric priorities that devalue play in policy and practice – pages 74–5. *Article into practice:* Youth justice and young people's rights to congregate on the street – pages 195–8.

Table 2.1 (Continued)

UNCRC Article	Questions related to practice and the UNCRC Article	A sample of sections from this book which concern the article and questions
Article 40 Every child or young person accused, or convicted, of committing a crime must be treated with respect and in a way that helps them to respect the human rights of others.	How to reflect children's rights to participation and protection in relation to youth justice? How to respond to tensions from a child rights perspective within areas such as capacity, capability and responsibility in relation to the UK's justice system.	*Article into practice:* Rights in relation to participation rights and practice within the justice system – pages 188–9. *Article into practice:* Respecting children and young people's decision-making within their experiences of UK law – pages 44–9, 188–97. *Article into practice:* Youth justice practices and challenges to respect for young people within practices such as ASBOs – pages 194–5. *Article into practice:* The impact of 'popular punitivism' on work with children and young people – pages 49–50, 188–9.
Article 42 The right to information about the convention.	How best to provide information about the nature of rights? How best to create structures and ways of working that enable children to act on their rights in a meaningful way within services? How to create effective structures and ways of working between children and adults in supporting and acting on information that is provided?	*Article into practice:* Examples of providing information to meet differences in age, understanding and communication – pages 49–50. *Article into practice:* Ways of working to develop structures and effective practice in work with children – pages 55–6, 77–8. *Article into practice:* Examples of peer work involving children and young people communicating, developing and using their rights – pages 43–56, 152.

The relationship between the UNCRC and the UK government may improve. However, in the interim, local authorities and organisations in the voluntary sector have produced a wealth of material that can be used to inform and support workers and children alike. This material is available in a variety of formats, and looks at issues such as making rights information available to different age groups or for children with learning disabilities. In relation to training staff, many organisations already engage with children's rights, and materials are available to support formal and informal training. Some service providers use such materials as part of in-service training or continuous professional development and organisations to support this work are also active in promoting awareness and skill in this area.

Examples of specific practices

Below are illustrations of the ways in which specific initiatives have tried to develop practice that reflects children's rights.

EXAMPLE 2.1   Consultation with young children

MacNaughton *et al.* (2003) initiated a consultation exercise with young children from birth to eight years. They used an action-learning model to assist 23 early childhood staff to consult children's experiences of their families and their care and education settings.

They used a combination of methods designed to enable each child to work with the language or process the child wanted to and could express themselves through. These included pictures and photographs as well as words. Most were three to five years old, with eight of the 137 being two years old or less.

The researchers worked with key questions:

* What do children think they need for their well-being?
* What do children wish for and value in their lives?

The children's views covered three areas of their lives: their experiences of family and home, of education and of care. In relation to their family and home, for example, the children's priority was to have a safe and caring family with whom to spend time, and most children felt safe with key people in their families. Many children also wanted a home in which members of the family have time together and time apart. The findings included the following:

> *Girl* – 'I feel special when I'm with my family.'
>
> *Boy* – 'I feel safe when I live in a house so the rain and thunder don't get you.'
>
> *Girl* – 'My family is special because they are always there for me.'
>
> *Girl* – 'Home is a place where I can be myself.'

The authors argue that this kind of approach reinforces the growing body of research evidence that young children:

- are quite capable of expressing their views on things that affect them and that they value;
- enjoy the opportunity to do so;
- can be encouraged and assisted in the development of the knowledge, skills and confidence they need to become active citizens who can participate actively in public decision-making.

(2003: 480)

They conclude that honouring children's rights to express themselves and their lives results in more effective policy; it creates a more inclusive community and moves us towards a healthy democracy. However, they also note issues concerning power and voice: it is crucial to engage with both as key challenges in relation to young children's voices being heard and empowered (2003: 466). Others reflect similar concerns regarding power and voice in relation to education. Jeffs considers the tensions between the notion of children's rights and what he calls the 'authoritarian, repressive and standardised school system' (2002: 55). His central argument is that the two are incompatible: children's rights to be consulted on their whole 'learning experience' (ibid.) are undermined by an approach which values uniformity and testing and which seems to have no place for children as active citizens. His conclusion is that schools, in their current guise, are 'contemptuous of [children's] opinions [and] the concept of democracy ... if we cannot create schools that respect the rights of children and actively foster democracy then we must not flinch from actively supporting alternatives that do' (ibid.: 57).

On a broader, strategic level, and as a contrast to Jeffs' views, the Canadian Association for School Health (CASH), a federation of 12 provincial/territorial coalitions, promotes the use of the school as a strategic site within the community to reach children and youth as well as adults. CASH has developed the idea of five key areas to focus on in developing youth involvement in public decision-making. Example 2.2 gives a brief summary of these areas to illustrate this approach to looking at efficacy in developing the right to be involved in decision-making.

EXAMPLE 2.2   CASH: Summary of five key areas in developing youth involvement in public decision-making

1 Relationship between youth involvement and organisation goals

This concerns examining and identifying the ways in which the organisation's existing aims or goals might relate to involving young people in decision-making.

2 The nature of the youth involvement

This involves considering and deciding on how participation might occur. Areas included here concern issues such as the frequency of involvement. For example, is it to take place only during the development of new ideas or initiatives or in evaluating work, or is it to be a permanent fixture within the processes of the organisation? This might also concern considering whether young people will participate as individuals or as part of a group involvement.

3 The processes to be used

This identifies the ways in which the organisation enables young people to participate. It involves a consideration of the ways in which participation is facilitated, for example whether activities to support young people will be of use, or whether training in the development of skills is necessary. This area also involves the organisation considering taking action to address any barriers which might hinder or prevent young people coming forward or taking part.

4 How participation relates to different types of decision-making

This entails looking at the different ways in which an organisation can involve young people within its structures and procedures. Examples include youth representatives on governing boards and regular committees and formal consultative projects involving young people.

5 The evidence of the impact of youth involvement

This involves identifying how the impact of any consultation or participation will be prepared for and communicated along with a consideration of how evidence can be sought to ascertain the impact of youth participation in the decision-making of the organisation.

(Drawn from McCall, 2008)

These examples illustrate the ways in which a child rights agenda has emerged, and show how ideas can be reflected in developing service provision and approaches to work with children. Within this work key areas can be identified as typifying the ways practice can reflect the ideas contained within a child rights agenda. Table 2.2 offers some key areas of this agenda as reflected in this chapter and links it to examples of practice in this book.

Table 2.2 Child rights agenda and implications for practice: illustrative examples

Rights agenda	Examples of implications for practice
Looking to see how children can be seen and engaged with as active, capable and as experts in their own lives.	Changing structures, management procedures and the day-to-day running of services from a child rights perspective. Developing ways of involving children in decisions about their bodies, spaces and futures. For examples see pages 103–6.
Changing adult roles and relationships with children in services and provision that try to address inequalities.	Changing decision-making processes to include children in decisions about themselves, events or issues that affect them or within organisations that work for, or with, them. Exploring the use of processes such as the role of advocacy within representation of children's views, opinions and decisions. For examples see pages 84–92.
Identifying and addressing the particular ways in which social divisions within society concerning areas such as poverty, race, gender, disability and sexuality affect children, rather than seeing their impact on children's lives as identical to their impact on adults.	Reviewing the nature and role of policy and practice and rewriting documents and guidelines from a perspective that connects child rights to the impact of other areas of inequality on their lives and experience of the provision. For examples see pages 117–20.
Way of perceiving children's lives and experiences from a child's perspective rather than from the perspective of adult ideas and opinions about what children see, want or need.	Enquiry through research into children's experiences and ideas about a part of their lives or service. Emphasising child-orientated ways of participating or communicating, such as play. For examples see pages 44–9.
Specific services that are designed with children in mind rather than adult services with no, or little, adaptation for children.	Spaces designed and created for children with input into the design and regulation or use of those spaces by children. For examples see pages 77–9.

Summary

This chapter has outlined the way a child rights perspective has begun to be reflected in policy and practice with children. It has given examples from the UNCRC and connected them to questions relating to practice with children, showing how they connect to areas of work with children contained in this book including education, law, play, early years and youth work. It has provided illustrative examples of the possibilities that a rights agenda can open up in work with children, as well as showing how tensions and problems within the engagement with rights can be understood. The following activities are intended to help reflect on the chapter and connect the content with practical work in settings with children.

Question 2.1   How can young children's participation rights be worked with?

Review Activity

The chapter refers to young children being quite capable of expressing their views on things that affect them and that they value, and that adults have a role to play in developing children's

- knowledge
- skills and
- confidence

and to involve them in this aspect of their rights.

1 In working with young children, what activities do you think could help create structures and activities to assist children to maximise their capacity to develop and communicate their views in ways that help them to understand their impact and effect?
2 Can you think of ways that adults working with young children might be helped to develop and alter their approaches to interacting with young children in response to these ideas and ways of working?

Question 2.2   How can rights help professionals see their work differently?

Review Activity

Take any of the areas described in Table 2.2 and think about how to relate them to your setting or workplace.

1 Consider the implications for staff relationships with children.
2 Consider any of the areas contained within the table that relate to changes in the way children interact with each other in relation to Unicef's comment that: 'If every child, regardless of their sex, ethnic origin, social status, language, age, nationality or religion has these rights, then they also have a responsibility to respect each other in a humane way' (UNCRC – see http://www.unicef.org.uk).

Further Reading

Alderson, P. (2000) *Young Children's Rights: Exploring Beliefs, Principles and Practice.* London: Jessica Kingsley.

Contains a good discussion of rights in relation to young children, alongside a thorough review of how ideas and concepts of rights relate to practice with young children in a range of contexts.

Moss, P. and Petrie, P. (2002) *From Children's Services to Children's Spaces: Public Policy, Children and Childhood.* London: RoutledgeFalmer.

A review of different areas of children's lives and of various arenas of provision. The book develops insight into the relationship between policy and practice, and into the relationships between children and those working with them. Particularly useful for looking at the ways in which inclusive relationships between children and the adults who work with them can be developed and understood.

Madge, N. (2006) 'Making things better for children and adults' and 'Findings and messages', in *Children These Days.* Bristol: Policy Press.

Good use of research with children, young people and adults to examine where contemporary tensions and difficulties lie in provision for children and young people, and to explore children and young people's perceptions of how they could be changed. Clearly presented and stimulating consideration of how improvements could occur.

3

Children's Rights: Social Justice and Exclusion

Gary Walker

Chapter Overview

This chapter will consider how children's rights as articulated through the United Nations Convention on the Rights of the Child (UNCRC) relate to the concepts of social justice and social exclusion within the context of examples of legislation in the UK. These terms are complex and dynamic, and it is important and useful to have a working definition of what they mean to underpin their application to children. Social justice and social exclusion are key concepts in discussions about equality and fair access to resources and services. The link between these concepts and that of 'child rights' is explored here. Specific examples are presented where particular approaches to working with children in different settings represent attempts to achieve social justice and reduce social exclusion of children.

Rights and social justice

United Nations Convention on the Rights of the Child

For children in so-called developed countries such as the UK, it may at first glance appear as if rights promoted under the UNCRC are well enshrined in law. There are many examples where children's rights are promoted and safeguarded. The Children Act 1989 deals with a wide range of issues including the right of children to be provided with support where they are deemed to be in need of additional help, and the right to protection from significant harm. The Education Act 1993 covers provision for children with special educational needs, giving statutory responsibilities to local authorities and governing bodies of schools to assess and provide support for those children.

Freeman (2000) provides a useful framework for understanding how children's rights are conceptualised within the UNCRC. He suggests that the Convention includes a commitment to:

- general rights (the right to life, prohibition against torture, freedom of expression, thought and religion, information and privacy);
- rights requiring protective measures (this includes measures to protect children from economic and sexual exploitation, to prevent drug abuse and other forms of abuse and neglect);
- rights concerning the civil status of children (for instance, the right to acquire nationality, the right to preserve one's identity, the right to remain with parents (where this is in the child's interests), and the right to be reunited with the family);
- rights concerning development and welfare (including the child's right to a reasonable standard of living, the right to health and basic services, the right to social security, the right to education and the right to leisure);
- rights concerning children in special circumstances or 'in especially difficult circumstances' (this includes children with special needs, refugee children and orphaned children, special regulations on adoption, the cultural concerns of children, rehabilitative care for children suffering from deprivation, and a prohibition on the recruitment of soldiers under 15 years of age).

It is interesting to consider the UNCRC declarations alongside some recent legislative developments within the UK to examine whether they do indeed fully meet and respond to the imperatives of children's rights in the context of two key concepts: social justice and social exclusion.

What is social justice?

Miller argues that social justice involves a commitment to ensuring 'each person gets a fair share of the benefits, and carries a fair share of the responsibilities, of living together in a community' (2005: 3). He goes on to identify four principles of social justice, as follows:

- Equal citizenship – every citizen is entitled to an equal set of rights.
- The social minimum – all citizens must have access to resources that meet essential needs.
- Equality of opportunity – life chances should not be contingent on factors such as gender, class or ethnicity but on motivation and aptitude.
- Fair distribution – distribution of resources can be unequal but this must reflect the contribution that has been made based on talent and effort, and free choices people make about their lives.

Here, social justice is interpreted as being inextricably linked to concepts of equality and fairness in which individuals are seen as having equal minimum rights and opportunity.

Social justice, children and the UNCRC

In the above definition and principles, the terms 'every person' or 'all citizens' are used, and this can be interpreted as including children and young people. It is an interesting exercise, therefore, to reflect on this and consider the extent to which children truly are considered as equal citizens with adults for the purposes of social justice. The immediate objection here may well be that children, particularly younger children, are too immature to fully understand what exercising their rights means, especially if these are coupled with responsibilities, as they are in the above definition. Archard (1993) has summarised this debate by identifying two positions on this issue: the 'caretaker' and 'liberationist' theses. The former takes the view that, due to their developmental immaturity, children should only be afforded rights of protection and provision but not participation; adults should make decisions on their behalf. Liberationists do not believe that this argument is strong enough to deny children participatory and liberty rights, and argue that children should be allowed and encouraged to exercise every possible right as early as possible.

Welch (2008) has charted the development of the notion of children as 'citizens' within the UK. First, she discusses the idea put forward by the 'Think Tank' Demos in 2003 that children should have a vote from birth and that this vote may be used by their parents until the child is deemed old enough to vote independently. While this was something of a radical idea, she presents a critique of this which goes even further. Katz (2003, quoted in Welch, 2008) argues that allowing a parent to vote on behalf of their child would only serve to undermine children's participatory rights, not support them. Instead, he argues strongly for local level consultation with, and real involvement of, children on a range of issues relevant to children: the state of local playgrounds, school dinner menus and so on. In this way, the view of children as 'citizens' is given true meaning as it is translated into action. This approach is supported by Alderson (2003, quoted in Welch, 2008) who states that the idea of proxy voting by parents runs counter to the UNCRC which states, *inter alia*, that children have a right to express a view as soon as they can form one.

Welch (2008) goes on to remind us that 'citizenship' became a statutory element of the National Curriculum in England for high school children in 2002. This focuses on children learning about citizenship and their responsibilities, but not their rights. Scott (2002, quoted in Welch, 2008) has criticised this as tokenistic, arguing that there is a contradiction in children learning about participation without having the opportunity to take part in meaningful decision-making. Taking this example of education further, Jeffs considers the tensions between the notion of children's rights and what he calls the 'authoritarian, repressive and standardised school system' (2002: 55). His central argument is that the two are incompatible: children's rights to be consulted on their whole 'learning experience' (ibid.) are undermined by an approach which values uniformity and testing, and which seems to have no place for children as active citizens. His conclusion is that schools, in their current guise, are 'contemptuous of [children's] opinions [and] the concept of democracy ... if we cannot create schools that respect the rights of children and actively foster democracy then we must not flinch from actively supporting alternatives that do' (ibid.: 57).

EXAMPLE 3.1   Democratic schooling

Apple and Beane (1999) present examples of four schools in the USA which cover the full age range from 6 to 16, and which have successfully constructed democratic and critical educational practices which guide their entire curriculum. Elements of this approach include:

- a curriculum negotiated with staff, parents and children;
- extensive community and child involvement at every stage;
- flexible forms of assessing children's progress;
- a commitment to anti-racist, anti-homophobic and anti-sexist principles;
- a deep concern for social justice.

In one of the schools, the aim is to develop the 'thoughtful person', defined as one who asks the following questions:

- How do you know what you know?
- From whose viewpoint is this being presented?
- How is this event or work connected to others?
- What if things were different?
- Why is this important?

In this school, children study a course entitled 'Justice: Systems of Law and Government' in which the essential questions raised are:

- How is authority justified?
- How are conflicts resolved?
- Are justice, morality and fairness synonymous?

Rights and social exclusion

What is social exclusion?

Walker and Walker provide a definition of social exclusion which distinguishes it from poverty. According to them, social exclusion is a 'dynamic process of being shut out, fully or partially, from any of the social, economic, political or cultural systems which determine the social integration of a person in society' (Walker and Walker, 1997, quoted in Byrne, 2005: 8), Mandipour *et al.* focus on social exclusion as a 'multi-dimensional process, in which various forms of exclusion are combined: participation in decision making and political processes, access to employment and material resources, and integration into common cultural processes' (Mandipour *et al.*, 1998, quoted in Byrne, 2005: 8).

For these writers, social exclusion, then, is a complex process involving the exclusion of some people or groups by the actions of other people or groups.

In a government document concerned with safeguarding children there is recognition of the link between social exclusion and parenting of children:

> Many of the families who seek help for their children, or about whom others raise concerns about a child's welfare, are multiply disadvantaged. These families may face chronic poverty, social isolation, racism, and the problems associated with living in disadvantaged areas, such as high crime rates, poor housing, childcare, transport and education services, and limited employment opportunities. (DfES, 2006: 185–6)

However, what this passage fails to do, perhaps, is to acknowledge that such social exclusion results from the actions of others, including the government in the form of certain social policies which it creates. The assumption within the passage seems to be that social exclusion is an unavoidable element of a neo-liberal society in which, necessarily, there will always be 'winners' and 'losers'.

Social exclusion, children and the UNCRC

We have already seen, in the government document above, one example of the link between social exclusion and children: the former can place constraints and pressures on parents which impact directly on the quality of children's lives. This impact can be long-lasting and significant. The work of Feinstein reminds us that 'high early achievers from disadvantaged backgrounds are overtaken between the ages of five and ten by poor early achievers from advantaged backgrounds' (Feinstein, 2003, quoted in Reed and Robinson, 2005: 285). Furthermore, even where children from disadvantaged backgrounds attend schools with few other children from similar situations, they do no better academically than children from disadvantaged backgrounds who attend schools with a high percentage of children from the same background as themselves (Gibbons *et al.*, 2005). This disadvantage continues into young adulthood, for as one study discovered, those entering work from marginalised groups found that the 'labour market offered insecure poor work with a pattern of benefit dependency both in and out of work' (Johnson *et al.*, 2000, quoted in Byrne, 2005: 104). It appears that social background is the overriding influence upon pupil achievement, employment and life chances. As Byrne says, where societies are unequal, 'social exclusion follows as night follows day' (2005: 114).

> ### EXAMPLE 3.2   Tackling inequality through childcare provision
>
> One way of tackling inequality and social exclusion is illustrated by Paxton *et al.* (2005) who demonstrate how the Scandinavian model for early childcare has managed to meet three complex imperatives:
>
> - sound child development;
> - maternal employment;
> - gender equity.
>
> These have been achieved through the provision of universal, good-quality childcare staffed by well trained, well paid and highly motivated workers. The effect has been to 'break the link between parental social class and income and children's outcomes' (Paxton *et al.*, 2005: 358).

There are several articles of the UNCRC which relate directly to social exclusion. Article 3, for instance, states that:

> In all actions concerning children, whether undertaken by public or private social welfare institutions, courts of law, administrative authorities or legislative bodies, the best interests of the child shall be a primary consideration. (UN, 1989: 3)

The term 'a primary consideration' needs some further discussion here. Clearly, this means that the interests of children are not the only, or the paramount, consideration but one main consideration, possibly to be addressed along with other competing considerations (Freeman, 2002). Perhaps it is this which allows the UK government, in a recent review of child support policy, for example (that is, financial support for children where parents have separated), to maintain as a key focus of the policy revenue income for the Treasury at the expense of improving the quality of children's lives (Green, 2006). Another clear example of this is government approaches that have chosen to maintain a close link between child maintenance (payments coming in from absent parents) and distribution (payments to families). The effect of this is that poor families in particular are penalised. Where an absent parent has been assessed as having to pay a certain level of maintenance, then, if the family is in receipt of state benefits, these benefits can be cut, pound for pound, to match the amount due from the absent parent. If the absent parent then does not pay, the child is left wanting while the parent with whom they are resident enters into lengthy legalistic procedures in an attempt to retrieve the 'missing' money from the absent parent. Green (2006) argues that if these are separated – if the government continued to pay the family direct the amount due, and then pursued the absent parent for the maintenance costs – this would alleviate real hardship for children. Given the close link between poverty and social exclusion, such UK government policy can be said to lead directly to the possibility that an imperative to ensure Treasury revenue overrides the interests of already disadvantaged children and exacerbates social exclusion of this group.

Another example of a contradiction between the best interests of the child, and wider government agendas linked to social exclusion, can be found within the service area of youth justice. Section 34 of the Crime and Disorder Act 1998, applicable to England and Wales, abolished the rebuttable presumption that a child over the age of 10 (but under the age of 14) is *doli incapax* or, literally, incapable of evil. In other words, where before the inception of this Act the prosecution had to prove that a child aged between 10 and 14 knew that what they were doing was wrong, this is no longer the case. The presumption became that the child did know it was wrong: that all 10 year-olds are capable of making such a distinction. This is quite explicitly laid out in the consultation document prior to the Act receiving royal assent, which states in the paragraph introducing this change that 'the Government proposes to reassert responsibility' (Home Office, 1997: 1). In removing this test of the child's moral maturity, which the government describes as archaic, illogical and unfair in practice, the distinction between children and adults is lost when it comes to criminal responsibility. To suggest, as the government does, that these modern changes are designed to ensure that no opportunity is missed to 'reform' the child, that they contribute to the rehabilitation of the child and, therefore, the prevention of reoffending is surely to employ a level of calculated doublespeak which George Orwell would have been proud to demonstrate in his dystopian novel *Nineteen Eighty-Four*. The change may be better understood in terms of pursuing an adult agenda, responding to adult fear of crime by young people and a determination to send a strong message to young people (and the electorate) that those who act outside a set of adult-prescribed socially acceptable norms will be dealt with harshly.

The idea of separate children's rights in this example seems to have been abandoned. As Macauley (2003) suggests, one might have expected the abolition of the *doli incapax* test to coincide with a rise in the age of criminal responsibility, but this is not the case. Muncie rightly points out that, far from bowing to pressure from the United Nations to raise the age of criminal responsibility to bring the United Kingdom in line with Europe, the government, in abolishing the *doli incapax* test, removed, for 10- to 14-year-olds 'an important principle which (in theory at least) acted to protect such children from the full rigour of the criminal law' (1999: 154). Thus, along with one of the lowest ages of criminal responsibility certainly in Europe, the government has, for England and Wales, reduced the safeguards for children caught up in the criminal justice system.

In taking this harsh line with young children who offend, the UK seems to be reinforcing the social exclusion of this group. Muncie (2004, quoted in Moss, 2008) demonstrates that severe punishment, including the use of secure placements, is ineffective in reducing reoffending rates, with these being between 70 and 80 per cent. As Moss concludes, perhaps the reason why the government persists with harsh punishments in the face of evidence that this clearly does not work is to reinforce to the wider society what is acceptable and unacceptable behaviour, and that this function of the system is perceived to be more important than true support and rehabilitation of children who offend and the upholding of their rights, which could be said truly to be in their best interests. As Muncie puts it, this 'reforming zeal' of the, then, New Labour government had led directly to children's rights being not only ignored, but 'explicitly undermined' (2002: 94).

A further potential clash between UK law and the UNCRC related to social exclusion, social justice and children's rights can be located within another initiative in section 1 of the Crime and Disorder Act 1998, that of the Anti-Social Behaviour Order (ASBO). These were introduced to tackle behaviour which '*caused or was likely to cause harassment, alarm or distress*'. The local authority or the police may make an application for an ASBO with respect to any person aged 10 or over. If approved, the order prohibits the named person from doing anything prescribed in the order. While being subject to an ASBO itself is not a criminal offence, breach of it is. ASBOs last for a minimum of two years and breaching it can lead to a fine or imprisonment. For young people aged 12 to 14, the latter can mean a secure training order; for 15- to 18-year-olds it could lead to a six-month custodial sentence. Furthermore, young people's personal details, including their photograph, can be widely circulated within a community along with a telephone number for members of the public to ring if they see the named person taking part in any of the prohibited activities.

Article 16 of the UNCRC states that:

> No child shall be subjected to arbitrary or unlawful interference with his or her privacy, family, home or correspondence, nor to unlawful attacks on his or her honour and reputation. (UN, 1989: 6)

While the UK government may adhere to the letter of this, in that by introducing the Crime and Disorder Act they have made lawful the use of ASBOs, it could be argued that they have undermined the spirit of this Article. By allowing the 'naming and shaming' of children subject to ASBOs, the government has also allowed children to be exposed to stigma, labelling and, possibly, even verbal and physical attacks. This must run counter to the spirit of Article 16, particularly when one bears in mind that the UK government refused to raise the age of criminal responsibility, so that children as young as 10 can be subject to such exposure.

For professionals working in the related fields of youth justice, youth work and social care, the state of affairs described here presents some serious challenges. An immediate one may be that while such workers want to see young people as capable, responsible and self-determining, they will also want to resist a call for such young people to face the consequences of their actions in the same way as adults are expected to do. The tightrope that workers may

need to negotiate is encouraging young people to be active, sentient participants in their own destiny while at the same time recognising that young
people may lack the experience or maturity, perhaps, to think through the
consequences of some of their actions. The key challenge here, therefore, is
how to encourage self-determination among young people without becoming
compliant in a culture which demands that young people face the full force
of adult law if their decisions cause them to fall foul of the justice system.

In healthcare, it is possible to find examples where professionals seem to
have struck the right balance between upholding children's rights to express
and follow through a wish in relation their treatment, and recognition that
some children's understanding of the complexities of their situation may be
limited. Alderson (2002a) demonstrates how very young children can participate actively in serious decision-making regarding their medical treatment
(see Example 3.3).

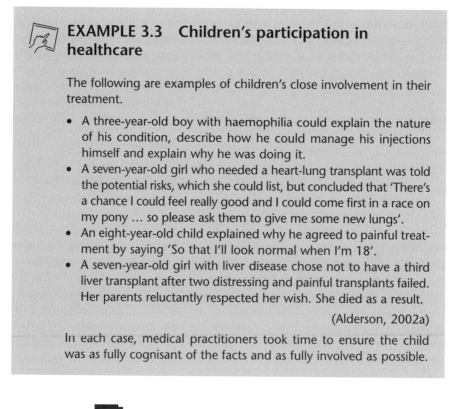

EXAMPLE 3.3   Children's participation in healthcare

The following are examples of children's close involvement in their
treatment.

- A three-year-old boy with haemophilia could explain the nature
  of his condition, describe how he could manage his injections
  himself and explain why he was doing it.
- A seven-year-old girl who needed a heart-lung transplant was told
  the potential risks, which she could list, but concluded that 'There's
  a chance I could feel really good and I could come first in a race on
  my pony … so please ask them to give me some new lungs'.
- An eight-year-old child explained why he agreed to painful treatment by saying 'So that I'll look normal when I'm 18'.
- A seven-year-old girl with liver disease chose not to have a third
  liver transplant after two distressing and painful transplants failed.
  Her parents reluctantly respected her wish. She died as a result.

(Alderson, 2002a)

In each case, medical practitioners took time to ensure the child
was as fully cognisant of the facts and as fully involved as possible.

Summary

The key issues to emerge from this chapter are as follows:

- how children's rights relate to the concepts of social justice and social
  exclusion;

- how the terms and concepts relate to areas such as equality and fair access to resources and services in areas such as youth justice or education;
- how concepts of social exclusion and justice can help understand tensions between legislation, policy and practice at national and local levels;
- how particular approaches to working with children in different settings can assist in achieving social justice and reduce the social exclusion of children.

Question 3.1   How might social justice and social exclusion be defined?

Review Activity

1 Think about your own setting. Are there examples where:

   (a) Children might not experience equal minimum rights and opportunity compared to adults?
   (b) Children are excluded from key processes in the setting, for instance in decision-making?

Question 3.2   Why are social justice and social exclusion important in understanding child rights?

Review Activity

1 Look again at the example of democratic schooling in this chapter.

   (a) What do you think are the strengths in this model of democratic schooling?
   (b) What might some of the challenges be in trying to implement it?
   (c) How might this model contribute to social justice in the long term?

2 Now look at the example of tackling inequality through childcare provision and consider the following.

   (a) Why do you think it is important to have childcare workers who are skilled, well paid and motivated?
   (b) What messages about the status of children might the provision of universal, high-quality childcare send to the wider society?

〰 **Question 3.3   How can practice with children address injustice and exclusion?**

Review Activity

1   Consider the example of children's participation in healthcare: adults took care to involve children as fully as possible in decisions and actions that affected the children.

   (a) What do these examples illustrate about the ability of children to participate in decisions about their lives?
   (b) What specific capabilities are being exhibited by the children here?
   (c) What lessons could the current criminal justice system in England learn from these examples? You might want to consider how the children in these examples were consulted about their futures in a meaningful way which took account both of their current levels of ability and maturity, and of their rights to be involved in decisions affecting their well-being.

Further Reading 📖

Franklin, B. (ed.) (2002) *The New Handbook of Children's Rights: Comparative Policy and Practice.* London: Routledge.

Something of a classic text now, this book contains rich and deep material on children's rights with sections on the law, case studies illustrating pertinent issues and encouraging children's voices, and a good range of international perspectives.

Hallett, C. and Prout, A. (eds) (2003) *Hearing the Voices of Children: Social Policy for a New Century.* London: RoutledgeFalmer.

This edited volume contains wide-ranging and challenging chapters covering issues related to children's participation across the following themes: enabling children's voices to be heard, the social policy context, children's services and resources for children. In doing so, it takes an international perspective to present a broad and thoughtful contribution to the field of child rights.

Archard, D. (2009) 'Every child's rights matter', in K. Broadhurst, C. Grover and J. Jamieson (eds), *Critical Perspectives on Safeguarding Children.* Chichester: Wiley-Blackwell.

The focus of this chapter within a thoughtful and erudite volume is on the extent to which the commitments of the UNCRC are present within the *Every Child Matters* agenda. It discusses some contradictions and tensions between the latter and a rights-based approach.

Participation and Provision across Disciplines: Child Rights for, and by, Children

Phil Jones

Chapter Overview

This chapter looks at child rights from the perspective of children. It concerns itself with children's knowledge of, and insights into, their rights. This is included in order to deepen the book's understanding of rights and to ensure the primacy of children's voices in our treatment of rights. The chapter aims to enable readers to gain the perspective of children in relation to our understanding of rights and their implications for living and working with children. These accounts will also be considered in terms of debates such as how children gain access to their understanding of rights, to information on rights and how this affects children's capacity to act on their rights. The chapter will consider how to source or develop materials to enable children to be aware of their rights. This will include issues concerning different ways of communicating and understanding, taking into account factors such as age, capacity or the potential of non-verbal language. The chapter will consider how information relates to *action* on rights in different areas of children's lives. This aspect of the chapter will draw on what can be learned from the experiences children and adults have had in different areas of provision. The chapter will explore children's perceptions, opinions and ideas about rights. It will examine some of the ways in which approaches to participation have enabled such perspectives to emerge.

Children's perspectives on rights

Recent ideas and practices can be seen to form a particular framework in engaging with children's perspectives on rights. Information for children about rights, and how to connect this to actual action, is seen as crucial in enabling child rights to become a reality. Attention has been given to children not only being made *aware* of the rights they have, but on encouraging them to be *active in claiming* their rights. In its review of twenty years of the UNCRC, Unicef sees this crucial aspect of the future of child rights in terms of empowerment:

> Children themselves ... must also participate in social progress. As the holders of the rights stipulated in the Convention, it is imperative that children know and understand their rights and are empowered to claim them. The Convention should be taught in schools, so that children can be advocates for themselves. Children also have responsibilities to other children under the Convention: learning about their own rights entails recognizing the rights of others. (Unicef, 2009: 70)

An emerging aspect of this area involves the inclusion of children's opinions and ideas about their rights. Rather than adults alone 'holding' and defining what rights children can have, children and young people are becoming involved in defining rights from their own perspectives. This chapter's approach will look at children's perspectives on rights within this framework: highlighting the importance of the relationship between *awareness or knowledge, action* and *children's development of their own opinions and ideas*. Communicating rights is not just about information and understanding: as the following sections will show, it is also about connecting knowledge with action and participation.

Working with children to develop their knowledge, understanding and ownership of rights

Until recently, the development of conventions such as the UNCRC and related laws policies or practices were all created by adults. There was no input from those whose lives were supposedly the focus of the rights being created, debated or acted on: children. In part, this related to the historical and cultural positioning of childhood within many societies. This perspective concerned issues such as the stereotyping of children as 'incapable', and assumptions that the best interests of children were serviced by adult decisions based on adult opinions and adult perceptions of children's position and needs (Alderson, 2000; Jones *et al.*, 2008). The neglect of children's perspectives has come about as a result of particular social constructions that estimated them as incapable of producing relevant, reliable or representative evidence (Mills, 2004: 31). This attitude is still at work within many aspects of different societies. For example, some organisations still speak of children's rights purely in terms of adult actions and responsibilities for ensuring rights are acted on, or talk of children's and parents' rights as if they are the same thing. The emergent position is one that sees children as being active in defining and acting on their rights. Adults and children, together, develop ideas and practices that concern rights.

Developing awareness of rights: new attitudes towards knowledge and capability

This position, of adults and children working together, reflects the fact that children, as they are born and develop, do so within structures such as families or communities and societies. A part of the role of these frameworks is often perceived as a benevolent negotiation between child and adult in relation to factors such as the extent and nature of care, and representation of the child's interests and education. An aspect of this negotiation concerns the ways adults and children handle the extent to which a child needs others to be in a relationship with them in areas such as care, protection, development, nurturing and learning as they inhabit the world around them. This process is described and understood in a variety of ways by different aspects of society. Adult psychologists often see this in terms of developmental processes, for example; parents might see this in terms of changes in care, love, mutuality or independence, while medical practitioners or lawyers might see this in terms of capacity or maturity in relation to areas such as decision-making or consent. Children might see this in terms of what they can and can't do, the opportunities and frustrations they encounter in the world they make for themselves and the world adults make for them. In many societies this relationship is bound by different traditions and transitions, usually created by adults for children. These traditions concern arenas such as the law, education, parental and familial assumptions, or regulations about how adults and children conduct their lives both in the micro world of family and the macro world of society (Franklin, 2002). These existing traditions are subject to challenge and change. The past fifty years have seen changes in many countries in traditional attitudes towards children's lives, for example, in pressures to include children differently, or to give them access to decision-making processes (Freeman, 2000). This involves children having a voice in what happens to them in areas such as medicine, education and family life.

The creation of access to information for children is seen as a key part of this. Access to *knowledge* – what rights mean and how they are available to children – has been the concern of much effort. Save the Children, for example, places the teaching of rights as a central aspect of education:

> Teaching about rights can be incorporated into learning across the curriculum. In broad terms, the UNCRC enshrines the following guiding principles for all children and young people in the UK:

- they have rights
- they have the right to be informed about their rights
- they should be given opportunities to exercise their rights
- they should be given opportunities to uphold their rights
- they should be given opportunities to advocate about rights.

(Save the Children, 2006: 7)

A parallel but separate aspect of this concerns the ways in which children can *act* on their rights and how adults respect and respond to their actions. Unicef links rights and responsibilities by saying that, though many of the rights in the UNCRC have to be provided by adults or the state, the Convention refers to the responsibilities of children in relation to rights:

- Children need to respect each others' rights.
- As the UNCRC says that children have a right to be protected from conflict, cruelty, exploitation and neglect, then children have a responsibility not to bully or harm each other.
- If children have a right to a clean environment, then they also have a responsibility to do what they can to look after the environment.
- Children's right to education is connected to an 'obligation' to learn and share their knowledge and experience with others.
- The right to a full life is connected to being responsible to others, for example those experiencing discrimination, to enjoy this right.
- Rights to freedom of thought, conscience and religion are connected to the responsibility to respect others' thoughts or religious beliefs.

(Unicef, 1989)

Children's knowledge and ownership of their rights

Research has revealed very different levels of *knowledge* of rights in different countries. In Norway, for example, a survey showed that children were aware of their rights from a variety of sources and indicated that organisations such as schools were active in ensuring awareness (Sandbaek and Einarsson, 2008). Research has revealed a much poorer level of awareness in the UK. Nearly twenty years after the UNCRC, the Children's Rights Alliance surveyed children's knowledge of rights and reported that the 'majority of respondents said they knew very little about the UNCRC' and of those that had '82% had not received this information through their school' (CRAE, 2008: 17–18). Clearly work needs to be done in the UK to enable access to information.

There are information sources for children, such as the 'Rights 4 Me' interactive website (http://www.rights4me.org). However, information is not enough on its own. Research into children's participation in areas such as social care meetings about their lives, or regarding what they think of the services and provision they receive, commonly report finding barriers to children acting on their rights. Enquiry often shows that though children 'consider it their right to see and be seen, to hear and be heard' in matters that affect them, they often:

- find the experience uncomfortable;
- feel ill prepared or unskilled about how to participate (for example, when and how to speak and how to be involved); and that
- when they give views or experiences they are listened to but their views are not acted on by adults.

(Lupton and Nixon, 1999; Thomas and O'Kane, 1999)

Information given to children about their rights may *contradict* positions in UK law where it does not follow the UNCRC, or the beliefs of their parents. An example of this is where information on child rights gives a child information about a UNCRC right which the UK government has refused them concerning not being smacked by their parents (see page 63–4). The discussion below includes examples of work which not only enable knowledge through information on rights, but give ideas for developing an understanding of a right and how it relates to taking action. They give children and adults ideas about how to create opportunities for change together.

One part of this is the creation of information that is accessible to children. Other aspects concern how to develop activities and ways of working that enhance children's understanding, their ownership of their rights and their capacities for action. Organisations such as the Child Rights Alliance (CRAE) or the Children's Rights and Advocacy Organisation (CROA: http://www.croa. org.uk) produce advice and working packs such as the 'Total Respect Training Pack' (CRAE) in order to increase children's and young people's effective participation in decision-making. These address issues such as communication skills for working with children and young people. *Children and Decision Making: Toolbox and Training Pack (*Thomas *et al.*, 1999) focuses on looked-after children's participation in decision-making. The pack includes a summary of the research, tools for direct work with children, training materials and a guide for use (Children in Wales: http://www.childreninwales.org.uk).

Other examples of this approach are *Decide and Do: Involving Younger Children in Decisions about Their Care* (Foster, 2000), a booklet designed to help practitioners develop and create opportunities for looked-after children under 12 years of age to participate in decisions affecting them, or *My Turn to Talk* (Lanyon and Sinclair, 2005), a guide for helping young people in care, aged 11 or under, to have a say in how they are looked after. These focus on decision-making, education plans, reviews and children's rights and can be used by children on their own or while working alongside practitioners. Organisations such as Unicef, for example, promote awareness of rights in schools. This is done within existing educational frameworks and approaches and the move from information to action is advocated in a particular direction. For more on this go to the Unicef website at http://www.unicef.org.uk/tz/resources.

What has been learned about communicating rights to children? Factors in this area concern responses to the kinds of 'barrier phenomena' identified above. They include:

- knowledge about rights involving a process to aid understanding rather than a list or learning by rote approach;
- the importance of developing a relationship with children to support their gaining knowledge;
- using a child-centred approach that recognises factors such as an individual child's capacities in understanding;
- the different languages that can be employed in communicating, taking into account factors such as age or issues such as concentration span and memory that may need to be considered in relation to differences such as learning disability.

An effective example of this is the *Convention on the Rights of the Child: Activity Book* (Willow, 2006), with material designed for young children such as picture activities to explore and express rights, matching images and rights statements, and picking a right and designing a superhero that has powers to make such right a reality. Images and text are used to help a child to see what they are entitled to in their home. This is an interesting example of the relationship between *knowledge* and *action* as the booklet gives a child information about aspects of the UNCRC which have not been implemented into UK law, for example, regarding smacking:

> Your family: the rights in the Convention on the Rights of the Child apply to you in your family. This includes the right to be heard and the right to be protected from all forms of violence (including 'smacking'). (Willow, 2006: 8)

Here the role of information is to familiarise a child with a right that the UNCRC says they should be entitled to, but which the UK government does not give them and which their family is not legally required to observe. The booklet suggests that an adult may assist in the reading of this book, and the information it contains is likely to help a child understand why they will not be subject to violence within a household that does not contain parents who smack. If it is read by an adult to a child within a home that does contain violence through smacking, then the information may be a catalyst for the child to ask questions and the parent to have to find a way to explain to their daughter or son why they are choosing to live with their child in a way that contravenes the UNCRC.

Publications such as *Get Ready for Change* (Gollub and Krapf, 2007), written with elementary and primary school age children in mind, contains projects and lessons designed to support teaching children's rights to this age group. The way their approach is structured is a common one and can be useful in considering how to approach this area of work. They define the conceptual framework that informs the projects and lessons as based in the process of learning *about*, *through* and *for* children's rights. Learning 'about' rights concerns students *knowing and understanding* what rights they have. The concept of learning 'through' rights concerns ensuring that students *can experience child rights* as principles that govern the classroom and the school as a community, while learning 'for' rights concerns encouraging children to *make use of their rights in their school life*. This is seen as 'training' for future roles as 'informed and active citizens in democratic community'. This concerns teachers, parents and children working together.

Rights need not be communicated in a 'one size fits all' manner. Research has revealed the usefulness of communicating rights in additional ways that enable children to respond to the differences they encounter in their lives. These might concern aspects of their lives in terms of gender, race, disability or sexuality. These do not supplant a general familiarity with rights, but rather seek to communicate the ways in which rights relate to different arenas of children's lives. This does not mean, for example, that communicating about rights in relation to disability is only of relevance to disabled children, but that all children may see the ways that rights relate to difference. This perspective also means that specific differences such as the ways in which rights relate to disabled children may, in particular, be of interest to them.

Children's ownership and action

Other differences in knowledge and action relate to *contexts*. Different aspects of rights may need to be communicated to children in different contexts, for example in relation to medical care, education or within legal contexts. This means that different areas of provision have commonalities, but that they may also have areas of rights that are foregrounded or are specific to their services. Hence in any consideration of children's knowledge and use of rights, it is important to consider context.

Research has revealed the importance of adults taking into account different modes of communication depending on context. A 'difference' here might mean that the specific application of child rights in hospitals may be different from the way they are applied in schools. However, additional factors may concern the different ways in which a child's needs in relation to communication are best met in the context. So, for example, feelings such as anxiety or power dynamics in terms of children's perceptions of their own status in relationship to adults such as nurses or doctors may need to be taken into account when looking at how children are involved in communication and action in relation to their rights in hospital. Here knowledge and action about rights is not seen as a piece of paper or an act but as a process which acknowledges the complexities and contexts of communication. Factors here might, for example, include whether a child is used to asking questions or asserting their views over those of an adult. Bishton reports of work using a variety of methods to communicate with children, enabling them to find a voice in ways that words alone would not have permitted. Diamond ranking, images and photographs, for example, are used. While they were taking photographs the interviewer asked children to indicate whether the object they were taking a photograph of was liked or disliked, and the interviewer made field notes of any other explanation the children gave of the photographs they were taking (Bishton, 2007: 7):

> Jessica expressed one clear dislike through all three methods. She said she disliked playing outside when it rained, in the thunder and clouds in the interview and diamond ranking; she also took a photograph of the outside playground in the rain. The other dislike that she revealed through the photograph taking and verbally explained to me while taking it was connected to another child in her class. Jessica took a photograph of Billy's chair and said she disliked having to sit next to him because he sometimes hurt her. (Bishton, 2007: 11)

Other examples of this include *Assert Yourself* (http://www.voiceuk.org.uk/publications.htm) concerning sexual abuse and the law for young people under 16 years of age with a learning disability. *Assert Yourself* is a DVD and booklet involving actors with learning disabilities performing work with an aim to encourage those with learning disabilities to be 'more assertive'. The importance here lies not in paying lip service to the idea of rights, but on communication reflecting the need to engage in a way that is meaningful to the child and which is truthful in the way it reflects organisational philosophies and practices.

Children's own ideas about rights

One important aspect of child rights concerns the ways that ideas and practices have begun to result not only in children being informed of their rights and how to act on them, but in them *developing their own views and ideas* about existing rights and their perspective on developing new rights. May has identified a need to broaden adult responses that involves moving from a position where child rights are conferred by adults to one where, if possible, children are empowered to be agents in their own lives:

> Ultimately the publications empower practitioners to ascertain, manage and represent pupils' voice, rather than encouraging practitioners to empower the pupils themselves. (May, 2005: 30)

The encouragement is to enable children to voice their experiences and opinions about the nature and application of rights, as well as to identify how children's critiques of rights can be developed to see existing rights differently or to develop new rights.

On the Get Ready for Change website there are examples of children's experiences and opinions (CRAE: http://www.getreadyforchange.org.uk/your-say/

archive/debate_1_whats_going_on_in_your_school/). They talk about their involvement in youth parliaments and student councils, and their experiences reflect children's ways of looking at rights and their communications about rights. Some argue that this perspective differs from that of adults, and that there is value in engaging with this emerging set of views. By 2010, for example, Ofsted had involved children in an exercise giving their opinions on rights in a way that included the opportunity for children to define new rights or areas of rights that needed different interpretations. This initiative engaged 1,834 children from a variety of different contexts – those attending a national children's conference, care services, residential schools and colleges. As referred to in Chapter 1, the report on the work stated that it positioned rights for children and young people as 'something you should always be able to do, to have, to know, to say or to be protected from' (Ofsted, 2010). Children voted on rights drawn from three sources: aspects of the UK's Human Rights Act relating to children; from the United Nations Convention on the Rights of the Child; and a list of ten 'extra things' that other children and young people had suggested should be made into rights for all children. The inclusion of the ten 'extra things' is reflective of the developments mentioned at the start of this section – where children and young people's own ideas are included alongside the adult-formed rights of the UK Human Rights Act and the UNCRC. The report identifies the following as examples of children and young people's own ideas about rights:

- 'Not to be bullied'
- 'To keep in touch with my parents, grandparents, brothers and sisters if I want to and they want to, wherever we all live'
- 'To enjoy myself now, as well as to prepare for the future'
- 'To be told about my past life if and when I wish to know'
- 'To be treated as an individual, not as one of a group of children'
- 'To make and keep my own friends'
- 'To make decisions for myself if I understand enough, whatever age I am'
- 'To do hobbies I want to do'

(Ofsted, 2010: 19)

In the light of the idea that children can have different perspectives on rights than adults, the report draws an interesting conclusion:

> The list clearly shows that some rights that are not already in the Human Rights Act or the United Nations Convention on the Rights of the Child, but have been suggested by children themselves in the past, are seen by children in our survey as more important than some of the Human Rights Act or Convention rights. (Ofsted, 2010: 19)

As an illustration of the ways in which knowledge and action can be accompanied by or followed by children developing new perspectives on their rights, Youth Rights UK has developed a *manifesto*. The organisation states its aims as including the provision of a commentary about matters affecting the rights of young people in the UK. Areas with which it is concerned relate to social justice, policing and surveillance in schools. Its website identifies the following:

> The tendency to always seek authoritarian solutions to social problems. For example new legislation that enables head teachers to issue fines to parents whose children do not attend school and imprisoning parents for failing to compel their children to attend school.
>
> The trend towards accepting surveillance as an everyday part of life; for example finger-printing systems used in schools for checking the register, and use of drug testing and sniffer dogs in schools. Surveillance de-personalises relationships and should not be an ordinary part of everyday life.
>
> Use of drugs to control hyperactive children. Understanding and time, not adult convenience and drug company profit should be the response to these children.
>
> We aim to challenge the excesses of power used against children and young people by accurate reporting of the facts, by argument and by protest. Currently we believe that protest should be within the law.
>
> (http://www.youth-rights-uk.org/manifesto.shtml)

Here is a clear example of the agenda being developed by children and young people, and of their taking debate, views and the advocacy of needed change into their own hands. The initiative aims at change, but from a young person's perspective – a statement of rights and action with new developments from their own view point.

Do adults limit how children see their rights?

One of the key ways in which child rights have been discussed and reflected in the content of this chapter concerns children being made aware of their rights and responsibilities. The emphasis here is upon communicating to children, enabling them to be aware of their rights. This is a major cultural shift. Information to date indicates that progress is both slow and resisted by some individuals and groups as well as by cultural attitudes towards children. However, some argue that information and access to participation in terms of rights is not enough on its own. This will not alter the lives of children enough in order to improve their situation and experience. One of the key challenges to the idea that information and participation is enough asserts that rights must be accompanied by major changes in the way society engages with children – a sea change of substantial proportions. The following text provides a way in to this debate. It comes from *Righting the Wrongs: The Reality of Children's Rights in Wales.*

> The necessary step-change in culture implied by UNCRC incorporation is even greater, and more complex, than that involved in ECHR incorporation ... Whether the current view is of childhood as a state of immanence, vulnerability, unruliness or innocence, it needs to change or at least develop to embrace the concept of children as rights holders whose rights must be respected and supported by the state in all its legislative, administrative and judicial manifestations. Such a change involves not only far greater support than ever before for children's participation in decision making on matters affecting them, but also a different approach to provision and protection. The potential of this latter aspect is captured with beguiling simplicity in a phrase used by the authors of a recent appraisal of 40 years of child and family policy in England and Wales: 'Children's rights as the acceptable face of redistribution'. The significance of such a change is hard to overstate. (Save the Children, 2009)

Here child rights are connected with wider ideas about children's position in society. Further discussion of this relationship can be found in Chapter 3. The ways in which children are encouraged to think about rights in the different spheres of their lives is important in this 'step-change in culture'. Those who seek or facilitate children's own opinions and perspectives on rights have agendas of their own: what are adult agendas? Some areas of rights are more comfortable for our society to attend to than others. So, in the current move towards children claiming rights, it is interesting to analyse where areas of comfort or discomfort are: where adults or adult organisations encourage child rights and where they do so reluctantly, or do not do so at all. Government initiatives and aspects of the voluntary sector seem to be far happier talking about children's rights in their communities or the services that provide them, but are much less at ease (and hence given less funding) encouraging children to be aware of rights in their families and how to take up a rights-informed approach in their dealing with their parents. In much literature child and family interests and rights are allied – as if they are the same: it seems to be both tougher and taboo to raise issues concerning children's rights within their family life, or how parents respect their children's rights (Jones and Welch, 2010). So, while there is an ever-expanding literature on how professionals should work with children in relation to their rights, often funded or initiated by government agencies, the arena of most influence on a child, that of the family, is often given a wide berth in government literature. This connects with a number of socially and politically complex areas, for example the extent to which the government can be seen by its potential voters to intervene in family life and the nature of that intervention (Frost, 2011). While it is now permissible within general cultural terms for a government to assert the need for education, there is unease about the extent to which a government can intervene in the home in relation to child rights (Welch, 2008). Similarly, though attention is given to areas such as gender and race, the discomfort that society presents in relation to children and young people's sexuality is less often mentioned (see Chapter 1 for more discussion of this area).

Summary

This chapter has considered how to source or develop materials to help children become aware of their rights, including issues concerning different ways of communicating and understanding, taking into account factors such as age, capacity and the potential of non-verbal language. It has considered how information relates to *action* on rights in different areas of children's lives, drawing on what can be learned from the experiences children and adults have had in different areas of provision. The chapter reviewed some of the perspectives which are emerging from children themselves, and explored children's perceptions, opinions and ideas about rights. It has included a discussion of effective approaches to participation which have enabled such perspectives to emerge.

Question 4.1   How are children made aware of their rights?

Review Activity

Consider the chapter's discussion about the relationship between *knowledge*, *understanding* and *action*, and the idea that 'communicating rights is not just about information and understanding … it is also about connecting knowledge with action and participation'.

1 Reflect on the ways in which children's knowledge of rights might be helped in your setting.
2 How might children be helped to make connections between knowledge and taking action in some of the ways adults work with children?
3 Consider the chapter's discussion of 'rights' and 'responsibilities'.

   (a) What are your views about the relationship between rights and responsibilities?
   (b) How would you introduce ways of enabling children to understand, and action, their rights into your work with children?

Question 4.2   How do rights relate to action in different contexts?

Review Activity

The chapter considered that: 'A "difference" here might mean that the specific application of child rights in hospitals may be different from the way they are applied in schools. However, additional

factors may concern the different ways in which a child's needs in relation to communication are best met in the context.'
Look again at Table 2.1 in Chapter 2.

1 How might you enable the children you are working with to become familiar with the rights in this table in a way that reflects their life in your setting?
2 Could you involve the children in thinking about the ways in which a right relates to their experience of the service?
3 The chapter gave examples of ways of engaging with rights that used a variety of strategies to connect with children's interests or ways of understanding, for example 'picture activities to explore and express rights, matching images and rights statements, picking a right and designing a superhero that had powers to make rights a reality'. How might you use different modes of communication to help children's awareness and understanding?

Question 4.3   What perspectives are emerging from children themselves?

Review Activity

1 Review the content of the chapter and identify examples of 'the agenda being developed by children and young people, and of their taking debate, views and the advocacy of needed change into their own hands and drawing on their own perceptions.'
2 How could you introduce these perceptions of rights into your work with children:

   (a) in relation to how you work with children?
   (b) in relation to children's awareness of their rights?

3 How could you help children reflect on, or debate, new areas of rights and responsibilities?

Further Reading

May, H. (2005) 'Whose participation is it anyway? Examining the context of pupil participation in the UK', *British Journal of Special Education*, 32 (1): 29–34.
A thorough overview of developments in children and young people's participation, with a clear review of difficulties which have been encountered, along with ideas and reflections on ways of working, including how organisational dynamics and processes relate to effective work.

NSPCC (1997) *Turning Points: A Resource Pack for Communicating with Children*. London: NSPCC.
A thorough and useful guide that examines ways of redressing adult orientated means of communication in work between adults and children, offering ideas that place the power of communication more in the child's hands. It includes ideas for children for whom verbal language is not the most effective way of communicating, as well as useful reflections on the importance of taking context into account.

Sinclair, R. (2004) 'Participation in practice: making it meaningful, effective and sustainable', *Children and Society*, 18: 106–18.
An effective analysis of initiatives in participation, containing research-based reviews of practice. This is of use in understanding why work concerning issues such as the role of adults can be useful and effective as well as understanding what can occur to hinder effective participation.

Treseder, P. (1997) *Empowering Children and Young People: Training Manual, Promoting Involvement in Decision-making*. London: Children's Rights Office and Save the Children.
A useful, practical guide with a number of valid and effective ideas which are applicable in many contexts. It gives ideas about activities, how to prepare and how to evaluate work.

Safeguarding and Protection: What Does a Rights-Based Approach Mean across Different Disciplines?

Gary Walker

Chapter Overview

This chapter will examine the relationship between ideas and practices concerning safeguarding children and a 'rights'-based approach to working with children. The chapter will draw on the experiences of specific disciplines such as teaching and social work, while also looking at rights-based issues from an interdisciplinary perspective. Contemporary developments in policy and legislation will be reviewed in relation to different areas of children's lives concerning their relationship to safeguarding and protection. The relationship between national legislation, policy, practical guidance and the meaning of a rights-based perspective in actual practice with children will be explored. The lived experience of workers and children will be examined in an effort to elucidate some implications of this complex relationship between 'safeguarding' and 'rights'.

What is safeguarding children?

The term 'safeguarding' first began to emerge in around 2003, when the then New Labour government introduced the *Every Child Matters* programme (DfES, 2003). One key aspect of this was a new emphasis on the idea of prevention: rather than waiting for a family crisis to occur and responding only to acute incidents of serious harm, professionals were now expected to step in early in the affairs of families to prevent any crisis from happening in the first place. A way to express this shift in expectation was to change the language that professionals were expected to use – away from 'child protection' towards the use of 'safeguarding children' and 'promoting their welfare'. One palpable example of the imposition of this new approach was that one key existing multi-agency structure for coordinating child protection activity at the local level – Area Child Protection Committees – was replaced by a new body – Local Safeguarding Children Boards – with wider powers and responsibilities.

Revised national guidance for all agencies coming into contact with children, *Working Together to Safeguard Children* (DfES, 2006), provided a full definition of 'safeguarding' by explaining its four elements as follows:

- Protecting children from maltreatment.
- Preventing impairment of children's health or development.
- Ensuring that children are growing up in circumstances consistent with the provision of safe and effective care.
- Professionals undertaking their role to enable children to have optimum life chances and to enter adulthood successfully.

What was commonly called 'child protection' was now conceptualised as only one part of a wider remit of safeguarding and promoting the welfare of children. The guidance went on to say that children need protecting when they are suffering, or likely to suffer, 'significant harm' and the harm is attributable to a lack of adequate parental care or control. Updated guidance published some four years later (DCSF, 2010) retained these precise definitions, but extended the basis for judging what constitutes 'significant' harm. Accepting that is impossible to set absolute criteria for 'significant' harm, the guidance states that in reaching decisions, consideration should be given to the:

- degree and extent of harm;
- duration of harm;
- frequency of harm;
- extent of premeditation;
- presence or degree of threat, coercion, sadism and bizarre or unusual elements.

This concept of 'significant' harm was first introduced in a major piece of childcare legislation, the Children Act 1989. It was designed to reflect an ideology about family life and indeed children's rights which was at direct odds with the new emphasis upon early intervention and support for children and families. Developed by the New Right Conservatives, the Children Act 1989 articulated the view that parents had the right to bring children up as they wished, and the state (in the form of professionals) had no right to intervene, unless children were at risk of 'significant' harm. Therefore, while the basic presumption in approach to child welfare has changed dramatically (from *laissez faire* to interventionist) the underpinning threshold for statutory involvement by agencies remains actual or likely 'significant' harm to the child.

Within this concept of 'significant' harm, the national guidance *Working Together to Safeguard Children* provided descriptors for the four categories of abuse which all agencies were to use in classifying any 'significant' harm which they might encounter. The details of these descriptors have changed over time, from the first version of the national guidance published in 1991 to the 2010 version, for example. These changes seem to reflect prevailing notions of which experiences are harmful to children. The 2010 versions of these descriptors are given in the following sections.

Physical abuse

Physical abuse may involve hitting, shaking, throwing, poisoning, burning or scalding, drowning, suffocating, or otherwise causing physical harm to a child. Physical harm may also be caused when a parent or carer fabricates the symptoms of, or deliberately induces, illness in a child.

Emotional abuse

Emotional abuse is the persistent emotional maltreatment of a child such as to cause severe and persistent adverse effects on the child's emotional development. It may involve conveying to children that they are worthless or unloved, inadequate, or valued only insofar as they meet the needs of another person. It may include not giving the child opportunities to express their views, deliberately silencing them or 'making fun' of what they say or how they communicate. It may feature age or developmentally inappropriate expectations being imposed on children. These may include interactions that are beyond the child's developmental capability, as well as overprotection and limitation of exploration and learning, or preventing the child participating in normal social interaction. It may involve seeing or hearing the ill-treatment of another. It may involve serious bullying (including cyberbullying), causing children frequently to feel frightened or in danger, or the exploitation or corruption of children. Some level of emotional abuse is involved in all types of maltreatment of a child, though it may occur alone.

Sexual abuse

Sexual abuse involves forcing or enticing a child or young person to take part in sexual activities, not necessarily involving a high level of violence, whether or not the child is aware of what is happening. The activities may involve physical contact, including assault by penetration (for example, rape or oral sex) or non-penetrative acts such as masturbation, kissing, rubbing and touching outside of clothing. They may also include non-contact activities, such as involving children in looking at, or in the production of, sexual images, watching sexual activities, encouraging children to behave in sexually inappropriate ways, or grooming a child in preparation for abuse (including via the Internet). Sexual abuse is not solely perpetrated by adult males. Women can also commit acts of sexual abuse, as can other children.

Neglect

Neglect is the persistent failure to meet a child's basic physical and/or psychological needs, likely to result in the serious impairment of the child's health or development. Neglect may occur during pregnancy as a result of maternal substance abuse. Once a child is born, neglect may involve a parent or carer failing to:

- provide adequate food, clothing and shelter (including exclusion from home or abandonment);
- protect a child from physical and emotional harm or danger;
- ensure adequate supervision (including the use of inadequate care-givers); or
- ensure access to appropriate medical care or treatment.

It may also include neglect of, or unresponsiveness to, a child's basic emotional needs.

(DCSF, 2010: 38–9)

The inherent complexities and tensions that arise out of these definitions for a range or professionals will be explored in the sections that now follow.

Safeguarding and children's rights

At first sight, it may seem odd that any notion of safeguarding would not have at its core a similar notion of the inalienable rights of the child to be free from harm. Of course, in its widest sense, safeguarding is precisely concerned with enhancing the quality of life for children, in order to expedite a positive passage to adulthood. Built into this, in the 2010 version of the national guidance *Working Together to Safeguard Children*, is the idea of 'action to keep the child in focus' (2010: 33), which includes the following:

- developing a direct relationship with the child;
- obtaining information from the child about his or her situation and needs;
- eliciting the child's wishes and feelings – about their situation now as well as plans and hopes for the future;

- providing children with honest and accurate information about the current situation, as seen by professionals, and future possible actions and interventions;
- involving the child in key decision-making;
- providing appropriate information to the child about his or her right to protection and assistance;
- inviting children to make recommendations about the services and assistance they need and/or are available to them;
- ensuring children have access to independent advice and support (for example through advocates or children's rights officers) to be able to express their views and influence decision-making;
- the importance of eliciting and responding to the views and experiences of children as a defining feature of staff recruitment, professional supervision, performance management and the organisation's broader aims and development.

This detailed set of actions builds upon an earlier development which cemented in law the need to consult with children. Section 53 of the Children Act 2004 amended sections 17 and 47 of the Children Act 1989, so that before determining what, if any, services to provide to a child under section 17 (who may be in need of support services to achieve or maintain a reasonable standard of health or development), or action to take with respect to a child under section 47 (who may be in need of protection), the wishes and feelings of the child should be ascertained as far as is reasonable, and given due consideration.

While this sounds commendable, considerable tensions remain here. First, when attempting to work within a general 'safeguarding' approach, either to promote a child's welfare, or to prevent impairment to health or development as defined in section 17 of the Children Act 1989, professionals have no right to impose themselves on the family. All this work is entirely voluntary, and dependent on the agreement, not of the child, but of the parents concerned. Thus if the parents of a particular child whom professionals feel would benefit from support and services do not share this view, and there is no evidence of 'significant' harm to the child, then the professionals have no option but to withdraw from the family, even if the wishes and feelings of the child are that they (the child) would welcome support. The rights of the child here are 'trumped' by the rights of parents to bring their child up as they wish (so long as they don't abuse them and cause 'significant' harm to them). The child has no independent right to receive support – the law conceptualises them as the 'private property' of the parents, and this 'ownership' of the child cannot be breached unless there is evidence of 'significant' harm. This could mean that, contrary to the notion of basic rights, a child could be left in circumstances which a range of professionals agree is harmful to the child and about which the child has expressed disquiet.

There is a further necessary distinction here, which emerges from the use of the term 'significant' harm. If there is something called 'significant' harm, this suggests there is also harm which is not significant. Only 'significant' harm elicits a statutory response from agencies, characterised by them imposing themselves upon families in order to protect the child. Therefore the law allows, as has just been demonstrated, for children to be left in harmful situations with no independent right to have this harm ameliorated – the child is, at it were, at the mercy of their parents who may or may not decide to accept any help that is offered.

Furthermore, under section 31(10) of the Children Act 1989, where 'the question of whether harm suffered by a child is significant turns on the child's health and development, his (*sic*) health or development shall be compared with that which could reasonably be expected of a similar child' (DfES, 2010: 36). In other words, rather than looking at the individual child per se, as a child rights perspective might do, and deciding what their particular circumstances and needs are, professionals here are forced to compare the child about whom they are deliberating with a child living, say, next door in very similar circumstances. This again serves to reinforce the notion that there is an acceptable level of harm to children, borne perhaps from poverty or some other disadvantage, which could result directly from central government social policy. Only when this harm becomes 'significant', however this is defined, can the child be protected. The rights of the child to live free from so-called low-level harm caused by poverty or other forms of deprivation do not seem to be inherent in the law, if large numbers of children live in similar circumstances. Once again, we see here the clash between an individual child's rights perspective and the perspective which places each individual child within a wider social context, and then defines what is acceptable for those living within that context.

Implications for professionals

The first key difficulty for workers across a range of disciplines and settings lies in the interpretation of the 'definitions' of abuse. Within the description of physical abuse, the word 'hitting' is used as one possible manifestation of abuse. However, 'smacking' of children is not unlawful in England, and parents retain the right, under section 58 of the Children Act 2004, to use the defence of 'reasonable chastisement' against any charge of physical abuse amounting to common assault, though not against charges of wounding, causing grievous bodily harm, assault occasioning actual bodily harm or cruelty. Therefore, when, say, a child tells a teacher they have been hit and there are no dramatic injuries, the teacher has to make a decision whether what they have heard and what they know about the child and the circumstances might amount to abuse or 'significant harm'. From a child rights perspective, the child, first, has no right to protection in law from 'reasonable chastisement' (an interesting phenomenon when one considers that the law protects adults from a similar level of violence), and, second, may well experience a further layer of 'harm' by the professional hearing about this physical punishment deciding that the situation does not warrant any further action in light of the similar experiences of many other children similarly unprotected by the law. Jones and Welch have commented that:

> The years since the UNCRC have seen tensions emerge regarding the relationship between ... spaces in children's lives and how they are governed. An example of this is the tension within the home space over the state's role and capacity to intervene regarding children's rights to protection and smacking ... The term 'abuse' within the family usually refers to physical and sexual abuse ... Instances of abuse within families are diagnosed as being pathological: not what 'normal families' engage in. One specific contentious area of potential abuse is smacking and, as this is still legal within the United Kingdom, it isn't seen as abnormal behaviour. (Jones and Welch, 2010: 25)

Of course, interpretation of key terms within definitions of abuse may well also cause professionals to be overzealous about certain issues, leading the child to experience an over-intrusive response by social workers or others. One possible aspect of emotional abuse, for instance, contained within the definition is that it may include 'preventing the child participating in normal social interaction'. This is clearly open to interpretation and invites such questions as:

- What is 'normal' when it comes to social interaction?
- Who does, or should, decide what is 'normal'?
- What level or types of social interaction that the child is deemed to be missing should be deemed significant here?
- Who does, or should, have the final say about these matters?

Should a particular worker, or group of workers decide that the lifestyle choices of particular parents may amount to 'significant harm' by limiting 'normal social interaction' then the family (and in particular the child of course) may well be subject to intense scrutiny and assessment which could ultimately lead to the child being removed from the care of the parents. In this situation, the child would have very few 'rights' to prevent this, although of course their ascertainable wishes and feelings should be elicited by the professionals concerned.

EXAMPLE 5.1   Charlotte

Charlotte is aged 5 and is in Reception class at school. She is the only child who is never allowed to visit other children's houses to play after school or during the holidays, and she is never allowed to attend other children's birthday parties or other celebrations. Both her parents are very shy and do not talk to the other parents at school. Charlotte is doing well at school, and does not seem unduly affected by being the only child who does not attend these social

(Continued)

(Continued)

events, although she is sometimes heard to ask her parents why she cannot go.

- What is your reaction to this scenario?
- Do you think Charlotte is being prevented from engaging in 'normal social interaction'?
- Do you think Charlotte is suffering, or likely to suffer, significant harm?

Perhaps the area in which professionals may find greatest difficultly separating out the everyday experience of children from a deeper level of harm which might attract the label of 'abuse' is that of neglect. Within the definition, a child may be deemed to be neglected if they do not receive adequate food, clothing and shelter. The problem here is that neglect is clearly linked to poverty. This is not the same thing as arguing that all poor parents neglect their children. Nevertheless, professionals faced with a child who they see, say, coming to school every day with less than adequate food or clothing will need to decide if this particular level of neglect goes beyond what one could reasonably expect a parent living in similar circumstances to provide. In other words, given that, even under the definition of poverty designed to reduce the number of children reflected therein (which excludes housing costs), at least 20 per cent of children live in poverty in England (Child Poverty Action Group, 2008) then these professionals would need to decide if what they are seeing is the consequence of what might be called 'acceptable' poverty, which itself reflects central government social policy on welfare and benefits matters, or something more directly linked to what might be termed 'inadequate parenting'. This can be a very fine line to negotiate, as the answer to this question is often far from clear. What is apparent, however, is that any notion of child rights which ignores the plight of, or normalises the everyday damaging experience of, large numbers of children living in long-term poverty is deeply flawed both morally and in practical terms. Within the new, wider definition of 'safeguarding children', if tackling child poverty is not a central plank, then any claims that all the attendant activity around this much vaunted phrase will ensure that children's health and development will not be impaired, or that their circumstances are consistent with the provision of safe and effective care, or that their life chances are optimised, are seriously compromised.

One specific area which falls within the definition of neglect is a failure to 'ensure adequate supervision (including the use of inadequate care-givers)'. This is an area where the tension between individual children's rights and the likely variable response from a range of professionals is well illustrated. What constitutes 'adequate supervision' is open to interpretation. The law does not set a minimum age at which an older child can 'babysit' a younger child or at which a child can be left alone. However, parents can be prosecuted if they leave a child in circumstances 'likely to cause unnecessary suffering or injury to health' (Children and Young Persons Act 1933). It is therefore no surprise that various professionals could well react very differently to very similar circumstances they may encounter in their work. Of course, workers would consider numerous aspects of the situation, including the specific ages of both the 'babysitter' and those being 'babysat', or of the child left alone, the maturity of the 'babysitter' or the child left alone, the duration and frequency of the arrangements, what support systems may have been put in place, and so on. Nevertheless, it is entirely possible that parents and children across the country in very similar circumstances could be dealt with very differently according to the level of seriousness that workers attach to the scenario they find. This form of 'postcode lottery' has significant implications for the idea of fixed children's rights, which could cut both ways – it could serve to fail to protect those who have a right to such protection (and hence leave some children at risk of 'significant' harm), or it could serve to impose intervention strategies upon families (and hence directly upon children of course) for whom such a response is unnecessary. Furthermore, within this milieu is the notion that, from a child rights perspective, children who are either 'babysat' or left alone at home have a right to a say in this. The position of the official national guidance, which seems to assume that children are inherently vulnerable, supported by the NSPCC (2009) who take a cautious approach to this issue, is somewhat at odds with the notion of children and young people being active, competent, thinking agents in their own lives, as espoused, for example, by James and Prout (1997).

The difficulty here, of course, is that a purely rights-based approach to an issue such as this is unlikely to find favour among professionals acutely conscious of the potential public and media backlash to any decisions where the child is knowingly left in a situation of some risk, even though the notion of risk reduction and elimination is likely only to lead to further erosion of opportunities for children to enhance their social, moral and emotional development. After all, the 'safest' place for a child to grow up would be within a cage.

The national guidance on safeguarding children emphasises the need to place 'child protection' within a broad approach to raising children in order that they meet the prescribed *Every Child Matters* outcomes. It states that

> children need to feel loved and valued, and be supported by a network of reliable and affectionate relationships. They need to feel they are respected and understood as individual people and to have their wishes and feelings consistently taken into account. If they are denied the opportunity and support they need to achieve these outcomes, children are at increased risk not only of an impoverished childhood, but also of disadvantage and social exclusion in adulthood. Abuse and neglect pose particular problems. (DCSF, 2010: 29)

What is striking about this paragraph is that there is *no* mention of children's rights. Indeed, in the entire document of 393 pages, there are only 10 individual mentions of the word 'right' or 'rights' within a context of child rights. This suggests that in official government guidance, the notion of children's rights is subsumed by a more powerful agenda hinted at in the above paragraph, in which children are 'safeguarded' in order to ensure they do not cause social problems for future generations.

However, a focus on prevention and broader 'child welfare' is generally to be welcomed. It carries with it, though, an inherent danger. To include 'child protection' within a wide interpretation of 'safeguarding' and to reduce it to only one of four elements of 'safeguarding' – protection from maltreatment – is to risk losing a sharp focus on child protection. Professionals, when faced with complex family problems that could, or actually do, include child abuse, may focus on the other three elements of 'safeguarding' in the belief that these together override the one element concerned with 'protection'. The link with child rights here is significant – if one of the inalienable rights of children is to 'grow up safe from harm' (DCSF, 2010: 286) then anything which potentially detracts from this is problematic. Furthermore, given that the law is very clear that professionals cannot intervene without parental permission unless any perceived harm is 'significant', then even this right to grow up safe from harm is somewhat compromised. It seems children do not have an absolute right to grow up safe from harm, since this right can be overridden by the wishes of parents, as long those same parents are not causing 'significant' harm.

Summary

This chapter has examined the relationship between ideas and practices concerning safeguarding children and a 'rights'-based approach to working with children. It has drawn on the experiences of specific disciplines while also looking at rights-based issues from an interdisciplinary perspective. Contemporary developments in policy and legislation have been reviewed in relation to different arenas of children's lives concerning their relationship to safeguarding and protection. The relationship between national legislation, policy, practical guidance and the meaning of a rights-based perspective in actual practice with children has been looked at, drawing attention to the complexities and contradictions within policy and practice concerning 'safeguarding' and 'rights'.

Question 5.1   What is the current national legislation, policy and guidance for workers on safeguarding children?

Review Activity

1   Think about your own setting and the safeguarding of children.

   (a) How is 'safeguarding children' specifically addressed? Write down at least three key elements of your setting's safeguarding procedures.

(b) Are you clear what your individual responsibilities are?

(c) Do you know where to look for a written policy on safeguarding within your setting? Have a fresh look at it, and see how many times children's rights are mentioned.

Question 5.2   What are some emerging tensions between these and the idea of a 'rights'-based approach to working with children?

Review Activity

1 In your own setting, what might be some of the tensions between the notion of clear rights for children and the safeguarding policy? You might like to consider the following.

(a) How children in your setting are given a voice to express their concerns or opinions.

(b) The extent to which these voices are heard in your setting.

(c) The power dynamics that exist between children, parents and professionals.

Question 5.3   What might be some of the implications of this complexity for professionals across different disciplines working directly with children?

Review Activity

1 Look back through the chapters in this volume. Make a note of the ways in which professional approaches across different discipline areas might vary in respect of safeguarding children for those involved in:

(a) play work
(b) education
(c) social work
(d) health
(e) youth justice.

2 Think about the core function of each of these professional areas and how this might link to a responsibility for safeguarding or for promoting clear child rights. Can you see any tensions or contradictions?

Further Reading

Broadhurst, K., Grover, C. and Jamieson, J. (eds) (2009) *Critical Perspectives on Safeguarding Children*. Chichester: Wiley-Blackwell.
Covering a broad range of issues, this edited volume takes a critical look at approaches to safeguarding children within the UK. Drawing on multiple perspectives, it discusses the strengths but also highlights some inherent weaknesses and tensions within current policies that relate to a safeguarding agenda.

Kirton, D. (2009) *Child Social Work Policy and Practice*. London: Sage.
A good introduction to child care policy and practice in the UK, this book touches on debates surrounding the complexity of multi-agency working and the tensions between the rights of parents and the effective protection of children.

Masson, J. (2009) 'Child protection,' in H. Montgomery and M. Kellett (eds), *Children and Young People's Worlds: Developing Frameworks for Integrated Practice*. Bristol: Policy Press.
This chapter within an edited book explores safeguarding from a broad perspective which includes how the various child support services may interpret similar circumstances in different ways, and the extent to which children can be active agents within a safeguarding process.

Part 2

Rights and Service Provision: Areas of Practice

The Child's Right to Play: Rhetoric or Reality?

Mike Wragg

Chapter Overview

This chapter will address the child's right to play from the playwork profession's perspective of child rights. This perspective will be developed from concepts of social constructionism, libertarianism, areas of rights-based discourse and current theory in the field of play and playwork. The UK government's apparent commitment to the child's right to play will be presented within an overview of social policy, set against the backdrop of the United Nations Convention on the Rights of the Child (UNCRC). Case-study examples of such policy development, its practical implementation and the inherent tensions and dilemmas therein will be explored. The chapter will assess the extent to which the UK government's rhetoric surrounding the right to play can be viewed as a genuine reality.

What characterises a playwork perspective of child rights?

Playwork occupies a unique position within the child-focused professions insofar as it is the only discipline to work exclusively with the child's agenda. As the only truly child-centred profession playwork adopts a distinct perspective of children's rights. The factors informing this perspective are identified within the chapter. The UNCRC provides the backdrop to government statements on intentions to make a reality of the child's right to play (e.g. DCSF, 2008h). Further evidence of such developments, both in policy and practice, will be evaluated from the rights-based perspective of playwork.

Despite the ratification of the UNCRC and subsequent national developments in relation to Article 31, children's opportunities to play in the UK have continued to diminish (for further details of the UNCRC and other rights related conventions and legislation see Chapters 1 and 3). Case studies of the practical implementation of this right will be analysed with a view to questioning whether the government's stated intentions can amount to anything more than rhetoric.

Children's rights: a playwork perspective

Playwork is the professional practice of working with children to identify and remove barriers to their play and in doing so it provides rich and stimulating environments in which children are in control of the content and intent of their play, and in which adult intervention serves only to facilitate that process (Brown, 2008). Playwork is characterised and distinguished from other professions concerned with the child by virtue of the fact that it works solely with the child's agenda. Unlike teaching, social work or youth work, playwork does not seek to educate or care for children. Nor does it concern itself with meeting or addressing externally imposed targets for development.

This is not to say that playworkers do not recognise developmental benefits for the playing child, simply that they do not regard facilitating these outcomes as their primary objective. This brief description of playwork does little to convey the broader nature and complexity of this unique means of practice; consequently further reading is suggested at the end of this chapter. However, six assumptions, rooted in a form of educational libertarianism, are offered as underpinning the perspective from which playworkers conceive children's rights, and in particular their right to play.

The intrinsic perspective of play

The first of these assumptions relates to the way in which the value of play is understood and articulated. Research and policy development over the last 30 years has tended to concentrate on the physical, emotional, social and cognitive developmental benefits of play (Meire, 2007; Brown and Vaughn, 2009). The emphasis on these benefits as instrumental to the development of individuals and communities has given rise to an interpretation of play known as the *utilitarian perspective* (Powell and Wellard, 2008). An alternative interpretation acknowledges the developmental benefits of play, but sees its primary value as being for its own sake rather than for its content or potential outcome. This understanding, often referred to as the *intrinsic perspective* (Hakarrainen, 1999) informs the occupational standards and first two principles of playwork. The second of these principles states that: 'Play is a process that is freely chosen, personally directed and intrinsically motivated. That is, children and young people determine and control the content and intent of their play, by following their own instincts, ideas and interests, in their own way for their own reasons' (Playwork Principles Scrutiny Group, 2005).

The 'being' child

The second assumption relates to the way in which playworkers conceive and value the child. Much in the same way as playwork values the immediate rather than the deferred benefits of play, playwork also values the immediacy rather than the deferred potential of the child. This is contrary to the dominant way in which children are valued and conceived in UK society: as future social and economic capital – a conceptualisation often referred to as the 'becoming' child. Playworkers value children in the here and now, as competent, capable and autonomous social actors in their own right – a construct known as the 'being' child (Hendrick, 1997; James *et al.*,1998; Mayall, 2005). Although playwork tends not to go so far as to concur with the view of some libertarians that children should be afforded equal *status* to adults, they do regard children as having equal *value* (Alderson, 2000). That is to say that while playworkers recognise that children's biological immaturity renders them more vulnerable and therefore in need of greater rights of protection from themselves and others, it does not render them any less valuable. Children's views are considered equally important to those of adults, and in cases which affect matters of their play, more so.

The minority group child

The third assumption recognises children as a minority group who are disadvantaged by imbalanced power relations between themselves and adults. This assumption underpins an approach which, unlike many other areas of child-focused practice, seeks to challenge rather than confirm these relations (James *et al.*, 1998).

The individual child

Within this classification, however, playworkers also recognise that there is no such thing as a singular childhood experience. Although all children are exploited and discriminated against to lesser or greater extents, these inequalities are distributed through gender, background, ethnicity and age (James *et al.*, 1998).

Voluntary involvement and non-coercion

The principle of voluntary involvement is fundamental to the philosophy of libertarianism and the approach of playwork. The provision of the right to play ought not to involve any formal requirement for the child to attend or participate. Children who do choose to attend should be free to come and go at their leisure. Playworkers actively seek to remove barriers to children's voluntary involvement (Cohen, 1995; DCSF, 2008d).

Anti-paternalism

The political and philosophical concept of paternalism is generally understood to reflect the patriarchal family system whereby the dominant figurehead, or father, makes decisions on behalf of his subordinates – his wife and children. To advocates of paternalism the wise and powerful figurehead acts benevolently towards the poor and disempowered. To its libertarian detractors this practice serves only to further marginalise and oppress the disempowered. From playwork's perspective of child rights, anti-paternalistic practice is the act of challenging the dominant view that adults' needs and wishes should necessarily take precedence over those of children, and empowering children by facilitating a process by which they can genuinely make their own decisions.

These assumptions form the way in which playworkers conceive child rights. From this perspective attempts to provide children with the right to play become invalid if they contravene any of these assumptions. At best these attempts may simply represent misguided acts of tokenism, at worst they may be deliberate manipulations of the child's right to play for adult gain. The following section, commencing with the UNCRC, will provide a brief overview, from the playwork perspective, of evidence in support of the government's stated intention to make a reality of the child's right to play. Four case studies born out of this evidence, two in policy and two in practice, will then be evaluated in greater depth.

The social policy context

In 1991, as described in Chapter 1, the UK government ratified the United Nations Convention on the Rights of the Child. Although the children's rights debate can be traced back to the 1920s and beyond the UNCRC is generally regarded as a watershed for child rights and was the first international treaty to seemingly place children at the centre of its intentions (Daniel and Ivatts, 1998). From a playwork perspective, the UK government's ratification of the UNCRC was warmly welcomed for two particular reasons. Firstly, in Article 31 ('*States Parties recognize the right of the child to rest and leisure, to engage in play and recreational activities appropriate to the age of the child and to participate freely in cultural life and the arts*'), the treaty ensured play's position on the political agenda by making it, for the first time in history, an explicit right of all children. Secondly, the absence of any reference within the treaty to 'investment' as a means of justifying the provision of child rights challenged the conceptualisation of the 'becoming' child which was so dominant within social policy and much rights-based discourse (Daniel and Ivatts, 1998).

Nevertheless the Convention was not received entirely without criticism. Although the concept of the child as future capital is not used to justify the provision of child rights within the treaty, rights are nonetheless paternalistically conferred by adults without discussion or consultation with children (Foley *et al.*, 2001). Furthermore, rather than addressing the differing rights and needs of individual children both globally and within nation states, the convention adopts a universal representation of the child, very much informed by white Western ideals. The convention was further criticised for its lack of binding enforcement. Despite the numerous UN Committees which are variously responsible for overseeing that nation states fulfil their obligations to the treaty, there is no legislative mechanism by which to enforce compliance; individual nations are responsible for implementation through the development and enactment of social policy (Daniel and Ivatts, 1998). The significance of this criticism was highlighted by the UK government's initial report to the UN Committee in which it stated that all its obligations were being met within the present social policy context and no further action was necessary (Foley *et al.*, 2001). However, things have moved on apace since that initial report in 1994, and particularly in the field of children's play.

In 2001, the Department for Culture Media and Sport commissioned a national review of children's play provision entitled 'Getting Serious About Play' (DCMS, 2004). The following year, based largely on the recommendations of this review, the Children's Play Initiative of the Big Lottery Fund was launched with £155 million allocated for its implementation. Of this £124 million was to be divided among every local authority in England upon the production of a local play strategy setting out how it would ensure free and accessible play opportunities for all children. A further £16 million was made available to third-sector play projects to do similarly, and £15 million was allocated to establish Play England, a national organisation to act as the government's delivery partner (Voce, 2008).

Subsequently, in 2007, the Children's Secretary unveiled a ten-year plan for children in England detailing the dedication of a further £235 million, the development of 30 supervised adventure playgrounds and high-quality training for 4,000 playworkers (DCSF, 2007). The Children's Plan was followed, in 2008, by a national play strategy which explicitly stated government intentions to make a reality of the child's right to play, as enshrined in Article 31 of the UNCRC (Unicef, 1989a). During this period play also became increasingly prominent in wider areas of social policy, perhaps most notably within the Early Years Foundation Stage Curriculum and a number of Public Service Agreements. On the face of things this unprecedented level of political support and public investment provides solid evidence of governmental commitment to make a reality of the child's right to play. However, when scrutinised from the playwork perspective of child rights a different picture begins to emerge.

EXAMPLE 6.1   Children and Young People's Unit

As well as being a fundamental principle of the playwork perspective of child rights, the assumption that children are capable of and have a right to make decisions on matters affecting them is enshrined in Article 12 of the UNCRC. The following case study evaluates this principle in practice in respect of the kinds of government commitment that can make a reality of the child's right to play.

In 2001 a Children and Young People's Unit (CYPU) was established within a government department: the Department for Education and Skills (DfES). In 2001–02 the CYPU carried out a major consultation on what would become the *Every Child Matters* outcomes framework for every child to be healthy, stay safe, enjoy and achieve, make a positive contribution and achieve economic well-being. The original consultation document contained the outcome of 'achievement and enjoyment' where the aspiration was defined as:

> Children and young people should have the opportunity to fulfil their personal goals and ambitions, to make mature choices about their future lives, to achieve success in their academic, social and cultural development, to be recognised, to enjoy the fruits of their achievement when they begin work, and have the means to engage in constructive play and leisure pursuits for their own sake.

The measurement of success would be through outcomes, including:

> Educational attainment; first employment and employability; engagement in the arts, music, sport and wider leisure activities; access to popular play and leisure facilities; engagement in community and voluntary activities; a sense of achievement and self-esteem (Children and Young People's Unit, 2001: 22).

The overwhelming priority of all children questioned was for more places and opportunities to play. However, when it came to representing these views in the final documents the combining of the outcome of 'enjoyment' with 'achievement' resulted in children's play taking a much lower priority than education (Hood, 2007).

Ignoring children's wishes and prioritising education at the expense of play appears as a recurring theme within social policy development. Despite children themselves having stated that increased opportunities to play would most improve the quality of their lives (Children and Young People's Unit, 2002; Camina, 2004; Children's Society, 2006) the UK government's third report to the United Nations Committee on the Rights of the Child, for example, contained only five paragraphs referring to that issue. This compared with 104 paragraphs pertaining to education (UK Government, 2007). Furthermore, it seems as though when play is made a priority it is only ever really in terms of its instrumental role in achieving 'more important' adult-oriented outcomes. Evidence of this can be found in documents such as the Early Years Foundation Stage Curriculum which makes much reference to the importance of play, but only as a *means* of enabling children to *learn* (QCA, 2000). Even within the Children's Play Initiative the intrinsic importance of play is diminished by the priority attached to it as an instrumental means of halting childhood obesity reflecting governmental health priorities as described in documents such as the Public Service Agreement (Comptroller and Auditor General, 2006).

EXAMPLE 6.2 Play area and a community centre

A small children's charity situated in an inner-city area received a grant from central government to refurbish a community centre. In accordance with the local play strategy part of the money was to be spent on the redevelopment of the sizeable area of land surrounding the building as a children's play area. A stipulation of the funder was that children should be consulted on the process. The playworkers responsible for managing the project sought to consult with children from as wide a range of backgrounds as possible. However, following an extensive period of outreach work the self-selected group of 12 comprised all boys of south Asian heritage aged between 11 and 14 years.

For three months the children and playworkers met regularly to discuss how the play area might be designed. The boys were given a budget and playground manufacturers and landscape architects were invited to the meetings to demonstrate the types of play equipment and landscaping options that would be available. These included all manner of climbing and swinging apparatus and undulating features with trees, shrubs, sandpits and streams. The children were also taken, at considerable expense, to view play areas in other parts of the country to help inform their decisions. They were then asked to design and construct a scale model of the way they wanted their play space to look.

When it came to the grand unveiling, the playworkers were shocked to find that the children's design involved simply leveling and tarmacking the entire area of land. When asked why, given all the money and opportunities available to them, they wanted such a barren play area the children replied that all they ever wanted to

(Continued)

(Continued)

play was cricket and that their design would provide the perfect pitch. Faced by this unforeseen response, the playworkers found themselves in something of a quandary. If they were to reproduce the children's design they would undoubtedly attract criticism from local residents and others with an interest in the development. But if they were to do anything else they would be compromising their principles and disempowering the children.

Ultimately the pressures of adult objections were given more power than the children's views and the space was redeveloped to include swings, slides, climbing-frames, mounds, shrubs, sandpits and a cricket strip.

In this instance those adult objections may have been reasonable – the finished article probably contained more play value for a greater number of children. Furthermore, unlike the following example, these objections related only to the children's vision of the play, not to the children themselves. The next case study demonstrates the implications for the child's right to play of an increasing societal intolerance of children which is so closely associated with our culturally embedded paternalistic attitude towards them.

 EXAMPLE 6.3   Play house and nursery

Children, who were playing in a play house in the garden of their nursery, had a noise complaint made against them by a neighbour who stated that he did so because he has 'human rights as well as anyone else' (Savill, 2005). In response, the local authority ordered the nursery to soundproof its play house and limit the amount of time that children were allowed to play in the garden.

Examples of this level of extreme intolerance of children playing are not uncommon. Most of the three million non-emergency calls made to West Midlands Police each year are complaints about 'anti-social behaviour'. Of those concerning children, the vast majority do not relate to a particular crime, but simply to children being in a public space (Gill, 2007). Unfortunately these complaints all too often lead to outcomes such as the following: in 2006, three 12-year-olds, none of whom had previously been in trouble with the police, were arrested and DNA tested for climbing a cherry tree on public land. In 2002, three teenage children were arrested, DNA tested, fingerprinted and locked in a cell for playing at being James Bond, using plastic pistols (Gill, 2007). What we see here, then, are examples where the UK government's own legislation on controlling the behaviour of children contradicts their stated ambition to promote play for children.

Summary

Despite the presence of the UNCRC and many years of policy development culminating in an explicit commitment to make a reality of the child's right to play, children are faced with fewer opportunities to do so than ever before. Access to the public realm, the preferred play environment of children, has become increasingly restricted. Research has revealed adult practices have resulted in the average distance that children are permitted to travel from their home without the company of an adult being reduced by 90 per cent since 1971. Those children who are afforded this luxury have to wait, on average, three years longer than their parents did (Hillman et al., 1993). Between 1971 and 1990 the proportion of 7- and 8-year-old children travelling to school by themselves fell from 80 per cent to less than 10 per cent (Layard and Dunn, 2009). These mounting restrictions on children's play are often cited as the necessary consequence of keeping children safe in an increasingly hazardous society. But it is not only within their preferred play environment that restrictions are being imposed on children's freedom to play. In recent years break times within secondary schools have been dramatically curtailed. Some schools have chosen not only to abandon free time within the school day, but also the informal play and recreational space that goes with it (Gill, 2007).

Compounding these restrictions in schools are the tests and measurements imposed on children which are more extensive in the UK than anywhere else in the world (Thomas and Hocking, 2003). Mounting societal intolerance of children is also a regrettable contributing factor. A poll conducted on behalf of the children's charity Barnardo's found that 43 per cent of adults thought that more needed to be done to protect them from children, 54 per cent believed that British children behave like animals and 35 per cent agreed that nowadays it feels like the streets are infested with children (YouGov – Barnardo's, 2008). Terminology, such as sick, evil and scum, which would be illegal to use in relation to any other minority group, is regularly found in the national media describing children. This was put into context by a report by the UN Committee reviewing child rights within the UK, which stated the UN was 'concerned at the general climate of intolerance and negative public attitudes towards children, especially adolescents, which appears to exist in the State party, including in the media, and may be often the underlying cause of further infringements of their rights' (UN Committee on the Rights of the Child, 2008: 6).

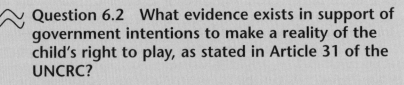 **Question 6.1   What characterises a playwork perspective of child rights?**

Review Activity

Referring to the six assumptions of the playwork perspective of child rights and the playwork principles (see http://www.playwales. org.uk/page.asp?id=50):

1 Consider any barriers to the child's right to play which may exist in your setting and think about any procedural changes you could make at your setting to ensure that all children have the right to play.
2 In relation to Example 6.1 why do you think the outcome 'enjoy' was combined with 'achieve'?

   (a) Consider which assumptions of the playwork child rights perspective were contravened in this example.
   (b) What does this say about the power relationships between children and adults?

Question 6.2   What evidence exists in support of government intentions to make a reality of the child's right to play, as stated in Article 31 of the UNCRC?

Review Activity

The National Play Strategy for England (http://publications.dcsf. gov.uk/eOrderingDownload/The_Play_Strategy.pdf) represents an explicit commitment to make a reality of the child's right to play. Referring to the definition of play used in this document:

1 Consider how closely it describes the play experience of children in your setting. Then *either*:

   (a) Think about how this definition could be incorporated into the play policy of your setting.

   Or:

   (b) Devise an action plan detailing the processes that you would go through to create a play policy ensuring that all children in your setting have the right to play.

2 Considering the processes and outcomes of Example 6.2 develop a consultation exercise to use with children to discover how their experience of play in your setting could be practically improved.

〰️ **Question 6.3   Can the evidence be viewed as anything more than rhetoric?**

Review Activity

Think about Example 6.3 and the summary of this chapter.

1 Consider what other factors, including other areas of government policy and media representation of children, might contribute to these attitudes and perceptions.
2 Think about what you could practically do to promote a more positive image of children to adults living in the community surrounding your setting.
3 Produce a flyer or poster to be displayed in your setting explaining the intrinsic value and importance of play.

Further Reading 📖

Brown, F. and Taylor, C. (2008) *Foundations of Playwork*. Milton Keynes: Open University Press.

An overview of contemporary play and playwork: it covers topics such as playwork identity, play environments, the role of the playworker, values and ethics, play and playwork theory.

Powell, S. and Wellard, I. (2007) *The Impact of National Policies on Children's and Young People's Opportunities for Play and Informal Recreational Activities in England: Report to the Children's Play Council*. London: National Children's Bureau.

Findings from a review of national policies and legislation show that recreational activities for children and young people regularly feature – but play is not always mentioned, even when policy documents are uniquely about children's free-time activities.

7

What Does the 'Voice of the Child' Mean for Children with Complex Learning and Communication Impairments?

Carol Potter and Chris Whittaker

Chapter Overview

In this chapter, we examine key issues relating to the rights of non-verbal children with complex learning and communication impairments to express themselves freely. We discuss barriers to self-expression and teaching approaches which seek to overcome these through the development of abilities in the areas of spontaneous communication and self-determination. We summarise the main features of the social model of disabilities challenge to the medical model, while highlighting the continuing debate concerning the role of impairment. The chapter will discuss evidence that adult attitudes and practices towards children with severe communication impairments can significantly reduce the children's opportunities to express their needs and wants. Exploring recent research in this area, we provide examples of practical strategies which have been shown to increase children's ability to initiate spontaneous communication. The concept of self-determination will be discussed, and the chapter will review the implications of research in this area for the teaching of children with severe communication impairments. Practical examples of approaches to teaching self-determination abilities are then discussed.

Complex learning and communication impairments: implications for children's rights

Articles 12 and 13 of the United Nations Convention on the Rights of the Child (1989) enshrine the right of children and young people to express their views and for these to be taken into account in decisions that affect their lives. This right is conferred on all children: 'irrespective of the child's or his or her parent's or legal guardian's race, colour, sex, language, religion, political or other opinion, national, ethnic or social origin, property, disability, birth or other status' (UNCRC, 1989: Article 2). To what extent can children who experience severe impairments in the area of communication, such as those with severe or profound learning impairments or children with severe autism, regularly avail themselves of these rights? Unfortunately, the answer to this question is almost certainly 'not as often as they should do'. We argue that the reasons for this attenuation of the children's human rights often reside in the quality of the communication environment that adults create around them, rather than in the children themselves.

Theory and research

Developments in theory and research in relation to those with complex learning and communication impairments have been influenced by social model of disability theory with its focus on rights and self-advocacy. The UK *social model* of disability originated as a challenge to the individualising *medical model* that placed the onus on people with impairments to adapt to mainstream society (Shakespeare, 2006). First-wave theorists developed the Marxist proposition that disability was structural oppression: a socially constructed product of exclusion under modern capitalism (Oliver, 1993). Oliver linked society's construction of disability as a 'personal tragedy' for 'afflicted' individuals, with the creation of 'dependency', both being an inevitable outcome of existing social policies. However, he argued that *independence/dependency* is a false dichotomy for, as social beings, we are all *interdependent*. Tregaskis defined disability as 'an artificial and exclusionary social construction that penalises those people with impairments who do not conform to mainstream expectations of appearance, behaviour, and/or economic performance' (2002: 457).

Oliver (1993) advocated direct action from disabled activists to assert their rights and predicted that their political strength would ensure success. Anti-discrimination legislation is now in place; the Disability Rights Commission was incorporated into the Equality and Human Rights Commission in 2007, ratifying Oliver's predictions, although much remains to be achieved (for further discussion of issues concerning this area see Chapter 3). However, this 'disability as oppression' analysis has been criticised, within UK disability studies, for marginalising the disabling effects of some impairments

(Shakespeare, 2006). Shakespeare's perspective was that 'impairment is not ... tragic and pathological. But neither is it irrelevant, or just another difference' (2006: 62). He argued for an *interactional* approach: medical, psychological, environmental, economic, political, where impairment is recognised as ubiquitous, with multiple ways to improve quality of life. Others have conceptualised the debate as advancing disability theory. Swain and French promoted an *affirmative model of disability and impairment*, 'expressed through resilience and resistance to the dominant personal tragedy model theory' (2008: 65).

Concepts of 'intelligence' and 'learning difficulty' are accepted as unproblematic within the medical model. However, Tregaskis (2002) claimed that the cultural creation of disability is seen most clearly in relation to learning difficulty, with the dominance of the medical model as the main instrument of exclusion. She interpreted learning difficulties as a sociological construct employing socially valued behaviours as parameters to label people as inadequate. Whittaker (2009) argued that, in the search for 'pure autism', non-verbal children, labelled as having severe autism and complex learning disabilities, have been regularly excluded from psychological research, conceptualising this as a form of methodological oppression. Recent genetic and behavioural research provides support for the existence of different autisms, which may prove to require correspondently different forms of intervention and further problematises the dearth of psychological research with non-verbal children with severe autism.

Self-advocacy, where disabled people run organisations and control research and social policy agendas, is a major tenet of social model theory and practice (Oliver, 1993). However, self-advocacy is problematic with non-verbal children with complex learning and communication difficulties. In the rest of this chapter we examine practical methods of supported advocacy through enhancing rights by means of spontaneous communication and self-determination. At a day-to-day level, it is often the case that the more severe a child's communication impairment is, the more directive adults tend to be in an effort to elicit some communication from the children. Such direction usually takes the form of excessive prompting, most often the use of questions. In this way, children are generally taught to *respond* to the promptings of others rather than to initiate communication themselves (Halle, 1987; Charlop and Haymes, 1994). The ability to communicate spontaneously is acknowledged as being vital to children's development and a communication is spontaneous if the child employs an *uncued, intentional* act to *initiate* communication (Chiang and Carter, 2008).

Spontaneous and prompted communication

There is a vital distinction to be made between prompted and spontaneous communication for two main reasons. Firstly, prompted communication allows children *only* to respond to the agendas and concerns of others, whereas spontaneous communication allows the free expression of those needs and wants which are most important to children themselves. Secondly, the ability to respond to the promptings of others and the ability to initiate communication oneself are different abilities and will require different teaching approaches. Unfortunately, this distinction is often not fully understood within many practice contexts. We argued, in Potter and Whittaker (2001), that prompt-based approaches may turn the children into *passive responders* rather than *active agents* who spontaneously express their own needs, exert control over their environments and develop as self-determined individuals. Enhancing a child's spontaneous communication then becomes, not a skill to be taught, but a human right to be celebrated and encouraged, as a vehicle for the child's liberation – and consequently should be a major educational goal. (For further discussion of this area in relation to the UNCRC and the European Convention on Human Rights see Chapter 1.)

Children with autism and little or no speech appear to be especially likely to experience impairments in initiating communication, yet relatively little research has been undertaken in this key area. Two studies reported very low rates of initiation (3 per hour) among children with autism with little or no speech (Pasco *et al.*, 2008; Stone and Caro-Martinez, 1990) while typically developing two-year-olds can be expected to initiate communication two hundred times in an hour (Wetherby *et al.*, 1988). It is important to note that neither of these studies took account of the nature of the communication environment in which these low levels of communication took place. In contrast, Potter and Whittaker (2001) undertook research in five special-school classrooms with 18 non-verbal children with autism. We examined rates of spontaneous communication and those aspects of the communication environment that might be influencing children in the development of self-initiated communication. We found that all children did communicate spontaneously to some extent, and that critically, the frequency and the nature of what they communicated depended on whether the communication environment was enabling or disabling. This is an important finding since it has often been assumed in the literature that children with autism exhibit low levels of spontaneity due to the nature of their impairment *per se*. We will explore some of the strategies which were found to be successful in facilitating spontaneous communication below.

Approaches to teaching children with severe communication impairments to 'express their views' spontaneously

There are a number of strategies which are important in enabling children with complex learning and communication impairments to begin to initiate communication. Here we will explore the use of prompting and the creation of communication-enabling environments. Halle (1987) stated that spontaneous communication occurs when individuals respond to naturally occurring cues in the environment. For example, a child would see a toy out of reach, realise that s/he wanted it and would communicate this, rather than being asked if they want the toy by somebody else. Halle (1987) developed the idea of a *continuum of prompts* from the most concrete type where, for example, an adult might physically prompt a child to make a Makaton sign for an apple, to the least concrete type where the adult would simply pause and wait for the child to sign 'apple' in response to seeing a bowl of apples on a shelf. Questions are frequently used as concrete prompts by adults to children with severe autism, but are rarely successful in eliciting a response (Chiang, 2009).

Once children have a communication system in place, such as pointing, signing or a picture-based communication system, adults must try to move away from more concrete prompts such as physical prompts and direct questions towards allowing children to communicate for items spontaneously. We found that the most effective strategy was a Minimal Speech Approach (MSA) where the adult uses pauses within a familiar activity to allow the child to respond, then no more than 2–3 word utterances, mapped directly onto the child's actions (Potter and Whittaker, 2001). Thus teaching children to communicate spontaneously without prompting is a crucial step in enabling to children to 'express their views' (Article 12). (For further discussion of Article 12 see Chapter 1.)

Being able to initiate communication is of fundamental importance because it gives children the opportunity to gain some direct control over their everyday environments, making their needs and wants known. Consider the following scenarios.

EXAMPLE 7.1   Snack time

Snack time – scenario 1

Five children with severe autism and little, or no, speech are sitting around a table at snack time. The adult is standing and offers children a drink by going round the table and asking each child, in turn, 'Do you want orange or do you want lemon to drink?', holding each bottle in front of each child. Each child waits his or her turn, having been previously taught to do so.

Snack time – scenario 2

Five children with severe autism and little, or no, speech are sitting around a table at snack time. The bottles of drink are behind the adult on a different table, out of reach but within the children's view. The adult waits without speaking for children to indicate their wants. One child points to the orange bottle and is immediately given the drink. The adult says 'orange' as the child takes it.

- What are children being taught in the first scenario and how are they being taught this?
- What are children being taught in the second scenario and how are they being taught this?

In the first scenario, children are being taught to respond to the communication of the adult and to wait their turn. They are learning that access to the drink is wholly determined by the adult offering it and that they should sit quietly until that offer is made. The adult is using a range of concrete strategies to prompt communication from children. The primary strategy is the use of direct verbal questioning which the children are very unlikely to understand given their severe receptive language difficulties. Yet they will reach for what they want, which the adult may interpret as a linguistic rather than a situational understanding. An immediate visual cue is also in use with the presentation of the bottles of squash directly in front of the children. However, the child's agency is denied, for access to the drink is dependent on their passive acquiescence, which is rewarded and therefore reinforced by the drink.

In the second scenario, the children are learning that they must spontaneously initiate communication to get one of the drinks which they can see *without* any concrete prompt from the adult to do so. In addition, they are learning that they do not have to wait their turn for a drink but rather can have the drink as soon as they ask for it. Children's access to the drink is therefore dependent on proactive rather than on passive behaviour. In this scenario, children, as autonomous active agents, experience more direct control over their environment than in the first. In the second scenario, the adult is not using direct concrete prompts. There are no verbal prompts, rather the sight of the bottles out of reach acts as a less concrete visual prompt and the adult sitting quietly transfers the onus of communication to the children. In this scenario, children are learning how to initiate communication rather than to respond to the communication of adults. There are clearly a number of teaching steps involved in moving children from the first to the second scenario, relating to the changing and withdrawal of prompts and the teaching of a communication system such as pointing and multipointing. For a fuller account of this Minimal Speech Approach, see Potter and Whittaker (2001).

In our view, it is essential that children are taught to communicate their needs and wants spontaneously, as the lack of such skills in adulthood can understandably lead to frustration and the development of less appropriate and more challenging behaviours. This, in turn, can lead to restricted lifestyles and opportunities for self-fulfilment and enjoyment, with Cederlund *et al.* (2008) reporting increased use of residential care in young adults with severe autism and limited communication. In this way, limited opportunities for children to access their right to freedom of expression may lead to even fewer rights as adults (Emerson, 2001).

Children's rights and self-determination

A related area of importance in enabling children with complex learning and communication impairments to enjoy freedom of expression as enshrined in the UNCRC's (1989) Articles 12 and 13 is that of self-determination.

What is self-determination?

Self-determination is a basic human right and refers to 'volitional actions that enable one to act as the primary causal agent in one's life and to maintain or improve one's quality of life' (Wehmeyer, 2007: 6).

Examples of self-determined behaviour include:

- making choices and decisions;
- solving problems;
- setting goals;
- having an internal locus of control;
- becoming self-aware.

(Sands and Wehmeyer, 1996)

Abery and Zajac (1996) argued that self-determination is a developmental process which starts soon after birth and progresses during the whole of one's life, and for this reason it is important to begin to teach it in early childhood rather than to wait until adolescence or adulthood. This is especially the case for children with learning disabilities who may take longer to develop new skills. Being self-determined has been found to improve the quality of life for individuals with intellectual impairments by increasing engagement (Keen, 2009), reducing challenging behaviour (Shogren *et al.*, 2004) and enabling individuals to become more actively engaged in the process of learning (Mithaug *et al.*, 2003).

Non-verbal children with complex learning and communication impairments: opportunities for self-determined behaviour

Despite the manifest benefits of developing abilities in the area of self-determination, opportunities for those with complex learning and communication impairments to be self-determined are often significantly restricted in a number of ways, and many children and adults are not involved in decisions which affect their everyday lives or later-life decisions (Morris, 2001). Morris (2003) noted that children with cognitive impairments who do not speak are especially unlikely to be included in any kind of participation in decisions which affect them. There have been some attempts to consult children with communication impairments in recent years about the services which they receive. For example, Lewis (2001) sought to gain the view of 12 young people with little, or no, speech on their experiences of respite care.

However, while there seems to be a developing interest in consulting disabled children on their experiences of services, much of the literature continues to relate only to methods and approaches used in gaining students' views (for example, Franklin and Sloper, 2009; Knight *et al.*, 2006) rather than on the actual findings where such approaches have been used in practice. Kirby *et al.* (2003) refer to participation as being a continuum along which the way in which children participate will be affected by their individual circumstances.

Why do disabled children have so little access to self-determined behaviour? In the UK, Franklin and Sloper (2009) cite the negative attitudes of adults who do not believe children capable of engaging in decision-making as well as the complexity of service structure and operation which precludes children's participation. A lack of training on how to involve disabled children is another important barrier. In the US, Wehmeyer *et al.* (2000) surveyed 1,200 teachers' views on barriers to self-determination for children with cognitive impairments. Key barriers identified were:

- a perceived lack of student benefit from instruction in self-determination (42 per cent);
- insufficient training or information on how to promote it (41 per cent);
- a more urgent need for instruction in other areas (29 per cent); and
- lack of teacher knowledge of curricular/assessment materials and strategies (17 per cent).

(Wehmeyer *et al.*, 2000)

It is noteworthy that this research took place in the USA where self-determination for children with cognitive impairment is an important issue. Since the advent of the National Curriculum in the UK, there has been little focus on this important aspect in relation to children with severe learning impairments due to an increased emphasis on a subject-centred approach, much to the concern of many involved in the education of these children (Carpenter *et al.*, 1996; Jordan and Powell, 1997; Whittaker and Potter, 1999).

Approaches to promoting self-determination

We will now discuss practical approaches to participation rights from the perspective of teaching self-determination skills to children with severe communication impairments. As indicated above, it is important to begin teaching these skills in early childhood. Capacity needs to be developed in area such as making choices, making decisions and learning how to solve everyday problems. How far children will make progress in each area will depend not only on the level of individual children's cognitive ability but also on the extent to which they experience frequent and appropriate opportunities to develop their skills. As was noted above, it is often the case that the greater the child's level of cognitive impairment, the fewer opportunities are presented for the development of self-determination.

Making choices

It is important that once children with complex learning and communication difficulties have developed an appropriate system of communication, such as pointing or signing, they are then quickly introduced to making choices on a regular basis throughout the day. It is possible to present children with frequent and varied opportunities to engage in choice-making, decision-making and problem-solving during, for example, snack time or getting ready for outdoor play. In a classroom context, we suggested that staff ask themselves a number of questions about the activities they present to children in order to identify ways of enhancing self-determination:

- Are there parts of an activity which children cannot do by themselves? If so this presents an opportunity for children to become aware of how to ask for specific help.
- Are there aspects of the activity which might allow for preferences to be made? If so there may be opportunities for choice, such as deciding where to sit, which computer program to use or which order to do tasks in.
- Is there a fixed time span for an activity or could children decide when to stop?

(Potter and Whittaker, 2001: 118)

Adults working with children should review a wide range of activities to assess whether children might be offered greater self-determination within them. For example, children could choose between games being offered to develop turn-taking skills, could choose where to sit, who to play the game with and how long to play it. Such an approach requires a shift in the locus of control within settings, allowing children to experience greater control of their everyday environments.

Problem-solving

Another important aspect of self-determined behaviour is the ability to solve problems. Wehmeyer defines problem-solving as 'using available information to identify and design solutions to problems' (2007: 34). Often, within classrooms for children with severe communication impairments, adults tend to overstructure the environment and activities, focusing on the product rather than the process of an activity, thereby unwittingly removing vital opportunities for children to learn problem-solving skills. For example, during outdoor play, non-fixed toys are often chosen by adults rather than allowing children to think about how they might communicate for these toys and retrieve them from relevant storage areas themselves.

A key strategy in promoting problem-solving capabilities in children with severe communication impairments is to problematise familiar activities and events so that children are required to reflect on them more deeply and take a more active part in the process.

EXAMPLE 7.2   Making a chocolate mousse

During a simple cookery session, once children are familiar with the routine of making a packet mousse, adults could gradually withdraw help so that by degrees, children are making more of the decisions themselves. For example, instead of adults opening a packet and pouring its contents into a bowl, children could be offered an unopened packet, thus setting up a problem which the children need to solve. If children are unable to open it with their hands, they could be offered a ruler or a pair of scissors, again requiring them to think more deeply about the nature of the task. Adults should then continue to offer non-verbal opportunities for children to reflect and make decisions. What should happen after the packet is opened? What utensils will be needed? Where are they? What is the order in which ingredients are put into the bowl? Adults can scaffold these problem-solving activities in a graduated way. For example, initially, they could offer either scissors or a ruler with which to open the packet. Later, they could expect children to remember that they need scissors and to go and find them. For those children who have significant problems with understanding spoken language, it is important to use a Minimal Speech Approach (Potter and Whittaker, 2001) where no more than two or three key words are mapped directly on to the children's actions. This requires the adults to think through the activity and plan how decision-making can be presented non-verbally, with appropriate pauses to give the children an opportunity for thinking and spontaneous communication. The aim of the activity is to promote self-determination – the production of a mousse is secondary, although a satisfying reward for the children!

Again, such an approach requires a shift in attitude, thinking and skill to execute. The activity will take longer and children's differing levels of ability will require adults to be mindful of each child's attention span and level of engagement. The grouping of children is a key factor here. It is most important that the activity, or at least the product of the activity, is intrinsically motivating for the children so that they are keen to solve the problems and reach their goal – in this case eating chocolate mousse!

The successful teaching of the abilities outlined above requires significant knowledge and experience in the complex area of communication impairment. However, the demise of initial UK teacher education courses in the area of severe learning disabilities in 1987–9, has resulted in a profession with little professional knowledge in this key area. Results from a survey conducted by Mroz (2006) of 294 nursery teachers revealed limited initial and post-qualification training in the area of language and communication development. More recently, a government-sponsored report concluded that Initial Teacher Training (ITT) provision 'is not preparing [trainee teachers] with the skills or the experience to meet the increasingly complex needs of SLD/PMLD [severe learning difficulties/profound and multiple learning difficulties] children' (Salt, 2010: 52).

Recommendations from this report, which include the need to develop additional training for teachers of children with severe impairments, appear to be have been accepted by the outgoing Labour government. We believe that they need to be implemented in full to ensure that children with severe communication impairments are taught in future by professionals who have the necessary skills and abilities to give them access to rights to freedom of expression, guaranteed by the United Nations Convention of the Rights of the Child (1989).

Summary

The key issues to emerge from this chapter are as follows:

- All children are entitled to freedom of expression, including those with the most severe communication impairments and additional complex learning difficulties.
- Access to this right for these children will require those teaching and working with them to have an in-depth knowledge of theory and teaching strategies which will promote both spontaneous communication and self-determination.
- Such approaches will require the development of communication enabling environments which will offer children frequent and meaningful choices within their daily lives.

These requirements have significant implications for initial teacher education which currently does not prepare students for the education of children with complex learning and communication difficulties.

Question 7.1   What are the theoretical foundations of the rights of disabled children?

Review Activity

Consider the chapter's discussion of the relationship between theory and practice on pages 83–4, for example Shakespeare's argument for 'an *interactional* approach: medical, psychological, environmental, economic, political, where impairment is recognized as ubiquitous, with multiple ways to improve quality of life' (see page 84) or Swain and French's discussion of an *affirmative model of disability and impairment*, 'expressed through resilience and resistance to the dominant personal tragedy model theory' (see page 84). Reflect upon your own beliefs, training and experience concerning the complex nature of the relationships between disability and impairment. How might your practice be disabling for the children that you teach?

Question 7.2   What are the implications of severe communication impairments for children's rights to self-expression and the adults who work with them?

Review Activity

The chapter connected Articles 12 and 13 of the United Nations Convention on the Rights of the Child (1989) concerning the right of children and young people to express their views and for these to be taken into account in decisions that affect their lives (see page 83). We argued that for children who experience severe impairments in the area of communication, these rights are not accessed as often as they should be. We discussed why this might be the case, proposing, for example, that 'this attenuation of the children's human rights often reside in the quality of the communication environment that adults create around them, rather than in the children themselves' (see page 83). The following activities are intended to assist practical reflection on these issues. Before undertaking them, please make sure you have gained appropriate permission of everyone involved in line with the policies of your setting.

1 Observe the interaction between adults and a non-verbal child with complex learning difficulties in your setting for one hour. How many times does the child communicate spontaneously – that is without any adult prompt to do so? Are these positive communications such as a request for an activity, or are they protests or rejections?

2 Observe each adult in your setting interacting with children with complex learning and communication impairments for 30 minutes. Make a list of the ways in which adults encourage children to communicate. What kinds of strategies are used most? Are these strategies which are likely to lead to children being able to communicate spontaneously?

3 Review the strategies outlined in this chapter to begin to develop a spontaneous communication enabling environment.

Question 7.3   What is self-determination and how does it relate to the needs of children with severe communication impairments?

Review Activity

Consider the chapter's argument that self-determination skills should be taught to non-verbal children with complex learning difficulties in

(Continued)

early childhood (see pages 89–90). The following activities are intended to assist practical reflection on these issues. Before undertaking them, please make sure you have gained appropriate permission of everyone involved in line with the policies of your setting.

1   Observe one or two children and the adults working with them for 20 minutes in three or four different settings (e.g. a group activity, one-on-one teaching, snack session, outdoor play). List the opportunities children have to make choices and solve problems.
2   Make a list of the activities which occur routinely within your setting and, for each activity, suggest ways of introducing choice and problem-solving on a regular basis, using an MSA if the children have severe receptive and expressive language difficulties.
3   Seek to introduce more choice-making and problem-solving opportunities and undertake another observation to monitor any changes in the presentation of such opportunities.

Further Reading

Campbell, L. (2002) 'Rights and disabled children', in B. Franklin (ed.), *The New Handbook of Children's Rights: Comparative Policy and Practice*. London: Routledge.
This chapter takes as its starting point the 'invisibility' of disabled children and explores their rights in the context of four of the UNCRC areas, namely right to life, right to protection, right to information and right to education.

Foley, P. and Leverett, S. (eds) (2008) *Connecting with Children: Developing Working Relationships*. Bristol: Policy Press.
This comprehensive edited volume is concerned with how adults relate to children and develop supportive relationships with them. A wide range of issues, including disabled children, are covered across the various chapters which are arranged thematically rather than by client group.

Thomas, C. (2007) *Sociologies of Disability and Illness: Contested Ideas in Disability Studies and Medical Sociology*. Basingstoke: Palgrave Macmillan.
More of a specialist book taking a sociological perspective, the reader will find here a rich discussion of many concepts related to disability. While not focusing solely on children, the book contains many general concepts which will advance the reader's understanding of the lived experience of disabled people.

8

Rights in Early Years Settings and a Young Child's Right to Silence

Caroline Bligh

Chapter Overview

Rights in early years settings have developed positions on areas such as participation and protection. This chapter will review these but will look at an area that is crucial but often overlooked. Where are the quiet places in an early years setting for a young child to retreat to, and does the early years practitioner understand the value of silence and the contribution offered by the silent child to the early years setting? Through an exploration into both positive and negative associations which are currently held between children and silence, the implications of a child choosing silence (as opposed to it being imposed from above) are examined in relation to early years practitioner understandings of silence. The intention is to paint an alternative portrait, through which the reader might feel empowered to reconsider preconceived perceptions of silence in relation to the rights of a child. Children's rights must also be accountable to cultural differences or otherwise they become the rights of some but not all children. Not only do children have a right to say what they think (Article 12) but they should equally have a right to think the unspoken word – silence. The chapter will explore the ways in which child rights feature in early years settings. On initial reading, 'the right to silence' does not appear to be in the UNCRC articles, and yet on closer inspection, 'silence' is clearly situated between the wording in Articles 14, 16, 29, 30 and 31. This chapter will explore the UNCRC and a child's right to silence in early years settings. Not all cultures value the spoken word as highly as those based in Western traditions in which every child is aiming to 'be a talker' (DCSF, 2008d). Is the potential in choosing the unspoken word as a meaning-making tool being unintentionally 'side-lined'? In examining the premise that to be silent is a fundamental right and a choice for children, the chapter will explore early years practitioners' work and their role in relation to this area of choice.

Introducing an early years perspective on children's rights

Let's consider this quote:

> Change happens, when those who don't usually speak are heard by those who don't usually listen. (Marshall, 2006: 1)

Responding to an inquiry headed by Lord Laming into the tragic death of Victoria Climbié (House of Commons Health Committee, 2003), the then Labour government introduced the *Every Child Matters* legislation (DfES, 2003) with the intention to illuminate the indivisible and universal rights of children. (For further discussion of this see Chapter 5). Deliberately not specifying a hierarchy of importance, the document was introduced throughout schools and early years settings with the intended outcome for every child (no matter what their circumstances) to have the support they need to:

- be healthy
- stay safe
- enjoy and achieve
- make a positive contribution
- achieve economic well-being.

Together, these egalitarian aims were launched as a 'holistic' framework of rights that (if fully respected) would facilitate an improvement in the health, welfare, development and active participation of all children (for further discussion of these aspects of rights see Chapters 1 and 2). Working with other professionals has been a new and sometimes challenging introduction for some early years practitioners who have been used to employing 'a mother hen' approach to 'teaching' where the class was treated as a self-contained unit, in isolation from what occurred outside of the four classroom walls. Sharing information with other professionals (multi-agency working) for the benefit of the child has not always been easy for practitioners. Not only have they had to relinquish sole ownership of the children in their care but in attempting to support a child in 'staying safe' through the sharing of the information on the child, the practitioner may have been inadvertently disrespecting a child's right to privacy (UNCRC, 1989: Article 12).

In 2008 the Early Years Foundation Stage (DCSF, 2008e) framework became statutory for children from birth to five years of age. This framework attempted to streamline and replace previous early years policies and frameworks with one manageable package with common principles that everybody involved in early years would be working towards the 'overarching aim of supporting young children in achieving the five *Every Child Matters* outcomes' (DCSF, 2008e). Hohmann's (2010) experiences were of early years practitioners being positioned at the forefront of delivery, and thus expected to demonstrate inclusivity of practice through actively participating in equality of opportunity and anti-discriminatory practice for all children.

As a former early years practitioner, my concern has been that what at first appeared to be a holistic, personalised approach to the welfare and nurture of children (based upon the four overlying principles of a Unique Child, Positive Relationships, Enabling Environments and Learning and Development) has become overshadowed by the 'top-down policing' of over-prescriptive documentation and continuous assessment, which has increased untold times the workload heaped upon early years practitioners. Included in this concern is the increased pressure from, and further accountability to, the local authority early years advisors and the Ofsted inspectorate which risks not only constraining good early years practice but also the implementation of the five *Every Child Matters* outcomes (DfES, 2003).

Areas such as participation rights are often stressed within early years provision. This includes the legal requirement to listen to young children under the Childcare Act 2006, section 3(5). The Act states, for example, that local authorities must have regard to any information about the views of young children in the planning and commissioning of services.

> For services to be successful and have a positive impact on young children's lives, the voices of young children themselves need to be listened to and actively taken into account. (HM Government 2006b: 11)

This perspective is stressed in a variety of ways within the Act, for example in active work using play and the arts:

> There are obvious practical difficulties in engaging this age group in meaningful consultation about strategic issues such as where Children's Centres should be located. However, projects and materials developed by the voluntary sector have shown how children under five can be consulted very effectively about their own experiences of services, through for example the use of painting, music, cameras and story telling. (HM Government 2006b: 11)

As can be seen in the above sample, this approach often results in young children's rights in early years being emphasised in terms of active communication:

Early childhood services have a crucial role to play in developing a listening culture which nurtures day-to-day listening and provides opportunities for young children to make decisions about matters that directly affect them. Local authorities are beginning to use the voice of the child to inform the design, planning and delivery of services, together with the voices of practitioners and parents. (http://www.participationworks.org.uk/topics/early-years)

Examples of this framework include Coppard (2004) on active methods for consulting young children about play provision and Cosh's (2005) work on consulting young children about their experiences of their provision. The 'Listening as a Way of Life' series of pamphlets (e.g. Clark, 2008; Dickins, 2008), similarly, looks at ways of working to increase communication and participation with young children in different areas of their lives, or in relation to different communicative capabilities.

McLamon, for example, has summarised this approach to young children's rights in the following way:

- All children aged from birth to eight years of age are important and unique individuals.
- They are not too young to show us what is important to them.
- Listen to what they are telling us through a range of methods.
- Reflect on what the children have said and take action where possible.
- What they tell us and how they feel is valuable to the adults around them.
- We, as adults, can facilitate change by involving children in the way in which we plan environments and activities.

(McLamon, 2008: 5)

While this emphasis on the interplay between listening, communication and participation is a crucial aspect of children's rights in relation to early years provision, it neglects to take into account an important arena of rights: those concerning silence. The following section offers an alternative way of looking at the rights detailed in Chapters 1 and 2. This chapter's discussions based around a young child's right to silence 'tease out' this fundamental *choice* from within UNCRC Articles 14, 16, 29, 30 and 31. Table 8.1 offers a way of seeing aspects of these articles in relation to silence and choice.

Each of these five UNCRC articles invites further exploration into the value placed upon a child's right to choose silence, the ways in which silence might be interpreted socio-culturally (Articles 14, 29 and 30) and, in particular, the value and respect (Article 14) placed upon a child's choice of silence in early years settings (Article 29).

This section presents contrasting manifestations of children's silence. The first is imposed silence from 'above' (a 'top-down' negative example, as above) and the second is when silence is positively and autonomously chosen (Cannella and Viruro, 2004; Viruru, 2005) as a 'bottom-up' agentive

Table 8.1   UNRC Articles in relation to silence and choice

UNCRC (1989) Article: area of concern	Reinterpretation, or emphasis, in relation to a child's 'right to silence'
14 The right to freedom of thought, conscience and religion	*Every child has the right to think* ... including the space and time to think alone or in silence
16 The right to privacy	*Every child has the right to privacy* ... including silence
29 The right to education	*Education must develop every child's personality* ... and create different kinds of spaces and relationships to enable this to occur
30 The right to enjoy their own culture, religion and language	*Every child has the right to learn and use the language, customs* ... of the people in the country where they live – including aspects which are non-verbal and which involve silence
31 The right to rest, play and leisure	*Every child has the right to relax* ...

action. It is perhaps unsurprising that, as a 'backlash' to the imposed silencing of children, worthy initiatives such as the Coram Family project (Lancaster and Broadbent, 2003) *Listening to Young Children* have emerged. The aim of this project has been to nurture respect for '*hearing* the voice of the child'. As such this laudable initiative has been presented as 'bottom-up' and agentive, redefining the portrait of a child from that of being passive to that of being autonomous (Edwards *et al.*, 1998). Clark and Moss (2001) encouraged early year practitioners to adopt the Mosaic approach into their early years practice, which by its design not only empowers children as decision-makers, designers and researchers in their own right (Kellet, 2010) but also empowers them to take ownership of their learning environment. Both of these offerings inspired willing practitioners to listen to both the spoken and unspoken words of children – through '*the hundred languages of children*' (Rinaldi, 2005).

However, following on from the success of 'listening to children' initiatives, the DCSF attempted to raise the status of 'speaking and listening' through the 'Every Child a Talker' (DCSF, 2008d) project. Unfortunately, this initiative reverted to a 'top-down approach' – instructing practitioners in how to make children talk both in school and at home. In the process of raising the status of spoken words, the importance of the *unspoken word* may have been forgotten, both as a cultural tool of learning and communication, and also as a place for privacy in thought and reflection. It can be seen that in attempting to raise the status of speaking and listening, the initial intentions of empowering children have since been misinterpreted and repackaged as strategic policies. In doing so, the position of power has shifted away from the child and removed a child's right to *choose* either the spoken or unspoken word.

Perhaps this disregard for a child's right to choose the unspoken word is due to current perceptions of silence, many of which are solely negative. For instance, when a young child does not speak, she or he may be considered as having a 'tendency to shyness', in need of 'bringing out of his/her shell' or as 'being 'troubled' in some way. The child may be temporarily withdrawing from a situation but is commonly described as 'sulking or being moody'. Indeed, in the arena of social work and/or child psychiatry, where physical or psychological abuse of a child may be suspected, silence may be considered as symptomatic of such a condition.

However, it should not be forgotten that silence also appears as a positive presence in most children's lives. Looking into my own childhood memories, I recall many periods of profound contentment when there was no expectation of or pressure put upon me to speak. The following auto-ethnographic case study presents four examples of when silence serves as a positive phenomenon in early childhood.

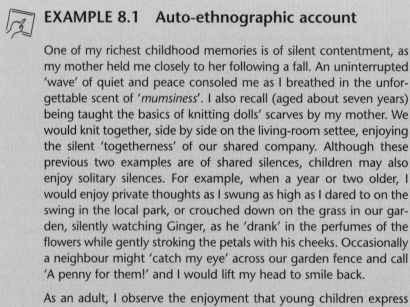

EXAMPLE 8.1   Auto-ethnographic account

One of my richest childhood memories is of silent contentment, as my mother held me closely to her following a fall. An uninterrupted 'wave' of quiet and peace consoled me as I breathed in the unforgettable scent of *'mumsiness'*. I also recall (aged about seven years) being taught the basics of knitting dolls' scarves by my mother. We would knit together, side by side on the living-room settee, enjoying the silent 'togetherness' of our shared company. Although these previous two examples are of shared silences, children may also enjoy solitary silences. For example, when a year or two older, I would enjoy private thoughts as I swung as high as I dared to on the swing in the local park, or crouched down on the grass in our garden, silently watching Ginger, as he 'drank' in the perfumes of the flowers while gently stroking the petals with his cheeks. Occasionally a neighbour might 'catch my eye' across our garden fence and call 'A penny for them!' and I would lift my head to smile back.

As an adult, I observe the enjoyment that young children express when playing both inside and outside activities together, through participation and engagement in shared, sustained thinking (Broadhead, 2001). The children are so engrossed in their situated learning activities that there is no time or need to talk, so silence becomes a shared practice which is distributed through and between the social actors – within a community of young learners.

The Early Years Foundation Stage does not address a child's right to silence

Examples such as those above demonstrate how accessibility to silent spaces should be a choice for all children. However, many pre-school children are expected and encouraged to spend their weekdays in intentionally highly stimulating environments (current daycare provision) where the emphasis is on a stimulating, educational and activity-based curriculum from the ages of birth to five years (EYFS: DCSF, 2008e). On the one hand, the EYFS (DCSF, 2008e) recognises the significance of providing enabling environments, yet it does not offer practitioners a clear understanding of a child's need to choose quiet spaces to ponder, nor why. Unfortunately, young children may miss out on silent spaces to 'just be' as they struggle for the attention of childcare workers.

Childminders were formerly chosen by parents who wished their children to be provided with a more relaxed and 'home-like' environment. However, rather than supporting, childminders in their provision of ample opportunities for young children to seek out silent spaces, childminders are now expected to follow the EYFS (DCSF, 2000e) and provide evidence of planned and stimulating 'activities' for children in their care for every hour of each day. Is it that silent spaces are viewed with suspicion?

> The exposure of many individuals, particularly of the Western culture to a relatively quiet soundscape can lead to a variety of negative emotions, including anxiety, terror, boredom, and loneliness. These negative perceptions of silence can perhaps only be adjusted through a greater personal understanding of the value of quiet, for the benefit of our own individual soundscapes and the good of our society. (de Geest, 1999)

What this quote aptly demonstrates, is that silence has an immensely important and yet clearly misunderstood and undervalued part to play in children's lives. It would appear that a child's right to *choose* silence should be given equal priority to that of choosing the spoken word.

However, current frameworks through which babies and children are cared for outside of the family community of practice are not addressing a child's right to silence. It is implied in the UNCRC Articles 14, 16, 29, 31 and 32, but not made explicit.

Whose right to silence?

This section discusses the question of whose right to silence is being determined? There is an implication in the question that there is an expectation of a spoken language. This may be the same monolingual language that ECAT (DCSF, 2008d) wishes children to speak (English) rather than a plurilingual representation of the world and cultures within a society.

The spoken and unspoken word (silence) are both thought of differently, depending on different societies or cultures and how value is placed upon them.

In many Western social and cultural traditions parents may display concern for a child who has been silent for several minutes. However, clear examples of radical cultural differences towards silence are plentiful. Tannen (1985) observed how silence may be perceived so negatively in some parts of Western cultures as to be considered a sign of social malfunction and to be avoided, or interruption is made, whenever possible. Western cultural traditions, therefore, may not only interpret the state of silence as awkward (Frykberg, 1998) but also assume successful communication to involve much conversation.

Silence as a means of communication may not be highly valued in such Western traditions and yet most people would agree that thought is an essential (yet unspoken) tool through which a young child mediates socio-cultural understandings of her/his 'world' and the communities of practice within it.

The highly regarded comparison study by Tobin *et al.* (1989) of pre-school children in Japan, China and the USA presented startling variations between the three cultures on how each perceived silence in relation to notions of power and the purpose of words. Whereas the Chinese pre-school emphasised diction, enunciation and memorisation among its top priorities in speaking, the Japanese pre-school encouraged language as a medium of group solidarity and shared social purpose (Tobin *et al.*, 1989: 189).

In sharp contrast to China and Japan, the American pre-school viewed the use of words as an expression of individuality, autonomy and cognitive development. From the results of questionnaires, 38 per cent of American parents placed communication skills as one of their top three priorities for their children's learning in pre-school compared to only 5 per cent of Japanese parents. However, not only did Japanese parents praise listening above speaking but their top priority was for their children to learn sympathy, empathy and concern for others, compared to that of only 5 per cent of American's and 4 per cent of Chinese parents.

Asa and Barnlund's (1998) cross-cultural study of verbal patterns among people of Japan and the United States also revealed silence as highly valued in Japan, with constant and uninterrupted verbal interactions considered highly unfavourable, shallow and to be mistrusted. In Japan, speech is not considered an appropriate medium through which to express and communicate profound emotions and thoughts. In addition to presenting private speech as an integral part of a young child's development (in English as an additional language learners), Saville-Troike (1988) also recognised the use of silence as a frequent, culturally widespread response to emotional intensity. Saville-Troike cites the Japanese word, 'haragei' – 'wordless communication' – in reference to preferred Japanese modes of communicating emotional issues (1988: 37).

Cultural variations such as these in the use of silence are as vast as the differences between languages. The meaning of each silence depends not only on the situation, but upon the value assigned by cultural convention to silence in each situation – not equally culturally distributed. If Western cultural beliefs and practices perceive speaking aligned closely to an assessment of cognitive development in pre-school children, then we are devaluing those children that in Japan are considered highly – those that are thoughtful and empathetic to others. However, Drury's (2007) ethnographic study of three four-year-old bilingual learners at home and school presents an alternative picture of silence, interpreted as an assertive, agentive action – not a passive or submissive response.

Viruru's (2001) nursery school study problematises the high status bestowed solely upon the spoken word as the main vehicle of human expression and communication. According to Viruru this is yet another example of Western adult majority culture imposing its cultural norms upon less dominant cultures and communities – and, in particular, children. Viruru asks whose interests are best served when spoken '… language is privileged over other modes of communication' (2001: 31). The ethnographic study, set in India, suggests that children 'engage in complex forms of communication that do not involve language' (2001: 31) and questions the common assumption in dominant Western adult discourses that the spoken word is 'almost overwhelmingly unilingual; however, most of the world's children use and live in multilingual environments' (2001: 31).

 There were striking similarities in these findings to that of Trawick who suggested that 'silence in relationships in India does not mean absence but is more of a tool that invites dialogue, probing and further understanding' (1990: 33). The children that Viruru 'interacted with also seemed to take the silence about my [Viruru's] presence there not as representing something forbidden but as an opportunity to share ideas and construct understandings for themselves' (1990: 33).

Adults raised within Western traditions or cultures may expect their children's lives to be full, active and stimulating, with speaking considered an integral part of this stimulating world. However, children also have a need to communicate by alternative and culturally appropriated means, and seek out the spaces in between the speaking, laughing and crying. Where are the *thinking spaces*, where a child can chill out, ponder, reflect and make sense of their world? Where is the respect for the child's unspoken multilingual word? Has the child who exercises their UNCRC right to be silent been neglected?

Early years practice and the right to choose

Morris states, 'Assume that all children and young people have something to communicate. It is up to us to find ways of understanding their views and experiences' (2003: 346). In this section the role of the early years practitioner in relation to issues about rights, understanding, communication and silence is reviewed. The currently implemented Early Years Foundation Stage

(2008e, 2008g) positively promotes the development of speaking skills in children, but does nothing to deter practitioners from viewing silence negatively. Silence is still imposed in early years settings as a means of control or punishment to isolate a child from their peers – such as sitting a child in the 'naughty corner' if a practitioner decides that a child has been 'misbehaving', or lining up in silence before the children are allowed to have lunch or play outside.

Burke's research into the solitary play of children with 'impairments' found that 'being alone was rarely seen as an undesirable or unwanted experience ... the children clearly sought and valued places to be by themselves ... to think and reflect; to be safe; to find privacy and solitude; to be autonomous and independent' (2008: 8). Alderson's work (2000) relates to these findings: describing how children communicate feelings of fun and pleasure in different ways according to their individual communication strengths. Morris states, 'Assume that all children and young people have something to communicate. It is up to us to find ways of understanding their views and experiences' (2003: 346).

Persistence in demanding that a child should be continuously communicating through the medium of talk strikes a surprising resemblance to that of the teachers who demanded silence of children in their classes because both reflect a 'top-down' approach to the application of silence that refutes a child's right *to choose*. Interestingly, the high status now given to children's verbal communication stands in stark contrast to the position in which silence is placed in music. In music the first and fundamental requirement is the ability to understand the significance of the silence between notes – not the pitch, nor the higher or lower notes, but the gap between notes.

In relation to a young child's spiritual development, Hyde (2008) believes that a young child needs spaces in between the frameworks of meaning to provide time for quiet, stillness and reflection. Whether or not silent spaces satisfy a child's need for spirituality or serve a meditative function is relative to this discussion – it is simply the choice of a young child to '*just be*' (silent) as a basic human right that is of importance.

On entering an early years setting there is an expectation of a cacophony of sounds awaiting the visitor, both from the children's voices and the actions that those same children are making while engaged in active play with sound-making paraphernalia such as interactive computer games and music-making instruments. This is considered normal and indeed desirable in the quest to 'stimulate' young learners and develop their linguistic and social skills. Practitioners are expected to encourage silent children to talk. Indeed, as previously discussed (see Part 1) initiatives in the UK such as 'Every Child a Talker' (ECAT: DCSF, 2008d) were conceived with the sole intention of encouraging every child to talk. With authoritative confidence ECAT makes explicit how an early years practitioner should encourage talking in the setting and the child's home: '... as well as practitioners talking expressively to children as a matter of routine in the setting, early years practitioners should be encouraging the same practice by parents at home ...' ECAT continues to direct: 'As practitioners, you will be talking regularly with parents about how well their child's language is developing and will be sharing their learning journey' (DCSF, 2008d: 3). I read these apparently 'helpful' instructions with a sense of discomfort. Where are children's rights in this document? Where is the child's agency, and who is taking ownership of the child's voice?

What must it be like for young children bounced from one activity to another, first in their setting and then to attend after-school clubs and other care settings, so as to accommodate the working routines of their parents? Creating a balance between the 'active life' and 'contemplative life' (Alerby, 2004) is a challenge, especially for children who have to demonstrate they meet outcomes through continual assessment against preprescribed learning goals.

Strozzi (2001) describes how, although many children arrive in a setting wanting to talk and to 'get on with things', there are others who may want to just 'be'. The practitioners at Reggio Emilia create spaces where children can just 'be'. 'This dimension of "being" (not becoming) is sought out in certain moments and is appreciated by both children and adults' (Strozzi, 2001: 65). Drawing upon current research, Lancaster and Broadbent (2003), Clark and Moss (2001) and Flewitt (2005) argue that the use of multi-modal methods of analysis can unravel *all* children's learning in early years settings, regardless of whether a child communicates through spoken or unspoken words. During the National Teacher Research Panel's initial study into what impacts upon the quality of children's creativity outdoors (Dimmock and Magraw, 2007), a number of illuminating (and unexpected) findings were revealed. One of the main findings was that appropriate use of silence and presence was an integral pedagogical strategy. In the study's conclusion Dimmock and Magraw state that, 'For us, the most exciting aspect of our finding is the place of silence in all of the above. Presence is not just about direct intervention; it is also about holding a silent creative space' (2007: 4).

> When interior dialogue develops, we are aware of self in a new way ... Just as adults nurture language; we also need to protect the interior spaces in which children come to know themselves. (Silin, 2005: 84)

From Silin's (2005) professional experiences within the classroom, his belief is confirmed that practitioners are often very skilled at helping children to express themselves but not always so good at 'reading' silences. Silin believes that valuing children's silence more often ourselves is important in helping children to develop their inner dialogue. He advocates making a 'space in the midst of the usual classroom chatter for silence to emerge' (2005: 88–5).

Finally, it is important for the early years practitioner to appreciate that language does not stand alone. Not only does it carry socio-cultural understandings of the communities with which it is connected, but in the early years setting it also carries power. The language of instruction in the setting is the dominant monolingual and academic discourse which is accessible to some, but not to all. The spoken language of the setting and classroom is also the carrier of governing political manifestos. For Conteh, the reader is encouraged to 'engage with the details of interaction in order to understand the bigger picture' (2007: 12) because, as Gee (2005) (cited in Conteh, 2007) argues, language can never be considered a politically neutral phenomenon – power is 'part and parcel of using language'. These wise words suggest to the early years practitioner that there is much more to communication and meaning making than simply the spoken word. Through 'silence' all children have the same opportunities to be heard, whether it be through painting, gestures or play – or simply choosing to 'just be'. Every child in an early years setting should have a right to silence.

A period of reflection

It is not only practitioners who need to become more reflective. Young children also need opportunities to be reflective, with time to consider experiences, to make connections and to ponder. Alerby (2004) asks, when do children have time to reflect on what they have done in school? Is there time to sit and listen to them and find out their experience? Alerby stresses the need for 'lived' time (2004: 7), that is time when children are given 'their own time' to think and contemplate and process the information from around.

> Perhaps it is because our individual soundscapes are so often crammed with a variety of sounds that compete and overlap each other that we become bewildered by these periodic moments of auditory space. (de Geest, 1999)

Summary

This chapter has reviewed early years and child rights in relation to areas such as participation and to the 'listening' agenda and its relationship to verbal and active communication. It has argued for re-evaluating a different perspective on these areas of rights. Silence may be difficult to comprehend: it is a misunderstood phenomenon and (in Western culture) little valued, and yet it serves as an invaluable tool for communication and understanding with young children. Theorising over *why* a child might be silent may be fruitless. Instead, perhaps the answer may become visible in answering the questions 'How does a child's right to silence fit in to a contemporary stimulating early years environment?' and 'Where are the quiet places where silence can be valued and nurtured?' Although current and opposing tensions are evident between a child's right to *choose silence* and *imposed silence*, the requirement for silence to be both respected and nurtured is presented as a fundamental *need* within all children's lives. Thus every child should have the right not only to seek out silent spaces (thinking spaces) in early years settings, but also to 'just be'.

Question 8.1 Are 'Children's Rights' currently addressing a child's right to choose silence?

Review Activity

1 Refer back to Unicef Articles 14 and 16. As you work through the following activities think about which of the above Unicef articles each practice activity relates to.

   (a) Can the children in your setting readily choose silent spaces?
   (b) Do children often have opportunities during the day to be alone, stand and stare?

2 If you recognise silence as an essential means through which a young child develops thinking and understandings of her/himself and the world around her/him, consider how you could provide an area of stillness (a thinking space) to 'chill', 'recharge' and/or 'just be' into your setting?

Question 8.2 Whose right to silence?

Review Activity

1 Refer back to the two UNCRC Articles 29 and 30. As you work through the following activities think about which of the above Unicef articles each practice activity relates to.

   (a) What changes could you make to support a child's right to be silent?
   (b) How will you share a child's right to silence with other colleagues and parents?

2 A young bilingual learner (Anyor) has started attending your reception class. She is in the initial stages of English as an additional language acquisition and is not yet speaking in class. Silence is a means for Anyor's communication and understanding – with herself, with important others and with the world around her. Reflect upon how you would best accommodate her learning during this initial phase of non-verbal speech.

Question 8.3   How do early years practitioners respect a child's right to silence?

Review Activity

1 Refer back to UNCRC Article 31. As you work through the following activities think about how UNCRC Articles 31 is related.

   (a) How do you 'listen' to a child's silence?
   (b) Demonstrate how you value children's private thinking spaces.

2 Reflect upon how, as an *affective* early years practitioner, you have attempted to support a child's right to choose silence in your setting?

Further Reading

Alderson, P. (2008) *Young Children's Rights: Exploring Beliefs, Principles, and Practice*, 2nd edn. London: Jessica Kingsley.
A clear and detailed overview of how the UNCRC applies to the youngest children, from birth to eight years of age. This includes a consideration of protection, provision and participation rights.

Clark, A. (2008) *An Introduction to How and Why We Listen to Very Young Children, Listening as a Way of Life Series.* London: ECU.

Clark, A. and Moss, P. (2001) *Listening to Young Children: The Mosaic Approach.* London: National Children's Bureau for the Joseph Rowntree Foundation and Department for Education and Skills.

Dickins, M. (2008) Listening to Young Disabled Children,' *Listening as a Way of Life Series.* London: ECU.
Detailed and useful introductions and overviews to key areas such as choice, listening, empowerment and rights-related approaches to young children.

Dimmock, I. and Magraw, L. (2007) *Silence and Presence: How Adult Attitude Affects the Creativity of Children.* National Teacher Research Panel, DfES Innovation Unit. Available at: http://www.standards.gov.uk/innovation-unit (accessed 18 June 2010).
An introduction and review of issues and practices concerning silence and creativity in work with children.

Education and Children's Rights

Jon Tan

Chapter Overview

The chapter will introduce readers to a rights-based approach to children's experience of education. Starting with a consideration of a number of key policies within the UK that relate to issues of children's and young people's rights, it then considers how practitioners are involved in the maintenance of rights within the school setting, focusing on recent policy reforms that place schools at the centre of provisions for children's and young people's welfare and education and involve significant changes in professional, multi-agency working. Following this, the chapter then considers another key aspect of a rights-based approach in education – the involvement of children and young people's voices within decision-making processes that relate to schools. It concludes that the issue of children and young people's rights represents an area of significant challenge within education policy and the work of schools, one that is made complex by potentially competing policy rhetoric. To help focus the consideration of the breadth of these discussions, this chapter will explore the *core policy and legislative framework that impacts upon schools' considerations of children's and young people's rights*. This helps us understand the policy context of rights when applied to the field of education, and enables us to gain an overview of government's expectations and institutional responsibilities. It will also consider *what the role is of schools and practitioners in the maintenance of children's and young people's rights in education,* to help us examine the complexities of the twenty-first-century school and the implications that multi-professional working has for educational practitioners. Finally, *it will ask how children's and young people's voices are heard within the policy and practice of education.* This section will consider the complex issue of the right of children and young people to be involved in consultation about education provision. It will explore some of the challenges, particularly the relationship between these rights and those of parents within a school standards agenda.

This chapter considers the policy and practice of children's and young people's rights as applied to mainstream compulsory education within the UK. Taking as a starting point the ways in which a significantly altered role for schools has been positioned by policy, it explores the implications and challenges of a multi-professional environment where traditional educative responsibilities have been ever more closely coupled to a social welfare agenda. Such developments in policy and practice have impacted widely, requiring a reconfiguration of school organisation, professional identity and the consideration of children's and young people's perspectives. Moreover, in the UK, such change has been effected across the sector as a whole, largely irrespective of the age range/phase of education to which provision is directed. The chapter examines some of an extensive range of key issues relating to rights and education, such as multi-professional working, accessing the curriculum, taking account of children's and young people's voices, and educating for rights as part of a social justice agenda.

Policy, rights and school professionals – a review of key issues

Considered as a major development in the recognition of children's rights, the United Nations Convention on the Rights of the Child (UNCRC, 1989) has prompted a policy response from successive UK governments since it was introduced in 1989. As discussed in Chapters 1 and 2, centred around four core guiding principles, the UNCRC established a broad landscape of rights associated with children, including rights in educational and welfare terms. These principles were:

- *Non-discrimination.* 'The convention applies to all children, whatever their race, religion or abilities; whatever they think or say; whatever type of family they come from.' (UNCRC, 1989: Article 2)
- *The best interests of the child.* The convention makes clear that '[t]he best interests of children must be the primary concern in making decisions that may affect them. All adults should do what is best for children. When adults make decisions, they should think about how their decisions will affect children. This particularly applies to budget, policy and law makers.' (UNCRC, 1989: Article 3)

- *Right to life, survival and development.* 'Children have the right to live. Governments should ensure that children survive and develop healthily.' (UNCRC, 1989: Article 6)
- *Respect for the views of the child.* 'When adults are making decisions that affect children, children have the right to say what they think should happen and have their opinions taken into account.' (UNCRC, 1989: Article 12)

In the UK, there is resonance with the UNCRC central aims within policy and legislation emanating from successive Conservative, Labour or alliance governments throughout the period to date. Indeed, there is much convergence and stability in the notions of universal rights for children and young people as expressed by policy directives such as the Children's Acts of 1989 and 2004, the far-reaching *Every Child Matters* programme of reform and the latest rendition of policy framework, the Children's Plan (2007). While the earliest of these policies, the Children Act 1989, established a legislative framework for the rights of children, more recently the emphasis has moved towards the development of policy principles and infrastructure that are largely needs and outcomes driven, with some notion of the safeguarding of these rights.

In many ways, the development of a rights-sensitive agenda within UK policy and practice can be understood at three levels of analysis. First, issues concerning children's and young people's rights and the interpretation of the UNCRC have given rise to what might be termed *provision-oriented responses*, characterised by governance of rights through the practice and policy of provision. Secondly, the ratification of the UNCRC in the UK, as discussed in Chapter 1, may also be viewed through a lens that foregrounds the significant mobilisation of policy and practice to address issues of *protection*. This has been a particularly strong emphasis within UK considerations of children's and young people's rights (see Chapter 5 for further discussion of rights and protection). Thirdly, such rights have also become manifest in the ways in which policy and practice have adopted a *language of participation*, stressing the importance of children's and young people's voices in consultation and decision-making (see Chapter 4 for more discussion on issues concerning participation rights). As themes running through the policy and practice responses to the rights agenda, provision, protection and participation have figured significantly within UK developments. Such themes resonate within the discussions of rights and education explored in this chapter.

Since 2002, there has been a growing consideration of inter-agency working as a cornerstone of children's welfare services, firstly in localised practice and service agreements through the Children's Fund (HM Revenue and Customs, 2002). The death of Victoria Climbié in 2000 and the subsequent inquiry led by Lord Laming (2003) brought the need for inter-agency practices into sharp relief. Commenting on what was considered to be '*a widespread organisational malaise'* (Laming, 2003: 4), the report estimated that there had been at least twelve occasions where authorities should have intervened and despite a range of professionals being knowledgeable of the risks to the child's safety, they had failed to do so.

Building from Laming's 108 recommendations, the development of initiatives such as the Every Child Matters programme centralised the notion of inter-agency working within the policy framework and established a core of principles that connect with UNCRC ideas of rights of survivability, development and involvement in decision-making, universally applied. The *Every Child Matters* (DfES, 2003) agenda, for example, can be seen to reflect these directly in its stated intentions:

> Children and young people have told us that five outcomes are key to well-being in childhood and later life – being healthy; staying safe; enjoying and achieving; making a positive contribution; and achieving economic well-being. Our ambition is to improve those outcomes for all children and to narrow the gap in outcomes between those who do well and those who do not. (DfES, 2003: 4)

At the same time, the programme brought closer together aspects of children's welfare and education and, in doing so, placed education professionals and schools at the heart of institutional responses. As Moss has argued, such trends in policy reorganisation of children's services have represented a shift away from what had been, up till then, a separation of health, social care and education services (Moss and Petrie, 2002). The re-emphasis of multi-professional approaches that involve partnership with parents and their communities has further interwoven institutional, parental and professional responsibilities to children and young people. Such a connection between professionals and parents is clear within the kinds of approaches developed:

> Early years settings, primary schools and the best secondary schools have done much to work with parents and involve them in their child's education. However, we have further to go to deliver our vision for all parents, especially in secondary school, and so:
>
> We will set out and consult on a new relationship between parents and schools and legislate if necessary in order that:
>
> - parents will be contacted by a staff member at secondary school before their child starts at the school;
> - parents will be able to attend information sessions at the new school;
> - every child will have a personal tutor who knows them in the round, and acts as a main contact for parents;
> - parents will have regular, up-to-date information on their child's attendance behaviour and progress in learning;
> - Parents Councils will ensure that parents' voices are heard within the school; and
> - parents' complaints will be managed in a straightforward and open way.
>
> (DCSF, 2007: 7)

In summary then, the policy framework within the UK has become increasingly one of complex interconnection. At the heart of provisions for children and young people is a core principle of professional collaboration and multi-agency identification of and responses to needs. Similarly, the expectations of successive governments have placed schools at the centre of much of this service provision, spanning welfare issues of health, staying safe and achieving economic well-being, alongside those of educational achievement traditionally associated with the work of schools and teachers. Thus, while the standards agenda continues to make significant demands on schools' resources, the broadening of responsibilities into other aspects of children's and young people's well-being has presented new challenges for education professionals. Putting schools at the centre of the provision in the delivery of a rights-driven strategy is not without its challenges. In each of the following sections we illustrate, through the use of case studies, two core principles of children's rights – non-discrimination in education and involving children in decision-making. In doing so, we then consider some of the challenges relating to how schools address children and young people's rights in education.

Reviews of rights-based approaches in education

Schools at the centre – a multi-professional approach

The following example documents how one local authority in the UK (Northumberland) introduced a Personal Development Centre to support a number of schools in the area. Working in partnership with a range of 'stakeholders' such as the police, social welfare and healthcare professionals and parents, this study foregrounds issues affecting young people's participation in education. Notably, it highlights the ways in which adaptations to the learning environment and to professional multi-agency partnerships are able to address barriers to children and young people's developmental rights.

> **EXAMPLE 9.1   The Personal Development Centre, Blyth, Northumberland**
>
> In 2008/9, Northumberland County Council established a Personal Development Centre (PDC) to work with schools and families in the area and to provide a different learning environment that supported children and young people who were considered at risk in terms of exclusion from school. As described by the National Strategies summary:
>
>> The PDC is a purpose-built classroom located in a building (formerly a school) in the centre of Blyth. It is co-located with the
>
> *(Continued)*

(Continued)

Blyth Education Support Team (BEST), which is a multi-agency team of professionals delivering a child-centred approach to a vast spectrum of social, emotional, criminal, psychological and health needs to ultimately reduce 'at risk' pupils from exclusion.

The PDC educates pupils for two days per week over a half-term (six weeks) or full-term (12 weeks) period of intervention. Pupils are referred to the PDC by headteachers from nine first schools and four middle schools in the town of Blyth. Referred pupils generally have social and emotional behavioural issues.

The PDC is a nurture-based classroom. It houses eight PCs and an interactive whiteboard, and has several teaching desks. In addition there is a fitted kitchen, dining table and cooking facilities which are used to enrich the alternative *Every Child Matters* curriculum.

The PDC has its own minibus transport which is used to educate pupils off-site. This helps motivate and develop career aspirations as well as broadening knowledge of the local environment. On the three remaining days, pupils work with a member of staff from the PDC in their host school in developing classroom-coping strategies that have been taught and practised in the PDC.

(DCSF, 2009b)

Clearly, the PDC is representative of the adaptation of the educational environment and the patterns of how professionals interface with pupils and their families in order to facilitate access to education. At the same time, the PDC in Blyth also operates as a centre-point for the coordination of a range of professionals through the Educational Support Team.

In a process such as that illustrated in Example 9.1, after the initial referral of a pupil by headteachers, an individual and their family might draw upon support through social services, healthcare professionals and the police. Such support may provide access to interventions to help family literacy in support of a child's learning, to address health and social care (e.g. children identified as primary carers) and to address behavioural issues. Perhaps most notably, it suggests a close, coordinated response from professionals that requires collaborative approaches to needs assessment, strategic planning of service intervention and forward planning that enables individuals and their families to make supported transitions beyond any short-life intervention.

Multi-professional approaches: some critical considerations

Example 9.1 provides a useful example of how education services have sought to reconsider the ways in which provision might be arranged to accommodate the needs of its children and young people. With issues of inclusion increasingly present in government policy, and in response to what may be seen as the non-discriminatory emphasis of the UNCRC, examples such as this exist as an indicator of how policy responses (though sometimes still within the remit of education) now draw on a range of practitioners. At the heart of this is, of course, the idea of *need*.

There is significant rhetoric within policy about the importance of providing services that are responsive to children's and young people's needs, provision that is tailored to that need. Yet, at the same time, one has to read beneath the surface of much education policy to see how children's and young people's rights are being addressed. As Henricson and Bainham (2005) commented in relation to *Every Child Matters* (DfES, 2003), for example:

> [It] makes scant overt reference to human and children's rights obligations. In terms of overarching aims, it is solely concerned with child outcomes and makes no concession to the independent entitlements of parents and families ... There is no discussion of the human right entitlement to respect for family life ... While we have seen that in practice this approach is largely followed, a strategic document of this nature should have made reference to such basic human entitlements. (Henricson and Bainham, 2005: 57)

What is, perhaps, more clear within the UK's development of policies to address children's rights issues is the movement towards a universal provision that is non-discriminatory and one that places schools centrally in delivery. Thus while much policy certainly places emphasis on education outcomes, these are bound up in a broader web of social provision that involves schools and their practitioners.

Taking multi-professional working specifically, the realities of this joining up of services is not without its challenges. Anning's research for the Economic and Social Research Council (ESRC) documents the tensions and impact on professional identities:

> For the teams to develop as learning communities, tensions arising from team members learning new roles and assuming new responsibilities and forging new professional identities had to be resolved. Roles included bridging or

> brokering knowledge exchange between agencies represented within the team structures and without. Changing roles could threaten professionals' sense of themselves as specialists where teams worked towards blurring boundaries of responsibilities to create generic (generalist) workers. On the other hand, individuals within teams spoke of the creative energy released by forging enhanced, or even multiple, identities within multi-agency teams, particularly when professionals felt that their career opportunities were enhanced by the changes. Others spoke of feelings of loss as their roles changed, in particular the loss of identity as a specialist. (Anning, 2005: 2)

Considering the principles of non-discrimination and development, one can illustrate how the concept of rights is embedded within UK education policy, particularly as part of the significant emphasis on inclusion. Here, the use of multi-agency approaches to secure such rights within education is exemplified by case studies of provision that are directed towards 'vulnerable', 'at risk' groups such as children from Gypsy Traveller communities. In the case of the Gypsy Traveller communities, schools often work in partnership with a range of educational and welfare services, and advisory and support teachers, coordinated through Traveller Education Support Services (TESS). At the heart of these coordinated approaches is the joint planning of provision, enabling a range of specialised professionals and interventions to assess need and to mobilise whole-school, classroom- and individually-based provision. The following is an example of the ways in which guidelines can reflect these relationships in order to address issues rights and social exclusion:

> The general principles of effective partnership strategies are similar to the process of joint planning carried out within schools between class teachers, Ethnic Minority Achievement (EMA) coordinators and/or SENCOs. This joint planning process may need to involve a range of partners – for example, in the case of Roma children who will be learning English as an additional language, the involvement of EMA support staff will be important. As well as providing individual or small-group support, it may be appropriate for the Advisory Teacher to work with the whole class to allow the class teacher to focus more closely on a group which includes Gypsy Travellers. This will give the teacher the opportunity to assess whether the child is achieving the learning objectives and whether subsequent learning objectives need to be modified accordingly. (DfES, 2003: 4)

Recent education policy has thus instigated fundamental changes towards schools being the locus of action for multi-agency intervention, and has suggested an orientation of schools as centres that are interconnected with individuals and community. The heavy reliance on education as the mechanism through which the children's rights agenda is taken forward has, nevertheless, met with criticism. As the Children's Rights Alliance for England (CRAE) responded in its considerations of the Children's Plan (2007):

> The delivery mechanism for many of the ambitious reforms set out in the report appears somewhat 'educentric', relying on assumptions that children are fully engaged in their school communities. While acknowledging that

schools are important centres around which to collocate and co-ordinate many services for children and their families, the needs of children who are disengaged from school must be adequately accommodated. (Children's Rights Alliance for England, 2009: 3)

Criticisms aside, while multi-professional working seems to answer well the need of policy to respond in a coherent and collaborative way, the challenges associated with inter-professional work and notions of professional identities and cultures perhaps require continuous professional learning to sit alongside everyday practice. Here, practitioners are *learning* to work together, and under ideal circumstances they exist as learning organisations. Just as professions learn to work collaboratively with each other, accommodating rights to be involved in decision-making raises further challenges for professionals to work with children, young people and families.

Working in consultation with children: schools and democracy

In the field of education, the notion of children and young people as active participants is not new. Indeed, the idea of their active involvement in the construction of meaning and knowledge has provided much of the foundation of progressive educational philosophy. In the years following the UNCRC, alongside emphasis on child protection and access to provision, the taking account of children's and young people's voices and involving them democratically in the relationship between provision and 'end-user' has gathered momentum. A report by the National Foundation for Educational Research (NFER) suggested that the accommodation of such perspectives through democratic processes has the potential to effect organisational change alongside positive individual developments for participating young people in such areas as individual self-esteem, confidence, behaviour and civic and political competence (Halsey *et al.*, 2006). While not confined to reviewing research literature that focused wholly on education, Halsey *et al.* (2006) nevertheless provide some weight to the idea that working in consultation with children and young people in organisations such as schools can have wide-ranging positive effects.

Example 9.2 illustrates the work of school councils as a means of involving children and young people in decisions. In accordance with the UNCRC's (1989) emphasis on the need for children and young people to be consulted and for their voices to be heard in matters related to them, there has been a significant growth in the use of school councils in the UK. Whitty and Wisby reported that almost 95 per cent of schools in England and Wales had a school council and over 60 per cent of teachers considered that they should be compulsory in England (Whitty and Wisby, 2007). Characteristic of such examples of giving children and young people a voice in educational decisions, the study in Example 9.2 considers a council as a democratic development, in many cases linked to personal, social education, citizenship and social justice.

> ### EXAMPLE 9.2   St Joseph's Comprehensive School, South Tyneside[1]
>
> St Joseph's Comprehensive School in South Tyneside, was one of seven school case studies reported in Davies *et al.* (2006), as part of the Carnegie Young People's Initiative supported by the Esmée Fairbairn Foundation. A comprehensive school of Roman Catholic denomination, the school consists of a student population of approximately 1,500 pupils, including those attending the school's sixth form. As reported in Davies *et al.* (2006), the majority of students are of white British heritage with the national statistical average of pupils receiving free school meals. The school council has elected representation of students from all year groups, council members being elected by their peers at the beginning of each academic year. New members are mentored by those more experienced. As a member of the South Tyneside School Council network and linked to the South Tyneside Youth Parliament, St Joseph's school council also has the opportunity to communicate with locally elected Councillors and other local government agencies.

The report published by the Esmée Fairbairn Foundation cites a number of examples of the school council representing young people's views, enabling them to have a democratic involvement in the shaping of school policies and practices. For example, students were involved in discussions regarding school homework practices, conducting research with the school community that resulted in further staff/student consultation in re-drafting policy with an emphasis on relevance, the connectedness between homework tasks and classroom work, and the importance of feedback. In other discussions with students, the school agreed to move towards a mixed-ability grouping for school organisation, following concerns about negative effects of a 'banding' system on motivation. Other initiatives, allied to the work of the school council, included fund-raising events, the organisation of an anti-racism week and links with the community through charitable activities.

In terms of impact, the evaluative work carried out as part of the Carnegie Young People's Initiative reported that:

> students spoke very positively about what they saw as the benefits of being involved in school decision making. For example, in reference to the homework policy consultation, they believed that their findings were of real benefit to both teachers and students ... The involvement of South Tyneside School

Council also promised to create better understandings and relationships among young people across the region, who tend to isolate themselves and have stereotypes about young people in other areas. Teachers and the Senior Management Team think that students could provide valuable contributions to environment and teaching and learning issues at school. (Davies *et al.*, 2006: 27–8)

Clearly, in this example, it is the impact of organisational practices that is emphasised. Here, the development of mechanisms for the consideration of children and young people's perspectives on school policies and practices have been utilised to inform decisions and practices at an organisational level. Relying on children and young people as evaluators and researchers is perhaps only one aspect of the experience generated by practices that involve children, young people and adults working collaboratively. Reviewing research evidence more generally suggests much wider benefits at organisational, individual and social levels (Halsey *et al.*, 2006).

Children and young people's voice: some critical considerations

The example of St Joseph's Comprehensive School stands as a good illustration of the ways in which school councils can operate to accommodate children and young people's voices in the school policy-making process. Pupils are involved in what seem to be core issues regarding school organisation and discussions of teaching and learning (e.g. homework policy and pupil class grouping). There is also some, though limited, reported evidence of school councils working towards broader awareness issues such as racism.

In response to government initiatives the majority of schools in England and Wales have established school councils as a means to achieve children's and young people's involvement in decision-making. While positive benefits and possibilities are often reported, Whitty and Wisby's work (2007) suggests that not all school councils enable student participation in decisions related to teaching and learning issues. As they summarise:

> Of the 2,417 pupils surveyed, a significant proportion attend schools which already have some form of provision for pupil voice in place. For example, 85 per cent reported that their school had a school council. Areas in which pupils had been able to input into decision making included anti-bullying initiatives and recycling policies. Only a small percentage (12 per cent) had been involved in decisions around teaching and learning. (Whitty and Wisby, 2007: 2–3)

Within Whitty and Wisby's research there is clear indication that children and young people's engagement in decision-making processes is only meaningful if it is *real* consultation that potentially gives over some degree of power to them. Perhaps their involvement in decisions concerning teaching and learning issues – found lacking by Whitty and Wisby (2007) – is a manifestation of traditional power relations between practitioners and students. The possible reluctance by professionals for such core decisions about school business to be subject to the uncertainties presented by children and young people's involvement may be indicative of central tensions in rhetoric about school standards, pupil and parental choice and practitioner professionalism (Henricson and Bainham, 2005). As Whitty and Wisby conclude:

> Despite the many potential benefits of provision for pupil voice, including school councils, the argument for school councils often lacks clarity. This means that school councils and related activities are often being introduced with insufficient strategic thinking in relation to the purposes they are meant to serve and without a clear idea of success criteria against which they can be properly evaluated. This can lead to neutral or even negative outcomes. The four drivers outlined in the research – children's rights, active citizenship, school improvement and personalisation – provide a starting point for thinking about aims and objectives for provision for pupil voice.
>
> Related to this, policy makers and schools should beware of viewing pupil voice as merely a means of supporting the current policy agenda. Genuine provision for pupil voice requires some power and influence to be passed to pupils, at which point it becomes unpredictable. Where this does not happen, there is the danger that pupil voice, and school councils in particular, could produce a cohort of young people who are cynical about democratic processes.
>
> (Whitty and Wisby, 2007: 4)

A number of studies have also made it clear that the effectiveness of school councils to operate as a means of student consultation and the promotion of citizenship education is greatest 'where there is a democratic ethos within the school and where teachers are committed to consultation, shared decision-making and to the promoting of the active involvement of young people in civic responsibility, through a range of learning activities supporting citizenship education' (Taylor and Johnson, 2002: 21). With citizenship education gaining in significance within the primary and secondary curriculum, coupled with a policy rhetoric for schools to draw ever closer to their communities, it is clear that taking account of the different 'voices' within the school environment represents a significant challenge. It is a precarious pathway between rights, responsibilities and entitlements that school leaders constantly navigate, responding to parental, student, curriculum, local and national governmental and practitioner agendas.

Children's rights and education: a political conundrum?

This chapter has considered some of the ways in which a children's and young people's rights agenda has been taken forward within mainstream school settings within the UK context. It is clear that the political landscape regarding rights has undergone significant changes since the CRC came into being in 1989. An analysis of UK policies related to children and young people shows considerable reform in the organisation of services concerned with welfare and education. Since 1997, New Labour's approach has consistently put education and schools at the centre of such provision delivery. Coupled with a political emphasis on partnership, community and choice, these policy emphases have suggested a closer relationship between schools, parents, students and their communities. In doing so, the role of the school has become extended, blurring any policy boundaries between aspects of health, social care, learning and development.

However, at the same time, a direct address of the United Nations Convention on the Rights of the Child within UK policy has been difficult to identify. Instead, children's rights have been taken forward in indirect ways as part of an outcomes-driven political agenda. Similarly, the 'space' within education where issues of rights and social justice might have been allowed to take the centre stage (e.g. within the curriculum and through socially just pedagogies) has become crowded out by a preoccupation with basic skills, literacy and numeracy.

Summary

There are, as this chapter has outlined, aspects of good practice where schools themselves have moved beyond conceptualising the children's rights agenda as being mainly about ensuring care, protection and the *right to education*, to addressing the relational dimensions between adult practitioners and children and young people. The development of the school as an organisation that *involves* children and young people as active citizens requires modifications to traditional power relations between teachers, students, parents and governmental agencies. Such modifications are fundamental and require difficult questions to be asked about the persistence of educational and social inequalities where certain voices are heard and others remain silenced. This is a significantly different conceptualisation of citizenship to that contained within the curriculum. As Mouffe states:

> This is a conception of citizenship which, through a common identification with a radical democratic interpretation of the principles of liberty and equality, aims at constructing a 'we', a chain of equivalence among their demands so as to articulate them through the principle of democratic equivalence. For it is not a matter of establishing a mere alliance between given interests but of actually modifying the very identity of these forces. (Mouffe, 1997: 70)

Perhaps, then, in considering the issue of children's rights as manifested within the UK education and political system, we should ask whether a policy preoccupation with outcomes rather than the direct addressing of social justice and children's rights is a political convenience?

Question 9.1   What is the core policy and legislative framework that impacts upon schools' considerations of children's and young people's rights?

Review Activity

1 In considering some of the tensions and issues concerning child rights and education the chapter comments on the 'precarious pathway between rights, responsibilities and entitlements that school leaders constantly navigate, responding to parental, student, curriculum, local and national governmental and practitioner agendas'.

  (a) Identify an example of 'rights' from within the chapter.
  (b) Identify an example of 'responsibilities' from within the chapter.
  (c) Identify an example of 'entitlements' from within the chapter.

2 In reading the chapter and drawing on your own experiences consider this 'pathway' and identify:

  (a) what you consider to be an example of where these different agendas come together in a way that works well;
  (b) what you consider to be an example of where these different agendas come together in a way that creates tension.

In both cases consider *why* you think the example works well or *why* there is tension. What implications for practice can you draw from your consideration of these examples?

Question 9.2   What is the role of schools and practitioners in the maintenance of children's and young people's rights in education?

Review Activity

1 Read through the chapter and note down what it says about the role of:

  (a) school policies and practices;
  (b) the ways professionals conduct themselves and their work with children.

2 Consider whether your setting can helpfully develop its ways of working in response to your notes about roles.

〰〰 **Question 9.3   How are children and young people's voices heard within the policy and practice of education?**

Review Activity

The chapter suggests that St Joseph's Comprehensive School in Example 9.2 'stands as a good illustration of the ways in which school councils can operate to accommodate children and young people's voices in the school policy-making process'.

1 Review Example 9.2 and consider whether you agree with this comment or not, taking into account some of the issues raised about children and their rights within education.

2 (a) What issues does the chapter raise as problematic in relation to school councils?

   (b) Consider these problematic areas in relation to the discussion of how to create effective participation in Chapter 4. Can you identify any issues which are important to take care of in school council work?

Note

1 This case study is taken from *Inspiring Schools: Case Studies for Change*, authored by Lynn Davies *et al.* (2006) and funded by the Esmée Fairburn and Carnegie Young People's Initiative. A full reference is provided at the end of the book.

Further Reading 📖

Moss, P. and Petrie, P. (2002) *From Children's Services to Children's Spaces: Public Policy, Children and Childhood*. London: RoutledgeFalmer.
An effective consideration of rights in relation to different disciplines including education.

Taylor, M. J. and Johnson, R. (2002) *School Councils: Their Role in Citizenship and Personal and Social Education*. Slough: NFER.
An effective overview of the nature and practice of school councils, including practical perspectives and considerations from different viewpoints.

10

Children's Rights, Identity and Learning: The Case for Bilingualism

Avril Brock and Jean Conteh

Chapter Overview

Bilingualism is a global phenomenon. The majority of children are growing up bilingually and most large cities around the world 'are abuzz with different languages being spoken' (Gregory, 2008: xiii). In the UK, patterns of migration for employment because of the expansion of the European Union have recently led to an increasing diversity of families, communities and therefore languages taking root. Similar trends can be seen in the migration of groups of people for protection from war and persecution, such as those from countries like Somalia, Burma and Afghanistan. Well-established, settled communities of bilingual British citizens, whose heritage is often in post-colonial regions such as the Caribbean and South Asia, need to have their language rights recognised and maintained. Many countries, Australia and Canada included, emphasise bilingualism as both a personal and national resource (Edwards, 2004). But government policies and practices in both early childhood education and in school settings in England often take a narrower view of bilingualism. They may promote the use of the languages of the home as a means of translation, interpretation and transition into English, but do not recognise the advantages and the benefits of becoming truly bilingual, for both their pupils and the wider society. This is not the case, as Edwards shows, in parts of Scotland and Ireland and the whole of Wales. However, there is no specific language education policy in the UK that upholds children's right to have a bilingual status. The main argument of this chapter is that, for children, the right to become bilingual is important both for academic success and for becoming a full citizen of the UK. This can be achieved through recognising both the language rights of children and their families and the responsibilities of education practitioners in supporting them. This chapter argues that promoting children's bilingualism is an essential element of their educational success. It contextualises concerns about language being at the heart of rights and illustrates the relationship between rights, policy and this aspect of children's lives. The chapter emphasises the importance of participation rights in relation to understanding and responding to bilingual children's needs on the part of those involved in developing service provision.

The chapter explores the current situation, highlighting the contradictions in policy, ideas for best practice and future developments within education.

There is an increasing acknowledgement that children are not merely the future workforce but are competent experts in their own lives with their own rights, and that their voices need to be heard. Children have complex lives, cultural experiences and identities which are not readily reduced to simple, statistically led categorisations (Ainscow *et al.*, 2007). Language is one key aspect of their diverse identities. Promoting and developing first and additional languages is an important means to ensuring that bilingual children are able to achieve their full academic and social potential.

The chapter contextualises the issues through an overview of research and theory which show the positive benefits of bilingualism. It also highlights the political influences that have underpinned decisions in education policy in England relating to the education and language provision for children defined as learning English as an additional language (EAL). It contains rich examples of the personal perspectives of children, parents and educators to illuminate the arguments. The chapter begins by setting up the argument that the rights of the child in terms of language and bilingualism need to be contextualised within family, educational settings, policy and professionals' expertise. Four examples of children and the ways in which they mediate their social interactions, learning and identities bilingually are included. These are taken from home, foundation stage, mainstream school, and complementary and other learning settings. Key issues are then explored, drawing on research and theoretical frameworks for bilingualism and bilingual education. These consider the children's experiences and point towards implications for policy and practice. The chapter then focuses directly upon rights issues: discussing the ways in which children's rights to be bilingual are represented legally and in educational policy, and mediated by their families and their educators. Implications for educational policy and practice are then considered. These include family involvement in learning, classroom practices and assessment of learners along with workforce education and development.

Framing the rights of the child

The UN Convention on the Rights of the Child (UNCRC) and the European Convention on Human Rights (ECHR) afford children the same range of civil, political, economic, social and cultural rights as adults. Children have an important place in the 'public domain of society and the private domain of the family', which is a site of diversity and a crucial part *of* society that requires respect and support *from* society (Children in Europe Policy Paper, 2008). Children need to be regarded as active participants in their own lives with the right to express views on all matters of concern to them (for details of this aspect of rights, see Chapter 1). Their needs, best interests and entitlements should be taken into account in any policy-making. Inclusive practice means that children should take part in decision-making processes (Nutbrown, 1996; Nutbrown and Clough, 2006).

The complex and powerful influences that home and community have on young children's educational achievements and individual well-being are well documented (Fabian, 2002; Brooker, 2002, 2006; Sylva *et al.*, 2002; Whalley, 2008). Parents and families are children's first educators and they have crucial roles in promoting young children's future development and educational achievement. All parents have the right to participate in decision-making regarding their children's education (Miller *et al.*, 2002), and there is a growing expectation that professionals work in partnership with families (for further discussion of this area see Chapter 9). The Early Years Foundation Stage (EYFS) curriculum (DCSF, 2008e) recognises that 'early support for children includes listening to families and taking part in a sensitive two-way exchange of information'. However, there is no clear understanding about how such principles can be applied to families' aspirations for their children's bilingualism, nor guidance for ways of supporting families in promoting the development of their children's fluency in more than one language.

It often falls to one or both parents, and possibly carers or grandparents, to nurture young children's developing bilingualism, enabling them to learn and maintain their first language through communicating with them on a daily basis. This input and interaction is crucial for encouraging language development in first and additional languages. However, parents in England who are trying to promote their children's heritage languages and develop their bilingualism/multilingualism frequently feel isolated and unsupported. There is often pressure from others, including the education system, to become proficient in the host language of a country, even at the expense of the first heritage language. Aims nurtured within the family are often undervalued by national policy, educators and the wider society.

This quote from 'Naheeda',[1] a young second-generation British-Asian, on the condition of her bilingualism demonstrates the difficulties often encountered by children and families where the first language is becoming subsumed into the host language of a country:

> Gujerati is my second language. It should be the other way but it's not. I never really picked up my home language, I picked up English first for some reason and then picked up Gujerati from friends rather than family. My parents spoke both languages at home, but I just picked the English up quicker. I do not even think I'm fluent enough in Gujerati to get by.

Cunningham Andersson and Andersson's (2004) research explores the issues families face when their children are growing up with two languages. They draw on interviews with 50 families from around the world, demonstrating the trials and rewards encountered by families who live in countries where their heritage language is in the minority. They find the single most important factor for language maintenance to be motivation, on the part both of parents and the children involved. In their view, bringing up children with two languages need not be difficult. The commitment and perseverance of parents is obviously key to success, particularly in countries like England, where there is as, as yet, little systematic support nationally.

While the first and most crucial site for the nurturing of bilingualism is undoubtedly the child's family and immediate community, once he or she enters formal mainstream schooling, the context inevitably widens and the range of influences increases. To nurture bilingualism in school so that it becomes a positive resource in learning, it is essential that, at all levels, teaching and learning take account of all the languages that comprise learners' repertoires. The professionals with whom bilingual learners come into contact thus need to have access to training and continuing professional development to provide them with the relevant professional attributes, skills and knowledge to ensure that this can happen. National and whole-school policies, the curriculum, teaching and learning strategies and resources all need to work together to make their contribution to a positive, supportive learning environment for the bilingual child. We explore these issues further below.

Vignettes

In this section, we provide vignettes of children's experiences, in both family and school contexts, which illustrate their bilingual capacities and identities, as well as some of the tensions involved in recognising their right to be bilingual.

Bilingualism in families

The following two vignettes illustrate some of the issues families face in attempting to nurture their young children's bilingualism, and show how support can be provided in settings from a young age.

EXAMPLE 10.1   Sanela: Tensions in supporting bilingualism – a mother's view

This example is taken from one interview of many undertaken for *Communication, Language and Literacy from Birth to Five* (Brock and Rankin: 2008: 38, 41). It demonstrates how difficult it can be for individual families to support their children's right to operate at a high level in two languages. Parents were asked to talk about their practices and the issues they faced in their children's early language development. Sanela moved to Bradford, England, from Slovakia to marry her English husband and when she had her first child, Sofia, she was determined to bring her up bilingually. She highlights the challenges involved. Living in England and being completely surrounded by English language and culture means that, although her family visits a few times a year, there are insufficient opportunities for Sofia to hear or speak Slovak:

> I just haven't got enough Slovak around me to use it, though I try to do so. Sofia has got a good vocabulary but she is not speaking it naturally like she is English. If I speak to her in Slovak, she understands me, but she is just not really responding in Slovak. I think it is purely because we don't have any family or friends nearby who would be speaking Slovak. So a few times a year when my family come over or we go there, it is not enough for her to be fluent in it. It is a shame because she has got the vocabulary, the interest and aptitude. It is hard, especially if I go out with friends, she hears me speaking English with friends. If my husband is at home, he is English and his Slovak is not very fluent – he does have some vocabulary but it is easy for us just to slip into English. So Sofia mostly hears me speaking in English. If I occasionally speak to her in Slovak for certain games or activities, she does understand but I don't think she considers it as my first or my natural language. She hears English so often and when she starts to go to nursery she will be even more exposed to English, but I will try. I have a friend who has two children aged four and two so we do try to see each other, but it is tricky as she is a nurse working nights, so we see each other only once a month which is not enough for them to be exposed to Slovak conversation. She is also married to an English man and she doesn't use her language much in front of her children.

Sanela and her friend both feel guilty because although they are extremely committed to developing their children's heritage language and enabling them to become fluent bilinguals, they are finding it increasingly difficult. They really want to speak to them in Slovak, but they feel quite isolated in 'this English culture' and its 'monolingualising' (Heller, 1995) ethos, and also because there just isn't enough exposure to the Slovak language.

EXAMPLE 10.2 Families' relationships with settings – the importance of outreach

This vignette derives from an evaluation undertaken in 2003 by the Department of Teacher Education at Bradford College for Bradford Early Years Services. The evaluation team comprised a college lecturer in early years and language and four bilingual students, whose participation was crucial to the success of the evaluation because of their ability to gain exceptionally rich data from the parents who had benefited from the project.

Bradford's 'Earlystart' Project (Power and Brock, 2006) was a five-year Single Regeneration Budget government-funded initiative aimed at helping young children from families where English was not their first language with speaking and understanding before they started school. The key aims of the project were to celebrate and value children's home languages as part of their identity, and to support bilingualism as a positive asset for learning. This was promoted through encouraging families to visit the settings and so benefit from the support that was available. One grandmother commented: 'We felt very welcome because the staff speak my own language and I enjoy bringing my granddaughter here'.

The outreach workers in the project spoke five languages between them – Bangla, English, Gurmurki Punjabi, Punjabi and Urdu. They promoted young bilingual children's language, learning and achievement through work that encouraged both home-based learning through play and books as well as sessions in four nursery schools. The following is one mother's view of the value of these sessions:

> Attending these sessions helps me to understand the importance of play; it has given me the opportunity to get involved in the trips and doing cooking activities. I particularly like borrowing dual language books because my husband can't speak English, but can read to our child in Bengali, which makes him feel involved.

The outreach workers identified many barriers facing parents in terms of their children's education. Some mothers felt disadvantaged because they spoke little or no English. They believed their children should be speaking English most of the time, and so felt they were unable to provide good pre-school education for their children. The outreach workers reassured parents that development in their first language was very important and that children would soon pick up English in school. This was confirmed by one mother:

> He is picking up a lot of English in comparison to other children who don't take part in the Earlystart project. In general

(Continued)

(Continued)

> his language skills have improved greatly. I also like it because they encourage my child to speak in our own language as well as English. I feel that this nursery values home language by helping to support bilingualism.

In this way both the family's and the individual child's rights to have their first language valued and their bilingualism nurtured were both being promoted. One of the project's main aims was to encourage mothers to talk with their children more, in order to develop home language skills and to boost everyone's confidence:

> Although I can't speak English I do help her look at books and tell the story in my own language and also we talk about the things that are going on in the book and tell the story that way. At first I was very shy to read to my son in public. I had to be on my own when I read to him where no one was listening and looking. I am more confident now and don't mind reading to him in front of other people.

The outreach workers acted as a bridge between home and school for mothers who felt intimidated because they spoke little or no English and so felt unable to come into school to discuss their children's learning. One grandmother commented that:

> ... we feel that we are more important. My other grandchildren used to attend this place; however, we were not that comfortable about bringing our children because there was no Punjabi-speaking staff and we didn't feel valued. I now feel I can speak and communicate with the staff and can understand how I can help.

Some parents had little or no formal education themselves in their countries of origin and did not understand the system in England. The outreach workers and staff involved in the project were able to support parents' access to information and knowledge about their rights to early education for their children. The outreach work enabled communication with parents in the security of their own homes, answering any questions they might have and encouraging parents to visit the school. The parents really appreciated the work of the outreach workers and teachers:

> It has helped the family become aware of how they could all help. The outreach worker also talked to my grandma, she was very interested in how she could help because my son is her first grandchild she wants the best for him.

The members of the extended families felt the benefits of the project and it achieved valuable results. However, as with many government initiatives, the funding was short term so there were difficulties in sustaining this good practice. Such work needs to be ongoing to maintain young children's developing bilingualism and cultural identity in both home and educational settings.

Bilingualism and learning in school

The following two vignettes illustrate ways in which individual bilingual children, given appropriate encouragement, can use their language resources to support their learning in mainstream schools, and the importance of this for their self-esteem and identities as learners. The first is part of an interview from a research project which explored the links children made between their learning in community-based 'Saturday classes' and in mainstream school. The second is an incident that happened to a 'language support teacher' in a primary school.

EXAMPLE 10.3   Sameena: 'performing identities'

Sameena is eight years old and bilingual in Punjabi and English. In her interview, she described what she did in a 'hot mental' activity (part of the National Numeracy Strategy) in her mainstream Year 3 class when her teacher asked her to count from 25 to 50 in fives. As she spoke, she varied the pitch of her voice to demonstrate how the counting in Punjabi was going on silently in her head while she said aloud the numbers in English that answered her teacher's question. In repeating the counting from 1 to 4 and then from 6 to 9 in Punjabi silently and saying the relevant number in English aloud in between, she always kept the numbers in both languages in sequential order:

> We had to count in fives, so I did it in my head in Punjabi then I said it out in English … Ek, do, teen, cha … twenty-five … chey, saat, aat, nor … Thirty … Ek, do, teen, cha ….. thirty-five …

This kind of skilled performance has been described as codeswitching (Conteh, 2007: 467) and is a common feature of the ways that bilinguals use their languages. But the notion of switching does not – perhaps – do full justice to the nature of the feat that Sameena is actually accomplishing, the way she is creatively and holistically using all her language resources at the same time to solve the problem set by her teacher. Garcia (2007: xiii) introduces the term 'translanguaging', a concept fully examined by Creese and Blackledge (2010), who describe it as:

(Continued)

(Continued)

> … the speaker uses her languages in a pedagogic context to make meaning, transmit information, and perform identities using the linguistic signs at her disposal to connect with her audience in community engagement.

The idea of 'performing identities' is clearly a significant one for Sameena in terms of the positive ways she has found to use her languages to succeed as a pupil in mainstream school, and also to participate in the Saturday class. She reported proudly to her Saturday class teacher that she had reached Level 3 (above expectations) in her KS1 Maths SATs (Standard Attainment Tasks) and that her bilingual counting strategy had helped her to do this. Her participation in the Saturday class was clearly very important in giving her confidence to use her Punjabi for learning in the mainstream class, albeit unknown to her mainstream teacher.

EXAMPLE 10.4   Mushtaq: the power of story

Mushtaq began his schooling in England at the age of nine, newly arrived with his mother from Bangladesh after the death of his father. They were to be looked after by his uncle, a restaurant owner in Bradford. A Hindu, Mushtaq was in the minority in the school that he joined where most of the pupils were Muslim. I met him for the first time in school one cold November morning. Unable to speak a word of English, he was assigned to my group for 'language support'. I was working with a group of about 12 children on a story, all of us sitting round a large round table in 'Room 3'. Mushtaq came into the class, he sat down next to Ali, the only other Bengali-speaking child, and spent the whole session in silence, composed and watchful. We carried on with our work on a West African traditional story. After the oral telling, each child chose a section to illustrate. While they worked, I worried about how to include Mushtaq, who sat in watchful silence. The session finished and the children went back to their classrooms.

The next morning, early, I was in Room 3 setting up for the day when the door opened and in came Mushtaq. Silently, with a smile on his face, he handed me a piece of paper covered in neat script. I took it from him as he went off to registration. I had no idea what it said, nor even what script the text was written in. I knew it was not Urdu; I had seen plenty of examples of that around the neighbourhood of the school. At a loss what to do, I walked along to the staff room, where I met the Hindu teacher who was in school that day to conduct inter-faith worship. Just in case he could help, I showed him the paper. His response was powerful, 'Who gave you this?' he asked excitedly and then went on to tell me that the text on the paper was written in Bengali and was a story about how the Sun and Moon came to live in the sky – the very story I had told my group the day before.

So, Mushtaq had given me back my story and in doing so he had shown me that he was highly literate in his first language. It turned out that Ali had re-told the story in Bengali for him and Mushtaq had written it down at home for me. Realising how proud he was of his literacy in Bengali, I asked him to help us write a dual-language book of the story where he provided the Bengali text and the other children wrote sections in English. We went on to produce several such books, which Mushtaq, on his suggestion, audio-recorded for other Bengali-speaking children to hear. From this, he began to learn to read the English sections for himself and then progressed to texts in English only. Within six months, he was one of the best readers in the whole class. The production of the tapes in Bengali had an incidental outcome for the other Bengali-speaking children in the school, at times an embattled minority in their relationships with the Punjabi-speaking majority. The tapes and books gave them pride in their own language, and Mushtaq became a strong role model for them. His confidence and pride in his literacy in his own language was a strong factor in raising the self-esteem and identity of the whole group in the school.

Theory, rights and bilingualism

The benefits for learning of being bilingual have been documented by many researchers (Brock, 1999; Cummins, 2000; Conteh, 2006a; Baker, 2007; Drury and Robertson, 2008):

> Irrespective of languages or geographical locations, children who acquire two or more languages from birth, or learn a second language after the acquisition of the first language, demonstrate strengths. (Drury and Robertson, 2008)

Cummins (2001), reporting empirical work going back over twenty years with French-English bilinguals in Canada, introduced the socio-cognitive theories of 'language thresholds' (pp. 104–8), Basic Interpersonal Communicative Skills (BICS) and Cognitive Academic Language Proficiency (CALP) (pp. 57–8) and 'linguistic interdependence' (pp. 109–12) into discussions about bilingualism. His theoretical models which have been developed over the years (Cummins, 2000) provide powerful explanations for many distinctive features of bilingual behaviour, showing how learning first and additional languages are linked, and how academic language – distinct from conversational proficiency – needs time to develop. This is affirmation of the efforts of parents, such as Sanela in Example 10.1 and the parents in the outreach project in Example 10.2, in nurturing their children's bilingualism. In upholding their right to be bilingual, one key aspect of Cummins' model is the need to recognise learners' whole experience of language as part of their 'common underlying proficiency' in whichever language they are using, and the ways in which their learning in different languages can work together to provide firm foundations for new learning and cognitive development. It is also, as Sameena's and Mushtaq's examples illustrate, a powerful aspect of learners' identities.

Recent research theorising young children's literacy learning (e.g. Gee, 1996; Street, 2003) is important for understanding the needs of those bilingual learners already literate in their first language, such as Mushtaq. This work has led to the 'many pathways' model of literacy learning (Gregory *et al.*, 2004), which has implications for the rights agenda. Literacy is reconceptualised, not as a decontextualised set of skills, but as different kinds of cultural practices. The research studies reported in Gregory's book, most of them focusing on bilingual learners, contribute to a *syncretic* model, where learning experiences in different literacies enable the construction of new insights and personal knowledge. It places at its centre the active engagement of all participants (families, educators and learners) and the need to recognise and value all the literacy experiences in which a child may participate.

A third field of research into the experiences of children in community-based schooling (Conteh *et al.*, 2007) is beginning to reveal evidence of the vital ways in which these settings provide for bilingual pupils – and their teachers – 'safe spaces' in which all their languages can take on full and equal roles in classroom interactions. In all large cities in England, there are a vast range of such settings, often called 'supplementary schools', teaching heritage languages and cultural practices: in Bradford, for example, there are just under 80 such schools. Martin *et al.* (2006) argue that 'these schools fill in the gaps and demonstrate the normality of multilingualism' for their participants. In these contexts, bilingual children have the opportunity to reclaim 'the specificity of cultural and social identity that (is) missing from mainstream schooling' (Hall *et al.*, 2002: 409) and construct their own strategies to support their learning, as Sameena shows. The research is revealing the importance of these schools and classes for the pupils and their families, often providing the sense of belonging and recognition of identity lacking in mainstream schooling (Conteh, 2010). This has strong implications for mainstream education and the upholding of bilingual children's rights in policy and practice.

The rights issues

Responding to bilingualism – a history of contradiction
There has never been clear recognition of the value of bilingualism in educational policy in England. While the Bullock Report (DES, 1975) had some

encouragingly enlightened things to say about bilingualism, schools and society, the Swann Report (DES, 1985) bequeathed us its 'education for all' ideology, the notion of equality of opportunity as the imperative to ensure that all learners experience the same educational provision. As part of this, Swann strongly advocated the end of mother-tongue teaching in mainstream schools, and of local authority support for supplementary mother tongue classes. This 'monolingualising' (Heller, 1995) ideology was strongly taken up in the National Curriculum, introduced soon after. Safford has identified 'the contradiction at the heart of education policy in England' for bilingual children, which has never been satisfactorily resolved. She suggests that there is an ambivalence towards bilingualism, which leads to two conflicting policy paradigms in the curriculum: 'the celebration of ethnic and linguistic diversity, and the universal model of language development and assessment' (2003: 8).

In her critique of National Curriculum provision for bilingual learners, Gregory reviews the research, and puts forward key theoretical principles to underpin a notion of bilingual learning. She points out that the National Curriculum took hardly any account of the research, and implies that it led to a denial of the rights of the bilingual child, suggesting that 'it is beginning to look as if *provision* of the same curriculum might not be adequate to give children equal *access* to it' (1994: 160, authors' italics).

Providing 'equal access' does not mean treating all children in the same way. It may seem common sense to expect that young bilingual children should be treated like any others and that they will somehow 'pick up' English from those around them when they begin school, but this does not take account of the complex interrelationships between first and additional languages that researchers such as Cummins explain in their work.

Corson (1993) spells out the negative implications for children's learning of policies that do not recognise bilingualism. Ultimately, they deny bilingual learners the means to develop cognitively to their full potential and open the door to educational underachievement at a later stage (Baker, 1996). For teachers working with bilingual children, the practical implications of such contradictory messages are complex and have been documented (e.g. Bourne, 2001; Safford, 2003; Conteh, 2006b). The failure to activate the positive cognitive implications of bilingualism for learning continued to be reproduced in official documentation in England at the beginning of the twenty-first century (see Barwell, 2004, for a critical review). However, there have recently been positive developments, including the DCSF-funded PNS/EMA (Primary National Strategy/Ethnic Minority Achievement) project, reviewed by Conteh *et al.* (2008), which led to the production of some excellent CPD materials (DCSF, 2006). Also, the current (2010), large TDA-managed research project is developing a national strategy for the workforce in relation to pupils learning English as an additional language (EAL) and supporting the piloting of approaches to training for students in initial teacher education. But there is a long way to go until bilingualism becomes a normal feature of classrooms in schools in England, and teachers have the knowledge, professional skills and confidence to enable them to empower their bilingual pupils as learners and as participants in dynamic multilingual communities and the wider British society.

Summary

We have presented evidence from research, theory and the lived experiences of children and their families to support the argument that children have the right to be bilingual. To conclude, we suggest that this stance has several important implications for educational and social policy, teacher education and development, and the notion of citizenship in a multilingual society. To promote bilingualism as a human right for children in British society, we need to find ways to:

- support families and communities in nurturing bilingual children's whole language development;
- develop recognition among educators of the importance of promoting bilingualism in educational settings;
- develop the appropriate professional knowledge and expertise to support all professionals working with bilingual learners;
- value the diversity of children's language and cultural experiences and what they bring to their learning in mainstream settings, including in assessment processes;
- promote awareness of the benefits of multilingualism for the wider society.

Baker (2007) argues that the decision to bring children up bilingually is important and promotes communication, culture, cognition, character, curriculum and cash advantages and so has long-term educational, social, economic and cultural consequences for children, their families and society as a whole. Children's social relationships, cultures and learning cannot be divorced from contextual variables such as language, culture, class, gender or ethnicity. Children need opportunities to drive their own learning and to gain the confidence to make decisions for themselves about the languages they learn and can use in different educational, family and cultural situations. As Drury and Robertson (2008) argue:

Listening to young children means listening to their bilingual voices.

> **〰 Question 10.1   Why does the whole-language development of bilingual children need to be seen as a right?**
>
> **Review Activity**
>
> The chapter argues that, for children, the right to become bilingual is important both for:
>
> - academic success
> - for becoming a full citizen of Britain

and that this can be achieved through recognising:

- the language rights of children and their families
- the responsibilities of education practitioners in supporting them.

1 Review the chapter and complete Table 10.1, identifying an illustration of each of these and justifying why you think the illustration links to the four key elements of the chapter's argument.

Table 10.1   Review activity for Question 10.1

Key chapter element	Illustration from chapter	Rationale why illustration connects to key chapter element
The right to being bilingual linked to academic success		
The right to being bilingual linked becoming a full citizen of Britain		
Recognising the language rights of children and their families		
Recognising the responsibilities of education practitioners in supporting them		

Question 10.2   Why is it necessary to listen to bilingual children, their families and practitioners in considering how to uphold bilingual children's rights?

Review Activity

Consider Examples 10.1 and 10.2.

1 List the ways in which children, families and practitioners are listened to in these examples and in particular.

   (a) the effect or impact that the acts of listening might have on the design or nature of service provision;

   (b) the effect or impact that the acts of listening have on the people who are consulted.

2 From these examples, try and draw a series of conclusions about *good practice* in consulting, listening and acting on what is heard.

〰️ **Question 10.3 How can the mainstream education system best uphold the right to be bilingual?**

Review Activity

1 The chapter quotes Safford's argument that there are two conflicting policy paradigms in the curriculum: 'the celebration of ethnic and linguistic diversity, and the universal model of language development and assessment' (2003: 8). Review the chapter's discussion of areas related to this contradiction and try to summarise the recommendations for *policy* and for *effective practice* that the chapter makes for the right to be bilingual.

Note

1 To protect individuals, all names have been changed in this chapter.

Further Reading 📖

National policies and resources

- The Primary National Strategy *Excellence and Enjoyment for Bilingual Pupils in Primary Classrooms* (DfES, 2006) is a set of professional development learning and teaching materials for primary bilingual children which promote the key principle of bilingualism being an asset and that first language has a continuing and significant role in identity, learning and the acquisition of additional languages.
- The *Multiverse* website presents bilingual and multilingual resources (http://www.multiverse.ac.uk).
- *QCA: Pathways to Learning for New Arrivals* (QCA, 2004) (http://www.qca.org.uk/8476.html) and *The Integration of Refugee Children: Good Practice in Educational Settings* (http://www.nrif.org.uk/Education/index.asp) are targeted at children who may be newly arrived in England but they are also extremely valuable for bilingual families in residence.

Professional organisations

- *NALDIC* (National Association for Language Development in the Curriculum) (www.naldic.org.uk) respond to current issues and produce articles and resources aiming to influence policy and practice, stimulate professional discussion and disseminate information to a wide audience in the education field.

- *The National Literacy Trust* is a comprehensive website (http://www.literacytrust. org.uk) offers support for families on communication, language and literacy.
- *Bilingual Families Connect* (http://www.bilingualfamiliesconnect.com) is a very accessible website resource for bilingual families where they can share and gain advice, become involved in a discussion forum and reflect on research from experts.
- *The Northern Association of Support Services* offers information about language acquisition and bilingualism with links to downloadable documents (http:// www.nassea.org.uk).
- Teachers can join the *EAL-BILINGUAL* e-mail list to access and share information, ideas and queries related to practice (eal-bilingual-request@lists. becta.org.uk).

Local authorities which provide resources and documentation to support children's rights to bilingualism

- *Milton Keynes* (http://www.milton-keynes.gov.uk).
- *Cambridgeshire Education Portal* has a range of *bilingual resources*, downloadable materials, links to other websites and contact details for both primary and secondary teachers (http://www.irespect.net).
- *Hounslow Language Service* (http://www.hvec.org.uk) has a mother-tongue section to help pupils maintain and develop their first language skills.
- *Kirklees LEA* (http://www.kirkleesmc.gov.uk) provides valuable websites and resources to promote children's bilingualism and supplies facts about rights and entitlements for families.
- *Haringey and Barnet* (http://www.barnet.gov.uk) provide useful information about families' rights and entitlements.
- *Birmingham, Leeds and Manchester* have developed valuable practical ideas and links for bilingual and EAL materials (http://www.emaonline.org.uk).

11

Rights, Health and Health Promotion

Diane Lowcock and Ruth Cross

Chapter Overview

This chapter will introduce broad principles and approaches to practice in relation to health and rights with a specific focus on rights as applied to health promotion for children and young people. The chapter starts by examining key principles of theory and practice underpinning health promotion which complement a rights framework, specifically empowerment and participation. It will look at some key issues in children's rights and health promotion drawing on central principles and how these are worked out differently with reference to mental and sexual health issues.

The idea that children and young people should have rights in promoting their mental and sexual health is uncontested from a health promotion perspective. However, the extent to which they actually see their rights realised may be limited in reality. The chapter will examine the extent to which children and young people might, or might not, be able to exercise their rights in these two areas. Research focusing on the experiences of children and young people in participation in the promotion of their own health reveals a range of benefits. The chapter will draw on examples from the wider literature to examine the nature of these benefits from the perspectives of children and young people and practitioners. Research with children and young people points towards ways of working that are more acceptable and effective in terms of promoting mental and sexual health. The chapter will examine specific ways in which a rights framework might be applied to both areas of practice and introduces debates about some of the key challenges therein.

Theoretical frameworks

It is useful to start with an overview of two key concepts in health promotion that are central to the discussion about rights – empowerment and participation. These are inherently linked. Arguably you cannot participate in anything to any degree without being empowered in some way. Participation can therefore be seen as a product of empowerment. The assumption is that the higher the levels of empowerment, the greater the level of participation (Tones and Green, 2004). In terms of a rights framework empowerment can therefore be seen as highly desirable.

A discussion about 'empowerment' and 'participation' is not uncomplicated. For instance, among others, Scriven and Stiddard (2003) highlight the difficulties inherent in the many definitions and interpretations of the term 'empowerment'. However, for the purposes of this discussion, it is viewed as being centrally concerned with ideas or beliefs about control or 'being in control'. In relation to health this means control over health in terms of both decision-making and health-related behaviour. However, as Tones and Green (2004) argue, empowerment can also be viewed as the way in which health is actually achieved. Issues to do with control clearly sit within a child rights framework when this is viewed as having control over what happens with, and to, you and being able to make a difference in your everyday experience (being listened to, having views acted upon, etc.). This directly relates to, for example, informed choice which is key to the areas of mental health and sexual health. The World Health Organisation revisited its definition of health promotion in 2005 in the Bangkok Charter to read 'the process of enabling people to increase control over their health and its determinants and thereby improve their health' (WHO, 2005). This refers both to the macro level – broader issues of children's rights with regard to health promotion – and the micro level – the day-to-day outworking and experience of health promotion.

In common with contemporary sociological perspectives on modern childhood the core principles of health promotion take the position that children are key players in their own lives, that they have their own voices which should be listened to, that they should be involved in decision-making and dialogue and that the exercise of the power of adults over children and the way that children respond to, or resist this, should be considered (Tilford, 2006; Prout and James, 1997; Dahlberg *et al.*, 1999).

Debate: to what extent do children have control over their health?

This kind of perspective foregrounds tensions such as to what extent children do, or should, have control over their health. For example, at a very simple level, a young child is likely to have very little control over what they eat and yet dietary habits in childhood can have a profound effect on health at both the immediate point in time and in the future. On the other hand, the media often highlights stories which they offer within a framework of children having 'too much' power and control. Control is very closely linked with autonomy. However, there may be some circumstances in which children may not be able to act in an autonomous way. This may be because they may lack the capacity or do not yet have the competence to make independent decisions (see Cattan and Tilford, 2006).

Laverack (2009) writes about different types of power. The types of power relevant to this chapter are 'power over' and 'power within'. 'Power over' is concerned with social structures where a person or persons has power over others, to make them behave in certain ways for example. This is pertinent to children and young people as adults are often in positions of *power over* them. In contrast to this idea is the concept of 'power from within' which is concerned with having a sense of control over what is happening to you and is tied up with issues to do with self-esteem and, clearly, empowerment. To be empowered is to be able to exercise *power from within*. Challenges may arise in promoting children and young people's health created by the tensions between the two different types of power.

The concept of 'participation' is central to any discussion about children's and young peoples rights' (Participation Works, 2010 http://www.participationworks.org.uk). When examining definitions of participation two main themes are evident: firstly 'being present and taking part' and secondly recognising that when young people participate what they say and do should be listened to and acted upon (Boyden and Ennew, 1997, cited in McNeish, 1999). This implies that children are perceived as autonomous individuals who have the inclination, skills and power to be present, take part and make decisions and that facilitators and practitioners value and are able to incorporate young peoples idea's and act on their decisions. Theoretical frameworks of participation can be useful when thinking about the application of a rights perspective. An example is Hart's ladder of participation (1997) which is specifically applied to children and young people and outlines a hierarchy where the higher rungs of the ladder involve true participation, i.e. child-initiated and child-directed (e.g. full budgetary and decision-making control), compared to the lower rungs which mask true participation for example, i.e. consultation (e.g. where young people are asked what they think but practitioners still have control of the agenda, budgets and decisions). Implicit within this hierarchical system is the notion that the highest rung on the ladder of participation should be the goal of young people and practitioners. This has been challenged by commentators arguing that a 'wheel' of participation maybe a more useful model (Davidson, 1998). In this framework types of participation are just viewed as different and all are available to be utilised by practitioners depending on the culture and context of work with young people (Treseder, 1996).

Hart (1997) adapted the original ladder of participation described by Arnstein in 1969. Arnstein was concerned with notions of power and although he did not specifically unpick ideas about power dynamics between young people and adults, it is clear that within a framework of children's and young people's rights, power should, at the very least, be shared with adults (Shier, 2001). It is useful to return to Laverack's ideas here. He also talks about another kind of power – 'power with'. This is seen to be a transformative process where power over is 'used carefully and deliberately to increase other people's power, rather than to dominate or exploit' (Laverack, 2009: 19). The end result is empowerment where the individual(s) concerned are able to take full control over decision-making processes. This type of power has implications where practitioners could use their 'power over' to increase young people's power.

Rights and health promotion: examples of contemporary discussion and debate

Two areas of health promotion have been selected to illustrate contemporary discussion and debate – mental and sexual health promotion. Mental health promotion will be examined because it has become an increasingly recognised issue for children and young people in recent years and is relatively neglected when compared with physical health. It will be considered in terms of positive mental health rather than a focus on mental illness (Rowling, 2006) and for the purposes of this chapter mental health promotion is defined in the most straightforward way – as health promotion focused on *mental* rather than physical health (Tilford, 2006). Sexual health occupies an almost unique position within the discourse of children and young people's rights. Almost no other topic evokes such strong political, legislative, social and moral reactions. Sexual health is defined for the purposes of this chapter as 'the acceptance and ability to achieve a satisfactory expression of one's own sexuality' (Naidoo and Wills, 2009: 4). Sexual health promotion (SHP) has been defined as 'the holistic process of enabling individuals and communities to increase control over the determinants of sexual health, and thereby managing and improving it throughout their lifetime' (Winn, 1996, cited in Lee, 2007: 5). Both these definitions have participation and implied rights of the child to govern their own life at their core.

This section of the chapter will focus on the extent to which children and young people may have rights when it comes to the practice of mental and sexual health promotion. While the notion that they *should* have rights that are realised is undisputed from a health promotion perspective, the extent to which they can exercise these rights in terms of their everyday lived experience is often limited. The Articles contained in the UNCRC that have particular relevance for sexual and mental health are summarised in Table 11.1 in terms of the dilemmas that are raised for practitioners.

Table 11.1 Relevance of UNCRC for sexual and mental health of children and young people – dilemmas for practitioners

Article	Article description	Sexual health	Mental health
3	Rights of 'best interest' * of the child is the primary consideration State to provide protection and care necessary for well-being ** of child taking into accounts rights and duties of parents Institutions should conform to standards established by competent authorities	What is the best interest for child? Who decides about best interest – the young person or parent or practitioner or joint decision-making? Protection against sexual abuse Protection against having sex 'too early' Provision of sexual health services and high-quality information What are the tensions between young people and parents? How does a practitioner deal with these tensions? Governing body requirements of practitioners	What is the best interest for the child? Who decides – child themselves, parents/caregiver, other figure in authority or power? Protection against psychological and emotional abuse Provision of services for mental health promotion and access to high-quality information and support At what point does the child/young person lack the capacity to self-care? Governing body requirements for service provision and support
6	Inherent right to life State ensures maximum survival and development of child	Rights of unborn child in termination of pregnancy vs rights of parents Provision of age specific SRE	The right to a mentally and emotionally healthy life Appropriate interventions at times of extreme distress
12	Freedom to express views in matters that affect them Views being given weight with age and maturity	Participation in education about sex and sexual health Provision of services and legislative frameworks in partnership with young people Development of policy, e.g. school sex education policy	Participation and consultation in issues to do with mental health and emotional well-being Partnership in provision in line with individual capacity

Table 11.1 (Continued)

Article	Article description	Sexual health	Mental health
13	Right to seek, receive and impart information (restricted if contravenes public order or public health)	Important for SRE, information about services and resources	High-quality information relevant to the individual child/young person available at the point of need Involvement of children and young people in peer support
14	State to respect right of freedom of thought, conscience and religion State to respect rights and duties of parents to provide direction to child Beliefs can be limited to protect public health and morals	Rights of child could be at odds with parents direction Who decides what beliefs harm health and morals?	Rights of the child/young person could be at odds if self or others are perceived to be at risk Rights of the child could be at odds with parents (issues of protection) Who decides what beliefs harm mental health?
17	Right of child to access information to promote well-being and health Especially focused at mass media	Access to unbiased accurate information about sexual health via leaflets, services, practitioners and TV	Access to unbiased accurate information about mental health services and provision
24	Enjoyment of the highest attainable standard of health and access to health care services To develop preventive healthcare and family planning education and services	If health is conceptualised as dimensional including sexual health and sexual pleasure children have a right to this Services for prevention of unplanned pregnancies and reductions in STIs SRE using lifeskills approaches	Rights to the highest possible standard of mental health and emotional well-being Rights to excellent and accessible service provision at the point of need Rights to preventive health care for mental health

*Best interest of the child is difficult to define but is usually considered to be what is advantageous to the child.
**Well-being is defined as a measure of happiness and can be achieved by developing a set of life skills that can be used to promote happiness.

Mental Health Promotion

Mental health receives particular focus in Article 24 of the UNCRC as follows: 'health is the basis of a good quality of life and *mental health* is of overriding importance in this' (United Nations, 1989). Article 12 of the UNCRC recognises the importance of considering children's points of view and experiences and this is in line with the underpinning principles of health promotion in terms of empowerment and participation. Tilford (2006) argues that, while there are differences of opinion as to when children are deemed competent to participate, their views can actually be considered from a very young age (at least from when language starts to develop) if the right kind of methods are used. This focuses on mental health promotion at an individualistic (or reduced) level; however, health promotion is centrally concerned with determinants of health and addressing health inequalities. Many of the challenges facing children with mental health problems could be argued to be systemic in nature (the experience of social inequalities such as relative poverty and discrimination for example). Therefore the degree to which children are actually empowered in a wider context in terms of their mental health may be limited.

Another challenge in terms of mental health promotion is the point at which intervention may be required for children and young people to prevent harm to either themselves or others. In these types of circumstances the rights of the young person concerned are likely to be overridden and not taken into account in the interests of safety or the 'duty of care' agenda.

Sexual Health Promotion

The UNCRC makes no explicit reference to sexual health although often sexual health is conceptualised to be one dimension of holistic health (Aggleton and Homans, 1987, cited in Naidoo and Wills, 2009: 4). Aggleton and Campbell (2000) provide one of the few commentaries relating to a rights-based framework for sexual health promotion for children and young people and highlight a number of tensions and ambiguities in policy and practice, particularly in school settings. The extent to which children and young people have rights regarding their sexual health in the UK is primarily influenced by legislative frameworks which draw on what is 'thought' to be morally and developmentally appropriate for young people. Legislation is governed by age limits, particularly the age of consent for sexual intercourse, in the UK set at 16 in 2000. Below this age, where young people's views and cultural norms conflict with parents and practitioners' thoughts about appropriate sexual activity and expression, frameworks of rights tend not to provide guidance about whose rights and responsibilities have greater weight. However, legal frameworks within the UK tend to emphasise the rights of the young person, although there are exceptions. Several well publicised cases discussed below have heightened moral panic relating to young people's sexual health including the rights of a child to consent for contraception and termination or pregnancy and the rights of school nurses to provide condoms and emergency contraception. This brings to the fore many tensions between rights enshrined in law and rights that are normalised within culture and community. As one young person succinctly puts it: 'It seems as if sex is compulsory but contraception is illegal' (Social Exclusion Unit, 1999).

The UNCRC articles relevant to sexual health are conceptualised within the following subsections.

Rights to Sex and Relationship Education (SRE) within the context of the family

Under the UNCRC Article 14, parents are able to direct children to exercise their rights and evidence suggests that where families have skills and are able to communicate appropriately about sex, is likely to be effective in empowering young people and ensuring fully informed decision-making about their own sexual health (Walker, 2001).

Rights within school SRE context

SRE is an imperative right enshrined within several articles of the UNCRC and many statutory frameworks and guidelines within state schools including the National Curriculum, National Healthy Schools Standard and Personal, Health and Social Education (PHSE and Citizenship). The quality and extent of SRE within schools varies widely thereby diluting rights of young people to seek and receive accurate and relevant SRE. Underlying this right of young people is the fact that parents can withdraw their children from SRE that lies outside the National Curriculum. So in this instance legislation favours the rights of the parents against the rights of the child. Sex education policies are in the statutory authority of the school governors, although some more progressive schools develop policy participatively with their pupils.

Rights within information context

Young people are entitled to have consultations, including information and advice, with healthcare professionals that are confidential (usually to the primary care team) and not passed on to any third party. Exceptions to this are if the young person discloses harm either to themselves or harm to another. However, teachers are not bound by similar professional codes of conduct and can disclose information to third parties, including parents. This has implications for teacher-led SRE.

Right to medication and treatment

Two main guidelines, developed under case law, govern the rights of young people to receive any contraceptive (including emergency contraception, contraceptive pills and barriers methods) and termination of pregnancy medical interventions.

The Gillick decision relates specifically to judgments about the competence of children to decide about their treatment in the absence of parental involvement. The test case came about when Victoria Gillick challenged a health authority circular granting authority to doctors to give contraceptive advice and treatment to young people under 16 (*Gillick* v. *West Norfolk & Wisbech AHA & DHSS*, 1983). After a protracted legal wrangle the ruling granted children the right to decide about their own treatment, without the consent of their parents, if they were considered to be Gillick competent, i.e. 'they can demonstrate sufficient maturity and intelligence to understand and appraise the nature and implications of the proposed treatment' (Wheeler, 2006: 807).

The Fraser guidelines relate to contraceptive advice and treatment only and allow healthcare professionals to provide contraceptive advice and treatment to under 16s but encourage practitioners to discuss how young people can involve parents in decision-making (Burtney *et al.*, 2004).

Involving children and young people in promoting their own health

There are many generic benefits to be gained when facilitating the participation of young people in the promotion of their own health. Halsey *et al.* (2006) provide an excellent review of evidence.

The most powerful benefit is that greater participation is implicitly linked to better health, although this relationship may not be directly causal (Runyan, 1998). Outcomes that are particularly related to mental health or sexual health are self-efficacy and feelings of power and control over their lives (Wallerstein, 2006). There appears to be a mechanism in which involvement develops young people's sense of self-worth and enhances decision-making capacity, although this mechanism is not well understood.

Benefits of participation are inherently interconnected (see Table 11.2) and all have the potential to lead to improved service and health processes and outcomes.

There are claims in the literature that the active participation of children in specific projects creates gains in a range of components associated with positive mental health such as self-esteem and self-efficacy (Hart, 1997). For example, a study in Johannesburg, South Africa, which evaluated a participatory action research project 'Growing Up in Cities', found that participation in the project had a positive impact on the children in terms of improved self-esteem, self-efficacy and locus of control (Griesel *et al.*, 2002).

Table 11.2 Benefits of participation

Context of participation

Information – provision of quality information to make informed choice
Consultation – respect for and use of young people's views
Representation – young people involved in planning and running project
Partnership – power-sharing of decisions with adults
Self-management – projects owned and managed by young people

Levels of participation

Participation in individual decision-making, e.g. decision to have sex
Participation in service development and provision, e.g. planning, delivery or evaluation
Participation in research, e.g. commission of or design of or doing of research
Participation in communities
Participation in influencing policy and public awareness

Adapted from Teenage Pregnancy Unit (2001).

In addition, a programme in Australia encouraging meaningful participation for young people in a range of activities demonstrates the ways in which resilience can be fostered which in turn has a positive effect on mental health (Oliver *et al.*, 2006).

Sexual health peer education projects have also demonstrated that peer educators and their participants increase their knowledge, attitudes and confidence about sexual health and also the peer educator's confidence about communication and interacting with groups (Strange *et al.*, 2002).

Good practice in health promotion from a rights perspective

This section will focus on the characteristics of good practice within a rights framework and will consider this from a practitioner's perspective highlighting some insights from examples of good practice. It will also consider some potential barriers that practitioners may face and how they might be addressed.

Context and levels of participation

The Teenage Pregnancy Unit (2001) provides an extremely useful framework when considering how to involve young people. This can be applied to any health promotion work for children and adolescents. They distinguish between different contexts of participation and differing levels of participation of young people (see Table 11.2). Good practice involves consideration of the most appropriate contexts and levels of participation within the specified resource framework. There is little point in aiming for self-managed projects if there is no budget for skills training for young people or where adult attitudes view all young people primarily in need of protection, not as autonomous individuals. The type and extent of participation needs to be considered in terms of what is desirable and achievable – not just from the professionals' perspective but also from the perspective of the children and young people themselves.

Facilitation and power-sharing

The challenge is to do things *with* children and young people rather than *to* them, allowing them to take the initiative; this requires a facilitative role (Scriven and Stiddard, 2003). In terms of mental health promotion maximising feelings and experiences of connectedness serves to counter isolation and give a greater sense of control (Oliver *et al.*, 2006). Partnerships with children and young people as well as different agencies are necessary with joined-up ways of working that encourage anti-discriminatory and inclusive practice. Children and young people should have a more participatory role in decisions that affect them in terms of sexual and mental health promotion and, promisingly, Cattan and Tilford (2006) point out that there are increasing efforts in this direction specifically in relation to mental health. However, they go on to say that there are still 'many situations where the approach to children is top-down and authoritarian and ... active involvement is not encouraged' (Cattan and Tilford, 2006: 94).

To facilitate consultation, representation and partnership practitioners need to create processes and structures that are more participatory in tone (Teenage Pregnancy Unit, 2001). The way that business is conducted may need to be radically overhauled. Agendas and meetings are not common structures for young people and may be too formal and disempowering for them, especially if meetings are dominated by adults and their agendas. If power-sharing with regard to decisions is to take place then clear terms of reference and decision-making structures need to be stated. If consensus methods are used to arrive at decisions, then obviously young people need to be thoroughly represented.

Practitioners can avoid working in a 'top-down' way with children and young people – that is, in ways in which their participation is minimal, tokenistic or even discouraged. The involvement of children at every stage – including commissioning, planning, implementation and evaluation – is key to this type of approach. As indicated in Article 12 of the UNCRC, consultation with children and young people is integral to this. However, Tilford (2006) concludes that, in many cases, no dialogue with children has actually taken place. In order to achieve this it requires creating opportunities for children and young people's voices to be heard, flexible and inclusive decision-making and investing in relationships.

Key messages for practitioners emerging from a review of the literature pertinent to looked-after children's views of mental health services (Davies and Wright, 2008) were that vulnerable children should be given equal choice and involvement in their treatment decisions and not miss out on the wider

NHS drive for service user involvement. In common with many other areas of health promotion the challenge for practitioners here is the balance between children's needs (for protection) and their rights (to have their views respected) (Davies and Wright, 2008). In keeping with a rights perspective McQueen *et al.* (1992) proposed that children be thought of as partners in health promotion whose opinions and perspectives about health are validated and whose competence to make and carry out decisions is appreciated. This is contrary to thinking about children as passive recipients of health promotion efforts on their behalf.

Engaging young people

One of the biggest barriers practitioners face is encouraging young people to participate. Often socially excluded, black and minority ethnic and young men tend not to participate. The use of incentives such as payment, provision of vouchers, tickets and accreditation of knowledge and skills are useful catalysts for young people at the early stages of involvement in projects. However, not all young people require this type of reward – simply being listened to and seeing change can be enough. Adults need to see their requirements for participation through the eyes of the young people. They should ask themselves questions such as: Will participation be enjoyable? What will I get out of participating? Is this issue important to me?

Information

One of the most important ways in which participation and empowerment might be facilitated is through access to accurate, timely and appropriate information to enhance decision-making and promote personal, social and cognitive skills. Children and young people have the right to correct information allowing decision-making to take place (Young Minds 2009). Both mental health and sexual health issues can be difficult for young people to seek information about due to embarrassment. Rights to information means that innovative ways of accessing health information anonymously can be helpful, for example making use of the Internet and telephone advice/help lines which can overcome barriers to information and facilitate seeking.

Safe and confidential boundaries

Knowing practitioner-specific boundaries around confidentiality is vital to working within a rights framework for young people. One of the most frequently cited barriers to not accessing services or to information-seeking is fear of disclosure of personal information to parents and other third parties. It is important at the outset to state clearly and in what circumstances confidentiality would need to be broken and when it could be guaranteed. This varies widely depending on the requirements of the governing body of the practitioner. Healthcare professionals are more able to ensure confidentially compared to school teachers. Above all young, people respect honesty and value adults keeping their word.

Peer-led work

Rowling (2006), among others, advocates the use of peer mentoring and peer support methods. These have the advantage that they are explicitly led by young people but facilitated by adults. Peer support has been useful in the context of mental health where peers are used as 'counsellors' and/or buddies (Nelson, 1995), and in sexual health within schools (Strange *et al.*, 2002) as part outreach and in communities with young people including the more marginalised such as young gay men (Kegeles *et al.*, 1996).

Working with parents

At certain stages in early childhood working to promote the mental and sexual health of the child will necessarily involve working with the parents or caregivers. The extent to which a child might actively participate in the promotion of their own health will depend on a range of factors including individual those such as competence and understanding and those to do with the wider context such as the physical and social environment. By working with parents it is hoped that children can develop autonomy, good self-esteem, assertiveness and decision-making capacity.

Setting standards and quality

A more recent theme of good practice driven by requirements to involve children and young people in all types of service is to develop standards of practice. One of the most useful flexible frameworks is Hear by Right developed by the National Youth Agency. 'Hear by Right is a tried and tested standards framework for organisations across the statutory and voluntary sectors to assess and improve practice and policy on the active involvement of children and young people' (Hear by Right at: http://hbr. nya.org.uk/). This allows organisations and projects to consider how participative their structures and processes are for their young clients. By using the toolkit organisations can develop an action plan to set and achieve standards.

EXAMPLE 11.1   Mental health promotion

At a conference in March 2009 designed for young people and by young people and organised by the charity Young Minds, children and young people were encouraged to share their thoughts and feelings about emotional well-being and mental health. The result-ing information provides a picture of the general principles of good practice from their perspective. Key aspects of practice included meaningful participation such as that which leads to change (see-ing something happen) and involvement at all levels of decision-making including strategic decisions. This was highlighted as being important for a number of reasons including feeling empowered, increased self-esteem and confidence, personal skills development and improved services (Young Minds, 2009).

The UK report *Transitions: Young Adults with Complex Needs* (SEU, 2005) highlighted the importance of taking into account the think-ing and behaviour of young adults as one of its three main themes. When asked about what an ideal service would be like with regard to support during difficult times the two most frequent points raised by the young people were the importance of joined-up work-ing (a 'holistic' approach) and the need for staff who understood and respected them and were prepared to listen.

Oliver *et al.* (2006) write about the Inspire Foundation, a not-for-profit organisation which works *with* young people. They have writ-ten a paper which brings together a wealth of information about the effects of participation on young people's self-esteem and con-cluded that participation is effective in building resilience (an important component of mental health). In the paper they discuss different ways that children and young people can be involved (participate) in a meaningful way, moving beyond the rhetoric that often accompanies a rights agenda towards real ways that children and young people may take part in promoting their own mental health. This includes an online service called Reach Out which con-nects young people with one another and provides information as well as signposting sources of support. Young people are engaged in all levels of the programme including decision-making and devel-opment of ideas. For further information about this see http://www.reachout.com.au.

EXAMPLE 11.2   Sexual health promotion

The Cupboard Project, based in Leeds, uses many of the character-istics outlined above as good practice. It is focused on young peo-ple who were identified as being in greatest health need aged 13–15, including those excluded from school, young parents, the

(Continued)

(Continued)

homeless and travellers. Young people attend different activities for 10 hours a week for a year, ranging from one-to one work, group work with other young people and 'Bling Friday', an accredited skills-based health behaviour peer education project. Young people participate in the management structures and evaluation processes of the project in addition to acting as advocates for the project nationally (through a National Youth Agency planning and dissemination event) and internationally (via a European Conference on *Every Child Matters*). Although this project is expected to feed into reducing teenage pregnancy is also has a focus on holistic health by encouraging skills for work within a volunteering framework, which will also improve health outcomes. More information about the project can be found at http://www.slhfa.org.uk/PAGES/Cupboard.htm.

The National Children's Bureau and the Sex Education Forum facilitated young people in the development of a Charter for Effective Sex Education, a recording 'Please Minister, can we have better Sex Education?' and a letter to the Minister for Education. This capitalises on the value and effectiveness of children and young people being expert witnesses about their own lives and their voices being more powerful than adults. It is one of the rare examples where young people are attempting to influence policy at the national level. This Charter can be found at http://partner.ncb.org.uk/dotpdf/open_access_2/sef_ypcharter_a4.pdf.

The Sex Education Forum also has a number of case studies many of which promote participation, empowerment and the rights of children and young people to positive sexual health http://partner.ncb.org.uk/Page.asp?originx_7634fg_83952689004939n25b_20073284534v. One case study is a peer mentoring project developed at a community high school in Northumbria, where year 12 pupils are trained in and then deliver a condom distribution scheme alongside a school nurse. This is thought to promote greater access to the services.

From the above topic-based examples, it is clear that working in participative (and empowering) ways offers practitioners opportunities to uphold children's rights (Sinclair, 2004). Furthermore, we would argue that participation and empowerment improve the health and well-being of children and young people. Further ideas about how practitioners can respond to the dilemmas posed by UNCRC can be found in Table 11.3.

Table 11.3 Addressing the dilemmas posed by the UNCRC: What can practitioners do?

Article	Article description	Ideas for sexual health	Ideas for mental health
3	Rights of 'best interest' of the child are the primary consideration State to provide protection and care necessary for well-being of child taking into account rights and duties of parents Institutions should conform to standards established by competent authorities	Encourage dialogue between children, parents and practitioners The Fraser guidelines specifically suggest that young people be encouraged to discuss decisions about contraception and sex with their parents To protect against sexual abuse, development of strong, safe and accessible points of disclosure To protect against having sex 'too early' or becoming pregnant 'too early' age-specific SRE from an early age both within the family and school context It is important to be aware of the duties and practices of your appropriate governing bodies through CPD updates and networks	A dialogue could take place here where the 'best interests' of the child are discussed which involves the child themselves depending on capacity State intervention may well be appropria⸋ in terms of protection and providing a dut⸋ care depending on the role that the par⸋ caregiver is able/willing to take Protection from psychological and emo⸋ abuse would be paramount Availability of accessible and high-qua⸋ information for mental health promo⸋ important and could be provided in ⸋ of non-threatening ways
6	Inherent right to life State ensures maximum survival and development of child	Legislation allows for termination of pregnancy at any age in England, Wales and Scotland However, there are excellent counselling services via general practice or Brook Advisory Clinics that can outline all the options for young people who become pregnant Termination is only one option In order for children to develop, including skills around informed decision-making, they need to become resilient and have access to relevant specific information This can be delivered within families, schools young people's organisations and/or be facilitated by peers	The right to a mentally and emotionally healthy life can be maintained through various ways of working which include anti-discriminatory practice and respect Appropriate intervention by the state at times of extreme distress may be necessary, particularly in situations where someone is at risk

(Continued)

Table 11.3 (Continued)

Article	Article description	Ideas for sexual health	Ideas for mental health
12	Freedom to express views in matters that affect them Views being given weight with age and maturity	Developing mechanisms for expression in a variety of ways This diversity allows the potential for all types of young people to be included Consider written, verbal, audio, use of drama and art, and electronic mechanisms Expression will be more valid if it is anonymous If the views of young people are sought then there must be some action taken in respect of their views Consultation without feedback and/or action is disempowering	Participation and consultation in issues to do with mental health and emotional well-being are important and there are various ways that this might be achieved, including forums and focus groups for example Partnership in provision in line with individual capacity should be encouraged at every level from policy-making downwards
13	Right to seek, receive and impart information (restricted if contravenes public order or public health)	Ensure that young people are aware of the numerous high-quality points of information Where young people have poor literacy they may need extra support and mentoring Audio feedback mechanisms are potentially useful Young people can impart information after training via peer education and mentoring schemes	High-quality information relevant to the individual child/young person should be available and accessible at the point of need Involvement of children and young people in peer support mechanisms to foster personal capacity and skills development

Table 11.3 (Continued)

Article	Article description	Ideas for sexual health	Ideas for mental health
14	State to respect right of freedom of thought, conscience and religion	Respect the rights of the child and the parent but prioritise the rights of the child	Tensions will occur when the rights of the child/young person are odds if self or others are perceived to be at risk which produces a challenge for practitioners
	State to respect rights and duties of parents to provide direction to child	This is enshrined in both the Fraser and Gillick guidelines	
	Beliefs can be limited to protect public health and morals	Sexual health and morality are inherently linked but by promoting more open and sensitive discussion about sexual pleasure as a right then subjective frameworks about moral panic may be reduced	The rights of the child could be at odds with parents (issues of protection)
			Generic education efforts aimed at breaking down myths and misconceptions about mental health issues in wider society such as public information campaigns
17	Right of child to access information to promote well-being and health	See Article 13	Provision of unbiased, accurate and relevant information about mental health services and provision that is appropriate to the level of understanding of the child and in an accessible format
	Especially focused at mass media	Encourage young people to work with journalists and media channels to promote images of children that reflect their lives and experiences	
24	Enjoyment of the highest attainable standard of health and access to healthcare services	Continue to develop evidence base of work by encouraging young people to be partners in research and evaluation	Practice that draws on evidence of what is effective in maximising the highest possible standard of mental health and emotional well-being for the child
	To develop preventive healthcare and family planning education and services	Children's voices are more powerful advocates for their services than adults'	Provision of excellent accessible services and information at the point of need as well as preventive healthcare for mental health
		Develop standards about involvement of young people in organisational and service commissioning, planning, delivery and evaluation	

Summary ☐

As this chapter has shown, health promotion work within the framework of the rights of children and young people has made progress, with great emphasis being placed on participatory methods of working and on valuing the voices of young people. Most of the work classified as health promotion tends to be centred on health topics as illustrated by the mental and sexual health examples within this chapter. As Cattan and Tilford state, 'Mental health promotion is a relatively new discipline' (2006: 1), and further exploration of children and young people's rights in relation to this area will be needed as provision evolves and the debate continues. The rights of the child within the context of sexual health are actually relatively strong both in legislation and practice, although attitudes of wider society about sexual behaviour and young people can somewhat negate these frameworks.

The topic-based approach to health promotion has an inherent weakness in that the wider, often more powerful, social and political determinants of health (e.g. poverty, social exclusion) can be neglected. Work that is going on involving young people at the micro-political level, for example in schools councils and the development of school-based policies and youth forums, is excellent but may not entirely address the wider determinants of health. Programmes of work that place intrinsic value on young people as active players within society, as equal partners with adults, would be welcomed. Aggleton and Campbell (2000) suggest that young people's health promotion should be focused on encouraging them to participate in society as whole rather than in specific topics. Young people could be involved in decision-making at a macro level where the most important determinants of health can be tackled.

∿ Question 11.1   To what extent do children and young people have rights when it comes to promoting their own health?

Review Activity

This activity is designed to help you think about your own values about the rights of young people and health promotion. It is important as a practitioner to understand your own values as a person and as a practitioner. These values are likely to impact on how you work with young people and how you work within a rights framework.

1 Examine at least two of the articles listed below that can be obtained from the Internet.

– BBC (2005) 'Mother seeks abortion rule change' [Internet], BBC News online. Available at http://news.bbc.co.uk/1/hi/england/manchester/4412354.stm.

- Clark, L. (2008) 'Schools to open sexual health clinics to hand out contraception and abortion advice without parents' knowledge' [Internet], Mail online. Available at http://www.dailymail.co.uk/news/article-1026600/Schools-open-sexual-health-clinics-hand-contraception-abortion-advice-parents-knowledge.html#.
- James, J. (2008) 'Why my son had the right to die' [Internet], Times online. Available at http://www.timesonline.co.uk/tol/news/uk/article4964094.ece.
- Paton, G. (2007) 'Anti-depressants given to four year olds' [Internet], Telegraph online. Available at http://www.telegraph.co.uk/news/uknews/1558203/Antidepressants-given-to-four-year-olds.html.
- Slack, J. (2006) 'Under-age sex: GPs must tell the police' [Internet], Mail online. Available at http://www.dailymail.co.uk/news/article-376308/Under-age-sex-GPs-tell-police.html.
- Sprat, C. (2009) 'Double tragedy drove "suicide pact" teenager to jump with friend from 125ft bridge' [Internet], Mail online. Available at http://www.dailymail.co.uk/news/article-1218214/First-picture-Neve-Lafferty-15-died-jumping-125ft-bridge-suicide-pact-14-year-old-girl-pupil.html.

2 Consider the following questions.

(a) What rights are contained within the stories? How do they link to the UNCRC Articles stated in table 11.1?

(b) How do you imagine you might feel about these rights as:

- a parent?
- an individual?
- a practitioner?

Are there differences in your responses within each of your identities?

Do you think your personal values compromise your actions as a practitioner within a framework of rights for young people?

(c) Examine the requirements as a practitioner of your own institution's governing body concerning confidentiality and children and young people (or use the requirements relating to school-based practitioners available at http://www.wiredforhealth.gov.uk/Word/confidentiality_policy_gen.doc).

Do you feel that the requirements of the governing body sit within a framework of rights for children and young people?

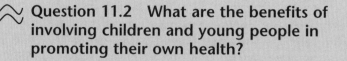

Question 11.2   What are the benefits of involving children and young people in promoting their own health?

Review Activity

1 Develop a mind map of some of the difficulties you would face in your practice when encouraging young people's participation either in a service development or in a health-promoting activity such as the development of a sexual health peer education programme or pupils' buddying system to address bullying within a school context.
2 How might you address these difficulties?

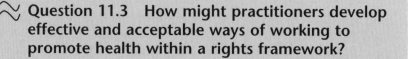

Question 11.3   How might practitioners develop effective and acceptable ways of working to promote health within a rights framework?

Review Activity

1 Look at the Reach Out website (http://www.reachout.com.au). Identify the ways in which the project is working in effective and acceptable ways in terms of a rights framework, drawing on examples that you can use in your practice.
2 Develop an action plan explaining how you can involve young people in health promotion activity that relates to your practice. Tools and templates for action planning can be found at http://www.alliance.brown.edu/pubs/changing_systems/teach_to_student/Action_Plan.pdf.

Further Reading

Cattan, M. and Tilford, S. (2006) *Mental Health Promotion: A Lifespan Approach.* Maidenhead: McGraw-Hill and Open University Press.
This chapter has drawn on aspects of this book to develop understanding of the issues of mental health promotion. The chapters of specific relevance to children and young people are those by L. Rowling and S. Tilford.

Oliver, K. G., Collin, P., Burns, J. and Nicholas, J. (2006) 'Building resilience in young people through meaningful participation', *Australian e-Journal for the Advancement of Mental Health,* 5 (1).

This chapter references this work and readers might be interested in exploring it in more detail. The paper makes reference to a range of different activities designed to enhance the mental health of young people that can followed up through the Inspire Foundation at http://www.inspire.org.au.

Teenage Pregnancy Unit (2001) *A Guide to Involving Young People in Teenage Pregnancy Work*. London: Teenage Pregnancy Unit.
This guide provides a user friendly and practice-based approach at different levels of participation. It contains activities that service providers and practitioners working in the field of sexual health could use when planning to work with young people.

The FPA has a number of excellent resources including leaflets and a training manual for young people, parents and practitioners working with young people, including marginalised groups such as teenagers with learning difficulties and lesbian, gay and bisexual adolescents. Available at http://www.fpa.org.uk/ Homepage.

Brook (Advisory Clinics) provides user-friendly and readable sources of information designed by young people, including a section of the rights of the young person for sexual health. Available at http://www.brook.org.uk/content/.

12

Social Work and Children's Rights: Promoting Young People's Participation in Social Work Practice and Education

Tracey Race and Alison Bennett

Chapter Overview

This chapter will explore the importance of a commitment to children's rights which is inherent in the value base of the social work profession. We will examine a theoretical model which enables us to recognise the tensions between the different and competing value perspectives that exist within UK childcare policy and how they influence social work practice. We will go on to describe the model of participation that informs our approach to teaching social work students about working effectively with children and young people. An understanding of emancipatory values and a commitment to human rights and to the General Social Care Council (GSCC) Code of Practice (2004) are central to contemporary social work. The legal and policy framework for practice with children and young people includes recognition of the importance of children's rights. Childcare policy is influenced by differing value perspectives. Social work practice is complex, often confronting difficult issues and ethical dilemmas within a context of limited resources. Contemporary social work practice presents many challenges and pressures for practitioners seeking to promote children's rights. A commitment to the value base of social work means that it is not enough to lecture about child-centred practice, children's rights and the importance of participation without modelling these principles in our practice as educators. The involvement of young people who have been the recipients of social work services in the development and delivery of teaching about social work with children and families enables young service users to have a voice in the training of the next generation of the profession. Their effective participation also provides opportunities for social work students to listen to young people and to recognise that they have an important contribution to make.

Understanding social work as a value-based profession

Social work is a value-based profession. It could be said that without this strong value base, this profession of values, there would be no profession, no distinct professional identity. Social work has its roots in Victorian philanthropy and a strong, historical tradition of promoting the welfare and best interests of service-users. Notions of rights – human rights, citizen's rights, children's rights – have always been central to the value base of social work. Neil Thompson sums this up well:

> Social work is one of the 'caring' professions, but also has a focus beyond caring alone, namely in the safeguarding of rights. In dealing with people who are socially marginalised and disadvantaged, social workers can often play a role in protecting them from abuse and oppression and the disregard of their rights. (Thompson, 2005: 184)

- What values do you think are fundamental to social work?
- Why are values important for social workers and how do they influence practice?

You may want to consider how values might underpin and influence the decisions and actions of social workers.

As the social work profession became established in the 1960s, the values articulated by Biestek (1961) were recognised as fundamental to social work's emerging professional identity. These values included a commitment to rights such as:

- *individualisation* – the right of human beings to be treated as unique individuals and to be respected as such;
- *self-determination* – the right of clients to make choices and decisions for themselves;
- *confidentiality* – the client's right to the protection of sensitive information.

These values have been described as 'traditional' values. Since the 1980s a more radical approach has developed within the profession, challenging the narrow individualism of traditional casework and emphasising the importance of the broader social and political context of social work practice. This 'radical social work' movement laid the foundations for emancipatory values, which include an inherent commitment to rights:

- *equality* – a recognition of structural inequalities based on social divisions such as class, ethnicity, gender, age, disability, sexuality, and the right of service users to equal opportunities and fair treatment;
- *empowerment* – the recognition of power imbalances in human relationships and social and political structures and the right of service users to gain greater control of their own lives;
- *partnership* – the right of service users to be seen as 'experts in their own lives' and to be involved in the planning, development and delivery of services and policies.

(Thompson, 2001)

When the GSCC was established in 2001 to regulate the development of the profession in England, including the introduction of the new Social Work degree, the value base was given fresh articulation in the Codes of Practice for Social Care Workers and Employers. In Standards 1 and 4 the importance of service user rights is given particular emphasis:

1 Protect the rights and promote the interests of service users and carers;
4 Respect the rights of service users whilst seeking to ensure that their behaviour does not harm themselves or other people.

(GSCC, 2004)

It is clear then that social work values, which include the promotion of service user rights, are fundamental to the professional identity of the practitioner. However, as indicated in the GSCC's Standard 4, the implementation of the social work value base is rarely straightforward and contains inherent tensions. These will be examined in due course in relation to social work practice with children and young people. However, it is essential at this point to look at what children's rights mean to the social work profession.

Social work and children's rights

Social work functions within a particular social context and according to the legal and policy framework of that time and place. As has been noted social work values are not fixed and immutable, they develop and evolve. The clear focus given to children's rights in the UN Convention on the Rights of the Child (1989), ratified by the UK in 1991, has had an important influence on social work (see Chapter 1 for more details on the UNCRC and other rights-related legislation such as the European Convention on Human Rights). Articles 12 and 19 in particular, outlining children's rights to express and have their views taken into account in all decisions affecting them and their right to protection from all forms of abuse, are central to social work practice.

The Children Act 1989 forms the legal basis of many aspects of social work with children and young people and incorporates the principles of the UN Convention. Key aspects of the Act are:

- the principle that the welfare of the child is the paramount concern;
- the duty of the local authority to safeguard and promote the welfare of children in need;
- as far as is consistent with the above, to promote the upbringing of children by their families.

(Allen, 2002)

In many ways the Children Act 1989 enhanced the rights of children and the attention given by social workers to children's rights. For example, the Act instituted statutory complaints procedures for young people, expanded their right to legal representation and exhorted social workers to seek the views of children prior to developing plans for their future. However, children's rights were just one of several value perspectives being enshrined in the Children Act 1989. Fox Harding (1997) highlighted four different value positions which coexisted in childcare policy at this time and which continue to run through the contemporary legal and policy framework for practice (see Figure 12.1).

In Figure 12.2 Fox Harding's (1997) model has been adapted to highlight how the value perspectives influence different approaches to social work practice.

Value perspectives in childcare policy

Laissez-faire/patriarchy Minimal state intervention	State paternalism/child protection The state has a key role to protect children
Parent's rights/defence of family The role of the state is to support parents	Children's rights/liberation Children's rights and views have central focus

Figure 12.1

Value perspectives in childcare social work

Laissez-faire/patriarchy Minimal social work intervention	State paternalism/child protection Core business of social work is to protect children
Parent's rights/defence of family Role of social work is to support parents	Children's rights/liberation Social work should promote children's rights and participation

Figure 12.2

The model in Figure 12.2 highlights some of the tensions inherent in social work practice. Despite a solid understanding of child care legislation and a strong value-based commitment to children's rights, social workers face many practice dilemmas. Consider different responses to the following ethical dilemmas:

- How should social workers protect children from parental abuse when they may express a clear wish to live with their parents? (*children's rights versus child protection*)
- Should social workers intervene when a young woman is expressing doubts about an arranged marriage? (*children's rights versus laissez-faire*)
- Should respite care be arranged to provide much needed support to exhausted parents when their disabled child is resistant to the idea? (*children's rights versus parent's rights*)

It has been noted that the approach to social work founded upon the Children Act 1989 and embedded in childcare policy is one which gives more prominence to the protection of children from abuse and to the protection of families than to the protection of children's rights (Fawcett *et al.*, 2004). The centrality of the duty to protect, reinforced by the language of law which defines young people requiring social work intervention in order to safeguard their interests as 'children in need' (Children Act 1989, section 17), can lead to an understanding of children circumscribed by their vulnerability, neediness and developmental dependency. (For other discussions of this area see Chapter 5.)

For many years, social workers have tended to define children's needs, to interpret their wishes and to decide what is in their 'best interests'. Often social workers come into a child's life at a point of crisis, so it is critical that they possess the skills to be able to communicate effectively with children. Children who come into contact with social workers at these critical times in their lives are likely to be those who are least able to articulate their wishes and feelings, and their very need for social work intervention determines that they are vulnerable in a range of ways. The opportunity of social workers to be able to promote a child's right to participate at these critical points can be understood as an uneasy position, where they are trying to balance competing values perspectives. Children have expressed the following views from their experience of working with social workers:

> Social workers need to understand more from a child's perspective about any situation ... [they need] understanding of a person's feelings and to understand that all children are different ... With children in care, they need to always know they have someone they can turn to and talk to ... You just want people to listen, understand and be there on a regular basis. (GSCC, 2008: 2)

Without having an accurate understanding of a young person's perspective the social worker will not be effective in responding to the needs or promoting the rights of the child.

One of the challenges of the social work value base is to maintain a clear view of the rights of the child, including recognition of their capability and agency and a commitment to enabling their participation in decision-making at every level, alongside fulfilling the duty to safeguard their right to protection from abuse and exploitation. This is in line with the judgment of Butler-Sloss, at the outcome of the Cleveland Inquiry, when she emphasised that 'a child is a person, not an object of concern' (HMSO, 1987: 245). There is a growing recognition that speaking with and listening to children is fundamental to ensuring their right to protection (Scottish Executive, 2004, cited in Warren, 2007: 99). Supporting and enabling young people to develop their sense of agency and autonomy is also recognised as central to promoting resilience and positive outcomes for children (Gilligan, 2009). Increasingly children and young people are playing an active role in the planning and delivery of services (Wright *et al.*, 2006). Enabling children to participate is the key to effective, value-based social work practice.

The contemporary context for social work practice

The election of the Labour government in 1997 marked the start of a significant shift in childcare policy. A major commitment of New Labour concerned the eradication of child poverty by 2020. This government also embarked on radical reform of children's services, through the *Every Child Matters* policy launched in 2003, which confirmed their agenda of seeking to ensure that all children reach their potential.

> Children and young people have told us that five outcomes are key to well-being in childhood and later life – being healthy; staying safe; enjoying and achieving; making a positive contribution; and achieving economic well-being. Our ambition is to improve those outcomes for all children and to narrow the gap in outcomes between those who do well and those who do not. (HM Government, 2004: 4).

The implementation of the Children Act 2004 confirmed the central theme of this *Every Child Matters* policy: that all children should meet the five key outcomes, and the requirement of professionals to support them to do this. For some key professional groups this meant that their roles and responsibilities were redefined and extended in relation to safeguarding and promoting the welfare of children and young people. This also reflected a growing emphasis that safeguarding children was everybody's business (HM Government, 2006).

While the publication of the *Every Child Matters* policy was consistent with the general direction of the government's childcare policy, it was understood to be a response to the publication of the Victoria Climbié Inquiry Report. Laming's Report (2003) confirmed that the key role of social workers is child protection. Child protection remains the 'core business' of children and family social workers.

This has been reinforced by later concerns following the death of Baby Peter Connelly in 2007. As information about the circumstances of his death came into the public domain, the effectiveness of our child protection systems and the ability of social workers alongside other professionals to protect children were again under scrutiny (Laming, 2009). The sorts of concerns being expressed were that children's social care organisations prioritise administrative tasks over direct contact with children and their families. There are estimates that social workers spend 70 per cent of their time in the office and only 30 per cent in direct contact with families (Laming, 2009).

The argument that the effectiveness of social work interventions is measured by ensuring that targets are met fails to convince social workers on the front line who struggle to manage the tensions of meeting agency requirements and managing databases when they should be spending time listening to and working with children. These sorts of concerns have been raised by Parton who described the UK child protection system as 'overly proceduralised, defensive and conflict ridden' (2006: 184). The dilemma for social workers working within this context is that the demands of the agency to demonstrate accountability for practice effectively compromises their ability to engage in meaningful relationships with children and young people.

It is evident that there are competing demands that influence how social workers engage with children and their families. To return to the Fox Harding (1997) model, for much of the time, social workers are operating in the domain of state paternalism and child protection. This may present conflicts with an approach promoting children's rights. Their professional values require them to acknowledge and address both of these positions.

Children's rights, participation and social work education

As social work educators we believe that it is central to teaching about children to take them seriously as individuals with rights and agency and not just to focus on their vulnerability and the duty to safeguard and protect their welfare. We promote the child's right to participate in planning, decision-making and every aspect of social work practice, as the foundation for child-centred practice. (For further examples of children's participation in articulating their rights see Chapter 4.) We recognise the many tensions for social workers in balancing competing rights in family work and the inherent contradictions in childcare policy. In order to address these issues in our teaching we promote an understanding of children's rights based on Arnstein's 'ladder of citizen participation' (1969). This model recognises that participation may be viewed as a process and that different levels may be realisable or appropriate in different situations. This perspective is useful in acknowledging that many children and young people are not voluntary service-users and may be resistant to social work involvement. Arnstein's model has been adapted by Hart (1992) to explore levels of participation work with children and young people. The levels are conceptualised as the rungs of a ladder from one to eight:

The ladder of participation:

8 *Young people initiated and decisions shared with adults*
7 *Young people initiated and directed*
6 *Adult initiated, shared decisions with young people*
5 *Consulted and informed*
4 *Assigned but informed*
3 *Tokenism*
2 *Decoration*
1 *Manipulation*

(Hart, 1992)

This theoretical framework is presented to student social workers as a means of assessing and evaluating children's participation in different aspects of practice. Students are challenged to consider a range of case scenarios and to develop ways of enabling children and young people to participate actively in different processes.

Consider different aspects of social work practice with children and young people. For example:

- a review for a looked-after child that is assessing the young person's progress in foster care and making plans for the future;
- a child protection investigation that is responding to concerns about a child's safety;
- an assessment of the needs of a child with complex disabilities that may recommend support services for the child and family.

How would you ensure that children and young people are able to participate in the process?

What would your involvement look like if the participation of the child was on the lower three rungs of Hart's (1992) ladder of participation?

How would your work be different if you were working with young people on the higher rungs of the ladder?

The participation of young people in social work education

In the development of a module entitled 'Children, Young People and Families', which provides foundational knowledge for social work students at the university where we work, we have sought to implement and model principles of children's rights: considering, for example, their participation rights. (See Chapter 1 for more details on the UNCRC and ECHR in relation to participation rights.) We have worked alongside practitioners from Barnardo's to establish a group for young people who have taken a key role in the development of the module. We have been working together since 2004 and have supported the young people, who have experience of being 'in care' or have had significant contact with social workers during their lives, to participate in the delivery of the module. The effective participation of the young people's group demonstrates to trainee social workers how much their future service users have to contribute. It is about participation in action in social work education.

The impact of the young people's participation in the module is best demonstrated by outlining a few examples of how they contribute to the module.

Charmaine

During one of the workshops we provide teaching about the concept of 'resilience', examining research and theory (Masten and Coatsworth, 1998) around the notion that some children do well despite significant adversity. The session includes a presentation by Charmaine, a member of the Young People's Service User Group. Charmaine is a wheelchair user due to cerebral palsy. She is also a performance artist and has published a book of poetry. She shares some of her poems and explains her own perspective on resilience. She tells of a caring grandmother who supported her through tough times and of enabling schools (both 'special' and mainstream) that encouraged her academic success. She emphasises that she sees her 'disability' as an asset rather than a hindrance most of the time and values her health and her creativity. Figure 12.3 is an example of one of Charmaine's poems.

Disability

When you say you have a disability
People might query your capability
Say you are a liability
Or question your stability

It can be hard getting about, wheelchairs
So many problems with accessibility
We need to tell the Council what those buildings lack
Nothing will change if no one dares!

Many people think if you are disabled
Your life's over before it's begun
That nothing can be done!
Don't prove them right and stop
having fun.
Because if you do
Then they have won.

Figure 12.3   Charmaine's poem

Charmaine epitomises resilience and her presentation puts vivid flesh onto the bare bones of the theory and research outlined in the lecture.

Consider a social work assessment of a child or young person with complex health needs or disabilities. In response to Charmaine's poem, how should a social worker listen to the young person and ensure they are taking into consideration their rights to:

- capability?
- access?
- fun?

Donna

Donna is a young woman who has had a significant amount of contact with social workers, particularly during adolescence. She provides 'testimonies' of her life experiences to allow students some understanding of her thoughts and feelings about surviving abuse from adults who should have cared for and protected her. Here is a short excerpt from one of the testimonies that was read out to the students:

> 'I just don't hate myself for it anymore and feel comfortable in my own skin. I just feel that if someone had noticed, I could have been saved a lot quicker. I believe that it is absolutely imperative for social workers to give 100 per cent to each and every one of their charges and to be trustworthy or the child just won't open up to them.'

Nikki

Nikki is a young person who lived for many years in the care system and experienced a number of placement moves. During one of the workshops, the lecture input highlights policy and practice issues around social work with looked-after young people. Nikki shares some of her experiences and highlights the difficulties of adjusting to many changes of allocated social worker. She emphasises the disruption caused by placement moves with no notice, explanation or preparation, possessions transported by social workers in black bin bags. Nikki has developed her own presentation to communicate to training social workers what she wants them to consider in their practice with young people:

Why is it important to be non-judgmental and open-minded?
Consider why it might be important to reflect on *how* you are forming opinions and perceptions as you read case notes from a file, for example. Why might it be important to reflect on what your own preconceived ideas about a child or young person might be? How might the examples in this section of the chapter relate to society's stereotypes of children or young people? How might getting to know an individual be an important factor in working with a child or young person?

Why should you not expect young people to trust you straightaway?
Reflect on why time and building a relationship is an important factor for children and young people who have experienced complex relationships with others. For example, some young people might have been hurt and abused and won't find it easy to trust people. How might time, repeated meetings and trust be important in developing effective relationships between workers and children and young people?

Why is it important to include young people?
Consider the different kinds of ways children might be excluded and included in the discussions of social work so far in the chapter. How do you think being included in decisions about their lives might be important for each of the young people included as examples here? Ask yourself questions related to inclusion; for example, would you like to have all your decisions made for you?

Learning from young people's participation in social work education

Through the four years we have been working with these young people we have learned a great deal about what it means to empower service users to be actively involved in social work education. An understanding of participation as a process, hopefully progressing up the ladder (Hart, 1992), has been helpful. The involvement of the young people has developed from leading one half-day workshop to contributing to all six full-day workshops, leading a range of activities and being part of the process of review, evaluation and ongoing evolution of the module.

The young people's own evaluation of their involvement confirmed that they considered themselves to be active participants in the process of planning and delivering the module. The young people were introduced to the ladder of participation (Hart, 1992), and asked to identify where they thought they were in relation to their involvement in the module. One person identified herself as at Level 5 – she felt that she had been consulted and informed; the others identified that they felt they were at Level 7, initiating activities with support.

Social work students have valued and learned much from these young people's involvement. The following comments are taken from the module evaluation process:

> Their stories were very moving. Was very honoured that they were able to share their experiences.

> As a second year social work student it really made me think about how I am going to become a more effective social worker.

The contributions made by the young people were very valuable and interesting, and one of the most beneficial aspects of attending the module.

Having the young people in to talk to us about their own views and experiences helped me really understand what the module was about and why it is so important.

Their experience will guide our practice.

One of the themes from student evaluation is the aspiration to be different to previous professionals, recognising the importance of listening to young people and upholding their right to participation.

Summary

In this chapter we emphasised the importance of children's rights as an inherent part of the social work value base. We examined the tensions around putting into practice a commitment to children's rights. We highlighted an approach to social work education that promotes and models young people's participation. Our aim is to train a new generation of social work practitioners who understand the central importance of listening to children and young people and promoting their rights.

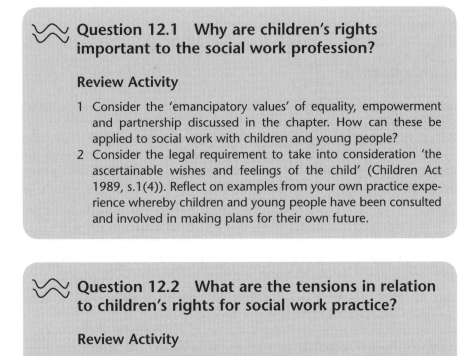

Question 12.1   Why are children's rights important to the social work profession?

Review Activity

1   Consider the 'emancipatory values' of equality, empowerment and partnership discussed in the chapter. How can these be applied to social work with children and young people?
2   Consider the legal requirement to take into consideration 'the ascertainable wishes and feelings of the child' (Children Act 1989, s.1(4)). Reflect on examples from your own practice experience whereby children and young people have been consulted and involved in making plans for their own future.

Question 12.2   What are the tensions in relation to children's rights for social work practice?

Review Activity

1   Reflect on Fox Harding's (1997) model of the different value perspectives that inform childcare policy and practice. From your own experience, can you think of examples of how these value perspectives have influenced social work practice?

(Continued)

2 Reflect on the contemporary context for social work practice, the current emphasis on the core business of child protection and the need to address targets and outcome measures. How can you ensure you promote children's rights in your day-to-day practice?

 **Question 12.3　Why is it important to promote the participation of young people in social work education?**

Review Activity

1 Reflect on Charmaine's poem, Nikki's questions and Donna's testimony. What have you learnt from listening to their voices that you can take into your practice with children and young people.

Acknowledgements

We would like to thank all members of the young people's group.

Further Reading

Bell, M. (2002) 'Promoting children's rights through the use of relationship', *Child and Family Social Work, 7* (1): 1–11.
Bell's interesting article summarises research exploring the views of children and young people involved in child protection investigations. She also discusses the importance of developing professional relationships with children and young people that promote their interests and rights.

Gilligan, R. (2009) 'Promoting positive outcomes for children in need', in J. Horwath (ed.), *The Child's World*, 2nd edn. London: Jessica Kingsley.
This chapter examines the importance of promoting the protective capacity of children through assessment practices which recognise the agency, energy and autonomy of the child and also seek to strengthen their social networks.

Hart, R. (1992) *Children's Participation: From Tokenism to Citizenship.* Florence: UNICEF International Child Development Centre.
In this text Hart develops and adapts Arnstein's (1969) ladder of citizenship in order to consider the participation rights of children and young people.

Warren, J. (2007) *Service User and Carer Participation in Social Work.* Exeter: Learning Matters, Chapter 6: 'Participation in practice: involving children'.
The focus of this text is on the centrality of service user participation as inherent in the social work role and value base.

13

Provision for Young People and Rights: Youth Work

Phil Jones and Alan Smith

Chapter Overview

Services and provision for young people are developed and created within a network of processes such as government decisions about spending and priorities in policy and practice, input from young people and the codes and guidelines developed by the organisations of the workers involved. Practice can involve relationships between adults and young people in relation to leisure, health, housing, education, training and employment. Activities can vary between group work and individual support and can take place in settings as varied as schools and colleges, neighbourhood or community centres, sports centres or through specialist projects. This chapter will explore the relationship between this area of provision and rights, focusing upon youth work as a particular aspect of services for young people. The chapter will look at the different ways in which rights are present in different aspects of services for young people, focusing on youth work. The ways in which young people see and describe their rights will be looked at in relation to different aspects of their lives and the services they use. Society's attitudes towards young people are contradictory and ambivalent, and tensions exist in the ways young people are seen and treated by policy and practice. The chapter will explore the implications of such tensions and their relationship to young people's rights.

The range of provision and young people's rights

Services for young people constitute a wide range of provision and involve connections between different agencies and sectors. Those providing these services are described in *Resourcing Excellent Youth Services* as 'a complex network of providers, community groups, voluntary organisations and local authorities' (DFES, 2002) normally aimed at those between 13 and 19 years of age. These services fall into two basic categories: services for young people which have many and various practices ranging from health to housing, and youth work which is a set of practices with a very distinct methodology and value base. Youth work covers a wide range of provision, but is underpinned by an explicit methodology and informed by a set of values. These include valuing young people's voluntary participation, seeking to tip balances of power in their favour, seeing and responding to them 'simply as young people, as untouched as possible by pre-set labels and prioritising and valuing their interests, current activities and emotional concerns (Davies, 2005: 22). As such, youth work starts where the young person is at, and responds in a way that is guided by young people's wishes.

This chapter will focus upon provision traditionally understood as 'youth work' located within the umbrella of 'youth services' but will also refer to other areas of general provision which serve young people. Different rights-based frameworks, such as conventions and policies, relate to young people: from the UNCRC with its remit to serve children and young people under the age of 18, to the European Convention on Human Rights. The chapter will explore the ways in which such frameworks concerning child rights can be related to youth work and youth services. It will concern itself with key threads through policy, debate and frameworks and guidance for practice concerning rights associated with provision, participation and protection.

How do rights relate to youth provision?

In many countries this area of practice relates to different arenas of young people's lives, ranging from welfare to education, from health and leisure to employment (Williamson, 1997b). The defined age range of 'youth' served also varies between different countries. The approach of the London Borough of Richmond, as a representative example (see below) of the UK framework, states that its services are for those between the ages of 11 and 25, with a 'priority age range of 13–19'. Likewise, different emphases are placed on the goals of youth work, often balancing national policy trends and financing with local needs or concerns and in response to the very different experiences, situations and 'multifaceted nature' of young people (Huq, 2009). Debates within youth work have often concerned issues such as the differences between the nature of centre-based models of provision compared to detached work (Crimmens et al., 2004), or a focus on individualistic development compared to communal change (Roche and Tucker, 1997), but each have agreed that the underpinning values have remained consistent. However, in recent years there has been an increasing emphasis on youth workers and youth services engaging with the problems of social exclusion (Jeffs and Smith, 1990; Ledgerwood and Kendra, 1997), where policy-makers and authority figures have frequently constructed the individual young person as in some way to 'blame' due to forms of 'deficit' or inadequacy, as opposed to accepting that social issues may have affected young people – a lack of affordable leisure activities or employment opportunities, for instance. (For further details of this issue and its relationship to rights see Chapter 3.) However, even where the policy agenda has focused on 'problematic' young people, there has been an attempt by youth workers to work with them through a voluntary relationship and across a wide range of issues that affect them, and these aims or values can be seen to relate to issues concerning rights.

The history and role of youth services has been critiqued by some as being problematic in its allegiance with the promotion of societal control and of correction: of redressing perceived deficiencies rather than encouraging young people to be active agents in their lives (Davies, 1999). Evans, for example, has commented that this was a response to 'the potential threat posed by the working classes at the time, by socialising young people into middle-class values and ways of thinking' (Evans, 1994: 180). This history is useful in considering the way contemporary youth work values have engaged with their relationship to the emergence of rights as a concept. The emphasis lies in framing youth work within empowerment, choice in provision and developing enabling relationships to enhance participation rather than ideas of deficit or control.

Developments involving users, policy-makers and organisations delivering or supporting the services have seen the emergence of principles and guidance which seek to permeate or underpin practice and relationships (Robb, 2007; Wood and Hine, 2009). These include *professional frameworks for practice*. Rights have, increasingly, featured in such principles and guidance and become part of the landscape within which relationships are formed between professionals and young people. One example of this type of emergent connection can be seen in a set of youth work values which have been developed. Table 13.1 below takes elements of these values and considers the ways in which a rights agenda can be seen to be a part of the way in which any proposed frameworks for intervention and relationship are understood.

National and international policies relating to these areas include, for example, the UN Convention on the Rights of the Child and its influence on youth services. Hackney Council, in London, for example, in its Youth Charter (2007) makes an explicit link between international, national and local policy and provision. It states that:

> The UNCRC acknowledges that those under 18 years of age have the ability, and therefore the right, to be involved in decision making. In November 2004 the Government published *Every Child Matters: Change for Children* which set out a national expectation that all services for Children and Young People involve them in taking decision about services and issues that concern them. (http://www.hackney.gov.uk/youth-charter-2007.pdf)

It then goes on to illustrate how its youth service works to meet the needs of the UNCRC and *Every Child Matters* in it policies and practices. Examples include:

- young people researching the effect of the services;
- being involved in the design of services;
- reviewing services on an ongoing, developmental basis.

This example shows the ways in which the UNCRC has affected youth provision through the local authority's *direct reference* to it within their aims and practice.

Table 13.1 is an illustration of a different way in which child rights are influential. The table presents in column 1 the *Resourcing Excellent Youth Services*'s (DfES, 2002) statement of youth work values. In column 2 we have created links with two key pieces of rights statements: the UNCRC and the Human Rights Act (HRA) (for fuller details of these see Chapters 1 and 2). In this way, youth work values can be seen to implicitly reflect a rights perspective relating to areas such as choice, participation and the voice of the young person.

The relationships in the table between youth work values and child rights demonstrate the way in which rights 'as a concept can create an impetus for change: their presence acts as a catalyst, a meeting point and a pressure for action' (Jones and Welch, 2010: 16). It also demonstrates the live interaction between rights and youth services: illustrating a 'rights-informed approach to how policies are created, and a rights-informed approach within the policies made that relate to how workers conduct interactions with young people. The former might involve young people in the creation of a setting's policies, the latter might concern the way adults engage with young people in areas such as choice or involvement in decision-making within everyday contact' (Jones and Welch, 2010: 19).

Given the wide range of youth services and the variety of professionals involved, there are specific aspects of the nature of practice and the relationship which are integral to the youth work process. These are most noticeable in the area of youth justice, or work with young people 'not in education, employment or training' (NEET), as their involvement with youth workers may not be 'voluntary' in the manner described by Davies, but workers will encourage their participation in an activity so that they retain an element of choice. However, other aspects of the roles professionals play across provisional can be seen to have parallels (Kehily, 2007; Robb, 2007). Examples of this are the concept and practice of 'reach' or 'contact' whereby the professional seeks to build a relationship with a young person; a key aspect of the relationships formed concerns supporting and enabling access to provision which can result in benefit for the young person. Rights-informed approaches to practice can be seen in a variety of areas of youth work, from community

Table 13.1 Examples of youth work values and a 'rights agenda'

Column 1 Youth work values (DfES, 2002: 6)	*Column 2* Connections to a rights agenda
Young people choose to be involved, not least because they want to relax, meet friends and have fun	Article 15, UNCRC: The right to meet people and gather in public
	Articles 28 and 29, UNCRC: The right to education
The work starts where young people are – with their view of the world and their interests	Article 31, UNCRC: The right to rest, play and leisure
	Article 11, HRA: The right to freedom of assembly and association
	Article 3, UNCRC: Adults should always try to do what is in the best interests of children whether undertaken by public or private social welfare institutions, courts of law, administrative or legislative bodies
	Article 12, UNCRC: Children who are capable of forming their own views have the right to express their views freely in all matters affecting the child, the views being given due weight in accordance with the age and maturity of the child
	Article 9, HRA: The right to freedom of thought, conscience and religion
	Article 10, HRA: The right to freedom of expression
It seeks to help young people achieve stronger relationships and collective identities – for example, as black people, women, men, disabled people, gay men or lesbians – and through the promotion of inclusivity, particularly for minority ethnic communities	Article 2, UNCRC: Children must be treated without discrimination of any kind, irrespective of race, colour, sex, language, religion or other status
	Article 30, UNCRC: The right to enjoy their own culture, religion and language
	Article 23, UNCRC: The right to a full life and to active participation in the community for disabled children

(Continued)

Table 13.1 (Continued)

Column 1 **Youth work values (DfES, 2002: 6)**	*Column 2* **Connections to a rights agenda**
It seeks to go beyond where young people start, in particular by encouraging them to be critical and creative in their responses to their experience and the world around them and supporting their exploration of new ideas, interests and creative ability	Article 13, UNCRC: The right to freedom of expression, including the right to all kinds of information and ideas Article 14, UNCRC: The right to freedom of thought, conscience and religion Article 9, HRA: The right to freedom of thought, conscience and religion Article 10, HRA: The right to freedom of expression
It is concerned with facilitating and empowering the voice of young people	Article 3, UNCRC: Adults should always try to do what is in the best interests of children whether undertaken by public or private social welfare institutions, courts of law, administrative or legislative bodies
It is concerned with ensuring young people can influence the environment within which they live	Article 12, UNCRC: Children who are capable of forming their own views have the right to express their views freely in all matters affecting the child, the views being given due weight in accordance with the age and maturity of the child Article 9, HRA: The right to freedom of thought, conscience and religion Article 10, HRA: The right to freedom of expression

action to leisure, from counselling to housing support. The National Youth Agency's *Act By Right* (NYA, 2004) is an example of this approach with its emphasis on participation and empowerment in the creation of five 'stages' relating to 'a journey' to enable young people to develop the knowledge and skills they need to take effective action on issues that concern them. The UK's National Council for Voluntary Youth Services, similarly, sees a key aspect of young people's rights being reflected in participation. This is linked to ideas of collaboration and decision-making. They advocate the notion of 'partnership' between adult workers and young people. This is connected to acts such as listening, identifying need and maximising the contribution of young people to any process. The role of workers in services is seen to be responsive to young people's opinions and concerns and the notion of partnership links this to services meeting needs and enabling society to benefit from young people's contributions.

A critical structure is created by them, drawing on these basic ideas. They describe a series of principles that should underpin youth participation, which can be summarised in the following way:

- The involvement of young people is voluntary – they are involved because they want to be, and have choices about how to be involved.
- Factors such as diversity are valued and participation is accessible to all – taking into account factors such as language.
- The relationships of those involved are based on equality and honesty.
- Organisations evaluate the way they work to ensure there are no barriers to young people being involved and participation is valued and views are acted on to result in impact and effect, and be visible in evaluation and planning.

(Adapted from *Principles of Youth Participation*, National Council for Voluntary Youth Services at http://www.ncvys.org.uk)

These principles are then embedded in the practice of the work. Key factors include:

- developing agreements within the organisation;
- raising staff awareness;
- developing goals with young people, staff and volunteers;
- developing ideas, involving young people into the process, plans, goals and necessary resources;
- looking at areas such as training and support for young people, staff and volunteers;
- work to include groups and individuals to ensure access and inclusion for young people with disabilities and ways to facilitate involvement, review and evaluate progress.

(Adapted from *Youth Participation: Getting Started*, National Council for Voluntary Youth Services at: http://www.ncvys.org.uk)

Many examples exist of young people engaging at various levels of policy or decision-making. Envision, for example, is a national education charity working with young people and the services which are provided for them. Their work relates to the rights agenda described earlier in this chapter, including areas such as active citizenship and youth-led campaigns challenging negative views and treatment of young people. The British Youth Council (BYC), for example, is led by young people for young people aged 25 and under. Their lobbying involves representing young people's right to provision, participation and protection though a variety of rights-based initiatives that challenge existing policies. Projects and campaigns include a concern with democratic rights, for example lowering the voting age in its campaign '16: A New Age for Democracy'.

For many young people, their involvement in decision-making may be at a local level, for example in relation to planning a residential or programme of activities. In this case, 'young people's participation can improve existing services or make demands for new services to address their needs' (Sapin, 2009: 139). Sapin goes on to stress that 'the degree of participation that young people are able to exercise may depend on the particular activity or organization' (2009: 143). An example from North West Leeds tells of a young woman, Kirsten, who was involved in a Positive Activities Youth Programme (PAYP) and through Youth Point (a local centre) she expressed an interest in 'Baby Reality'. She talks of the importance of starting a group, the friendliness of those involved as being of value, along with the work leading to a qualification. She refers to continuing the work beyond the life of the initial group and the momentum leading to her feeling empowered enough to start a new group for girls (http://www.breezeleeds.org).

Young people's perceptions of their rights

Recent developments have seen an increase in the recognition given to children and young people's *own views* on their rights, rather than on adult definitions or approaches to the nature and implementation of children's rights (Jones and Welch, 2010).

As already stated, organisations have emerged, created by and for young people, to represent and lobby for rights-related causes and issues at the national and local government levels and in specific services or projects. These both encourage and represent young people's perspectives on rights or rights-related issues. They can be seen to reflect rights in all three broad areas of participation, provision and protection, and to reflect the concerns about rights as described in the above excerpts from young people. Examples of national levels of work include Envision (http://www.envision.org.uk), the British Youth Council, UNICEF Youth Voice and Participation Works (http://www.participationworks.org.uk), whereas Hackney local authority is an example of local government level engagement. It consulted young people about their services and created a series of key messages with these young people in terms of how they saw the relationship between their rights and locals services. An example of this is described by them as:

> Young People have the right to be involved and have a say over services that they use or decisions that affect them. In the case of school inspections, school councils acting as representatives of their peers are involved with assessing how well the school is doing. (Hackney Council, 2007: 5)

This is enshrined in both the United Nations Convention on the Rights of the Child (UNCRC) and the Hear by Right standards. Their research revealed that:

> 75% of young people interviewed knew they had this right
> BUT, 61% felt that this right was not always 'acted upon'.
>
> (Hackney Council, 2007: 6)

Themes raised by young people themselves about the practice of rights emphasised involvement in participation through having a say, the need for information, training and support and the need to reflect differences and diversity in designing and implementing any initiatives (see Hackney Council, 2007, for details).

As the next section will show, critiques of current rights by young people and suggestions for new developments are crucial in developing rights, in order for them to avoid being static and out of touch with the very people they seek to represent and affect.

Tensions and difficulties in relation to youth services and young people's rights

Authors such as Charlton have pointed out not only the importance of rights within this sector, but also the tensions and contradictions within policy, cultural attitudes and service provision:

> The majority of young people take their responsibilities and rights as citizens seriously and this is essential if the UK is to retain belief in freedom and rights. Unfortunately, some of the policies related to social control and social welfare undermine the principles of rights and justice and this is not lost on young people. The most blatant example of this is the use of ASBOs. (Charlton, 2008: 106).

One area relating to rights concerns the ways in which the user-led approach emphasising young people's rights to participation identified in much of the practice referred to in this chapter is, potentially, being challenged or threatened by policies initiatives which are led and funded by externally imposed targets and outcomes, for instance the 'reach' and 'recorded outcomes' in Transforming Youth Work. Charlton's concerns are reflected in a young person report from a workshop organised by the Department for Children, Schools and Families (DCSF), the Children's Rights Alliance England (CRAE) and UNICEF UK feeding into the UNCRC committee review of the UK's response to the UNCRC. The group she was working in raised a number of issues, including their experience of mosquito alarms being used by shops: these emit a sound designed to affect only young people's hearing due to its high pitch. The following is from her account:

> The key problems we discussed included negative stereotyping of young people, mosquito alarms, police searches and age discrimination – ... The MP in our group was very surprised to hear what is actually happening to UK children and young people. I talked about police searches, where young people walking through a public place, can have to walk through metal detectors if the police deem them to 'look a bit dodgy' ... and the horrifying use of mosquito alarms ... Most of the group felt this was a severe violation of human rights, such as the right to freedom of movement, as well as being a clear example of age discrimination. (British Youth Council at: http://www.byc.org/media.php)

Table 13.2 draws on such issues, identified by young people, along with this chapter's consideration of key ideas and practices concerning young people's rights.

Table 13.2 Young people's rights: ideas and practices

Rights-related ideas in relation to youth work, young people's services and provision

- Rights need to be reflected in the values and practice of youth services and provision
- There can be a vital relationship between international, national and local policy and practice
- There are important parallels between rights as described in the UNCRC and HER and the values and frameworks for practices of youth work
- Rights relate to different areas of young people's lives including areas of provision, participation and protection
- Information about rights and how to act in response to them is important for young people and those who are involved in their services
- Young people are active agents in their lives, capable of valid judgements and opinions
- Young people's perceptions and opinions about their rights and how they are reflected in service and provision are important in offering a particular perspective that may differ from adults' ideas and interpretations
- Diversity and equality need to be addressed to ensure that access and involvement reflect difference and ensure that participation is accessible to all
- It is important to engage with tensions between policy and practice in areas such as confidentiality and issues such as ASBOs, which challenge young people's rights

Rights-informed practice in relation to young people's services and provision

- Young people's rights to provision should be reflected in responsive varied practice that reflects young people's views and needs
- Training for organisations, workers and young people is a component of developing awareness of rights and how to act on them and how to develop them
- Information about rights, how to act on them and organisations that relate to the implementation of rights is important to be provided in meaningful, accessible ways for young people and those involved in their services
- Young people's rights to provision, participation and protection should be reflected in involvement in the design, implementation and review of services and provision
- Rights need to be built into the review and evaluation of service provision
- Young people's perspectives on developing their rights into new areas are to be practically encouraged and engaged with

Opinions within the workforce reflect these issues in terms of rights, confidentiality and young people. Crimmens *et al.*'s research (2004) revealed that many workers were concerned about the effects closer involvement with crime control and community safety initiatives could have on 'the ways they were perceived by the young people, the public, partner agencies and local politicians'. They also questioned youth workers' involvement with recording and monitoring young people not necessarily involved in criminal activity, but 'not choosing' to be involved with wider youth support services. Their report revealed the following tension:

> Connexions aimed to involve street-based youth workers in identifying, supporting, tracking, and sharing information about hard-to-reach young people who were out of education, employment or training. Some street-based youth workers were concerned about this, having previously worked on the basis that confidentiality between the young person and the worker or project was sacrosanct. Subsequent government guidance (*Transforming Youth Work*) and the White Paper on anti-social behaviour have identified the Youth Service and Connexions as key members of Crime Reduction Partnerships, and appear to suggest a more directly controlling role for both. (Crimmens *et al.*, 2004)

Rights, confidentiality and the relationship between workers and young people are identified clearly here as an area of tension. The emerging issues identified in the previous two sections can be seen to present a series of new directions to show how rights are continuing to develop and feature in the lives of young people and those working with them.

Similar tensions exist for workers at the local/project level, where they may be engaging young people in decision-making activities about a programme of events or a residential, but ultimately budget constraints immediately limit what is and isn't possible. This is often beyond the workers' immediate control, but can jeopardise the way in which young people engage in future decision-making activities.

Summary

The challenge for youth work practice is to balance the desire to encourage young people to take an active role in the decisions that affect them, individually or collectively, and to promote their active participation in practice, while being tasked with meeting targets for engagement or learning outcomes. Frequently, the wish to include young people, and the time taken to work with them in a meaningful way, is seen to be counterproductive to the decision-making process, although most workers see the benefit in this form of practice. At this point, many workers take a pragmatic view about what they believe to be a meaningful engagement and how best this serves the rights of young people at all levels of society. In adopting this pragmatic response, workers stress the view that many things get decided through an 'elected' body, and therefore do not represent the opinions of the majority of citizens. However, on key issues which may affect individual rights, a greater level of consultation takes place, so why should youth work be any different?

As an area of practice, youth work is based on a set of values which, this chapter has shown, are firmly embedded within the rights agenda, and when practised at their best reflect the empowerment of young people. Given that the age range of those engaging in youth work overlaps the voting age, it is right that young people are encouraged to have a say in the decisions that affect their lives. By engaging young people in making informed choices, they are developing an understanding and set of skills which are needed to be an active citizen, and in turn promote a more fair and just society. By stressing the importance of a common value-base at the heart of professional practice, it doesn't matter what the context is in which the worker is engaged or whether the funding requirements are creating an artificial focus on targets or learning outcomes as the practice itself will retain its focus on fairness, equity and rights and this will translate to the way a young person experiences youth work.

Question 13.1   How do rights relate to youth services, in particular to youth work?

Review Activity

1   Given the values expressed in Table 13.1 (page 179) how do these relate to your daily practice, and think of an example where one of the 'values' was more significant than the outcome for a young person?
2   How might a worker:

  (a) balance the need to achieve externally given targets, or
  (b) meet with a young person through a court requirement

  with an explicit value about voluntary relationships?

Question 13.2   How do young people see their rights?

Review Activity

1   Reflect on the different areas identified in Table 13.2

  (a) Consider whether you agree with these as a statement of rights
  (b) Consider the ways in which the youth work you are involved in or you see described in this chapter can reflect or respond to young people's ideas as summarised in Table 13.2.

〰️ **Question 13.3   What tensions or difficulties exist in relation to youth services and young people's rights?**

Review Activity

The chapter referred to Crimmens *et al.*'s research (2004) which revealed that many workers were concerned about the effects closer involvement with crime control and community safety initiatives could have on 'the ways they were perceived by the young people, the public, partner agencies and local politicians'.

1   How do you see this research in relation to rights?
2   Go through the section of the chapter on 'Tensions and difficulties in relation to youth services and young people's rights'.

   (a)   List the tensions identified there.
   (b)   Look at the list of tensions and see how they relate to the list of values and references to the UNCRC and HRA in Table 13.1.

Further Reading 📖

Banks, S. (2010) *Ethical Issues in Youth Work*, 2nd Edn. Abingdon: Routledge.
A wide ranging account of youth work practice, and the challenges and dilemmas faced by workers in the light of government policy and current public attitudes towards young people.

Davies, B. (2005) *Youth Work: A Manifesto for Our Times.* London: National Youth Agency.
An overview of youth work, including a detailed consideration of values and practices in relation to the themes of rights raised within this chapter.

Robb, M. (2007) *Youth in Context: Frameworks, Settings and Encounters.* London: Sage/Open University.
An effective consideration of key issues in developing and understanding a range of practices, and a useful text on values and ways of working in relation to empowerment.

14

Youth Justice and Children's Rights

Daniel Marshall and Terry Thomas

Chapter Overview

This chapter will explore children's rights in relation to the changing and seemingly ever more punitive UK government policy and legislation in relation to the behaviour of children and young people. The tensions between this tougher approach to children and other overarching principles and legislation based on child welfare and rights will be discussed. Developments involving successive governments since the early 1990s will be considered along with some of the wider drivers for them. Key features of the current criminal justice system will be examined along with the ways in which children and young people's behaviour has been conceptualised and then translated into legislation. The extent to which the current criminal justice system undermines or upholds children's rights will be evaluated.

Key developments in criminal justice policy and legislation affecting children and young people

It has become a truism that each generation sees the behaviour of its young people as somehow worse than anything that has been experienced in the past. Pearson's work tracks our social concerns on the 'problem of youth' over the last 150 years and shows how everything was always 'better 20 years ago' or 'before the war' – regardless of which war we are talking about (Pearson, 1983). The problems caused by the 'misbehaviour' of youth can be approached in various ways, and the UK has currently decided that it wants to do so mainly through the criminal justice system rather than any educational or welfare-orientated approaches. Today we have a very interventionist and punitive youth justice system dealing with children and young people.

The criminal justice system as a whole has long taken age as a factor in dealing with offenders. The long-standing convention has been to categorise 'young people' as aged 14 to 18 years and those below 14 as 'children': the Children Act 1989 makes no such distinctions and for legal purposes all under 18's are regarded as children. The age of criminal responsibility is set at 10 years. The orthodoxy is that a new attitude to 'law and order' started in the early 1990s. During an interview on 10 January 1993, for example, Shadow Home Secretary Blair famously declared that we should be 'tough on crime, and tough on the causes of crime' and the then Prime Minister Major added his view that it was time to 'understand a little less and condemn a little more' (8 October 1993).

The politicisation of law and order that followed had the effect of bringing political parties together in a convergence of policies. As Garland pointed out: 'the centre of political gravity has moved and a new consensus has formed around penal measures that are perceived as tough, smart and popular with the public' (Garland, 2001: 14). Criminologists coined the phrase 'popular punitivism' and this new attitude came to bear on all youthful misbehaviour that varied from the criminal to the almost normal. Young people have always pushed boundaries to their limits as a part of growing up and finding their feet in the world. More young people than ever have come into contact with the UK youth justice system to the extent that it has been said we are actually criminalising our children: 'Normal adolescent behaviour is being criminalised because of the "over-zealous" treatment of young people ... incidents which used to be regarded as high-jinks or normal adolescent behaviour 15 to 20 years ago, are being seen as criminal activity now' (YMCA, 2006).

Morgan, former chair of the Youth Justice Board, said that children as young as 10 are being labelled with the 'mark of Cain on their foreheads because of a misplaced hysteria over teenage crime' and cited examples of swearing in the playground and breaking windows as leading to court (Jones, 2006). The campaign group NACRO believed we are criminalising children for trivial matters (NACRO, 2008) and even chief police officers expressed their 'concerns about criminalising young people' and giving them criminal records for little more than a phase they are going through (House of Commons 2008: Ev 79, Q489). Politicians may believe they represent the punitive public opinion on young offenders and, to some extent, this has been confirmed by academic studies (see, for example, Maruna and King, 2009); these same studies also reveal that the public has an understanding of deep-rooted causes such as poor upbringing, deprivation and poorly behaved siblings (Maruna and King, 2008). At a practitioner level both research and theory has challenged the prevailing cold climate (see Case and Haines, 2009; Hopkins-Burke, 2008; Muncie, 2009). In such a climate how are children's rights maintained when they come up against the youth justice system? Here we take the youth justice system to mean the interactions with, and decision-making by, the police, prosecution agencies, the judiciary, the prison service, the probation service and children's services (see Burnett and Roberts, 2004; Souhami, 2007).

Key aspects of the current criminal justice system

The age of criminal responsibility

The age of criminal responsibility in England and Wales was set at 10 in 1963 and is the lowest in Europe. In Scotland the age is eight but offenders go to a hearing rather than a court. Children and young people may be brought before a youth court in England and Wales between the ages of 10 and 18. This very low age in itself could be construed as a denial of children's rights to not have their behaviour criminalised at such an early age. (For further discussion of issues concerning age and rights in this area see Chapter 2.) Other countries have much higher ages of criminal responsibility such as France where it is 13, Germany where it is 15 and Sweden and Italy where it is 16. Behaviour that in this country is interpreted as crime is dealt with in these countries as a child welfare or child protection matter, without recourse to the criminal justice system. This criminalisation process can be seen to be using the youth justice system to respond to social and personal problems within UK society (Scraton and Haydon, 2002). The four UK Children's Commissioners have jointly recommended that our age of criminal responsibility should be increased (UK Children's Commissioners 2008: recommendation 103) and so has the United Nations Committee on the Rights of the Child (UN, 2008: General Comment no. 10, para. 16). At the moment none of the political parties is willing to act on the Commissioners' views and the criticisms of the UNCRC's Committee on governmental failure to act on children's rights in this matter. (For other criticism of the UK government's lack of action on certain areas of child rights see Chapter 1.) The Children and Young Persons Act 1969, ss. 4–5, had stated that the age of 10 would be raised to 14 – but the relevant sections were quietly repealed by the Criminal Justice Act 1991, s.72, never having been implemented. In 1998 the Crime and Disorder Act, s.34, appeared to some people to be actually *lowering* the age by repealing the concept of *doli incapax*. (For further discussion of *doli incapaxi* see Chapter 2.) *Doli incapax* was the doctrine that said that prosecution in the youth courts of anyone between the ages of 10 and 14 had first to show that children of that age knew what they were doing was wrong. Taking away the concept of *doli incapax* meant that all children over 10 *did* know what they were doing (Bandalli, 1998).

Key aim of the youth justice system

The Crime and Disorder Act 1998 was an important development in the relationship between young people and the state in this area. It set out the key aim of the youth justice system for the first time:

(1) It shall be the principal aim of the youth justice system to prevent offending by children and young persons.
(2) In addition to any other duty to which they are subject, it shall be the duty of all persons and bodies carrying out functions in relation to the youth justice system to have regard to that aim.

(Crime and Disorder Act 1998, s.37)

In itself this aim was somewhat negative in that it contained no reference to the welfare of children and young people and, in particular, no reference to the 'welfare principle' carried in the Children and Young Persons Act 1933. The 1933 Act (s.44) held that criminal courts must always have regard to the welfare of the child in all decision-making. Section 44 is still applicable today and an opportunity had been lost to reaffirm its importance by restating it in the new 1998 aims. This omission in an age of 'popular punitivism' and the removal of the *doli incapax* doctrine was seen as a bad omen for children's rights.

Policing the streets

The police are the keepers of the 'Queen's peace' and that peace is often represented as *order* on the streets and in public spaces. Young people with nowhere else to meet are prone to use the streets. Social gatherings of young people are not always seen as 'social'. Sometimes they are seen as anti-social and the streets become a site of potential conflict between police and young people. (For further discussion of this area of rights see Chapter 12.) Private companies and retailers have tried to disperse groups of young people using technology known as the Ultrasonic Teenage Deterrent Device or 'the mosquito'. The device emits a high-pitched disconcerting sound that only young people can hear. We might imagine a greater outcry should such a device have been targeted at any other social group. The *Buzz Off Campaign* was organised to try and get them banned (NYA, 2008).

The police do have powers of dispersal given to them by the law, and they do have powers to apply for certain areas to be made subject to curfews that young people are not allowed into after a given time (Anti-Social Behaviour Act 2003, ss.30–36).

These local child curfews were originally in the Crime and Disorder Act 1998, s.14, and applications for a curfew area had to be made by local authorities. Curfews were directed at the under 10s and the stated rationale was to protect the welfare of these children. In practice no local authority ever applied for any. The governmental response was to simply raise the age limit to 16 and allow the police also to make applications (Criminal Justice and Police Act, 2001, s.49); as one observer at the time put it, 'the unspoken assumption is that the police will be more eager to apply for curfews than the local authorities have proven themselves to be' (Walsh, 2002). The Anti-Social Behaviour Act 2003, ss.30–6, made it even easier for the police themselves to authorise curfews and within a few years some 400 curfew areas had reportedly been authorised (Barkham, 2005).

EXAMPLE 14.1   'W' and curfews

In 2006, a 15-year-old referred to as W challenged the Metropolitan police's right to use their powers to enforce curfews which allow police to remove anyone under the age of 16 from a public place between 9 p.m. and 6 a.m. if they are not accompanied by an adult, even if they are not suspected of behaving badly. W argued that these powers were 'arbitrary' in that they covered young people not actually doing anything wrong. He further argued that the police should not be allowed to treat him 'like a criminal' just because he was a young person. The Court of Appeal agreed, declaring the powers to be only permissive, not coercive. In other words, police could only take young people home if they agreed and could not remove them to their home against their will.

What are some of the key issues here? You may want to consider:

- What might be the presumption about young people out at night within this legislation?
- How are the rights of young people construed in this legislation?
- What might the decision of the court say about how the original legislation was written by the government? Although curfews were packaged as supporting the welfare of young people, the court here appeared to argue that the effect of the legislation was not related to welfare. Is the implication of this that curfews might instead reflect a preoccupation with appearing to be 'tough' on young people?

At the police station

Children have the same two rights as adults inside a police station – to have a solicitor and to have someone informed of their whereabouts (Police and Criminal Evidence Act 1984, ss. 56 and 58); the police must also try and find out who is responsible for the welfare of a detained child or young person (s. 57). (For further discussion of this area in relation to the UNCRC and the European Convention on Human Rights see Chapter 1.) The Home Office Code of Practice on police detention regards children as one of the 'vulnerable' groups detained by the police who are entitled to have an 'appropriate adult' with them during a police interview – this might be a parent, social worker or someone from an 'appropriate adult' scheme who is there to observe, facilitate and see fair play (Home Office, 2008; Pierpoint, 2006).

Children and young people may be photographed, fingerprinted and swabbed for DNA samples if they have been arrested; this is all done in the interests of helping police make identifications. Since 2006 *every* offence has been made arrestable, however trivial it might be (Serious Organised Crime and Policing Act 2005, s.110). This has become another contributing factor to the increased criminalisation of children who committed minor offences but became major contributors to various national databases. Examples of media attention related to this issue include the case of a 12-year-old having a 'tiff' with another 12-year-old at school ('Cops DNA-test boy, 12 over playground tiff', *The Sun*, 1 March 2004) or a 13-year-old who threw a snowball at an off-duty policeman's car and was held in a police station for four hours ('Snow joke', *Daily Mail*, 4 February 2005).

Fingerprinting is now done electronically rather than with the ink covered pads of the past, and matching and retrieval is much faster using the IDENT 1 national fingerprint database (Thomas, 2008a). DNA samples are stored on the UK National DNA Database (NDNAD). In 2008 126,972 samples were added on children and young people aged 10–18 (Hansard, HC Debates, 21 April 2009: cols 596–7W) and overall an estimated 1.1 million DNA samples were being stored on children and young people, with about half of these being on innocent children who had been arrested but not prosecuted or who had been subsequently acquitted in court (Sturcke, 2009; Thomas, 2008b). An 11-year-old boy known only as 'S' successfully challenged the police retention of DNA on innocent people in the European courts. The European Court of Human Rights ruled that indefinite DNA retention breached Article 8 (the right to privacy) (*S and Marper* v. *UK*, 4 December 2008, ECHR 1581). The Home Office response was a consultation paper in May 2009 proposing samples be kept on 'innocent' people for just six years or twelve years depending on the seriousness of the crimes alleged; it seemed a half-hearted answer and no differentiation between adults and children was made (Home Office, 2009: paras 6.17–19).

Summary justice and out of court disposals

Some punishments may be administered out of court; such disposals have included the Police Caution, the Conditional Caution, the Fixed Penalty Notice and the Penalty Notice for Disorder, usually in the form of a fine. In the past, police cautions to young people avoided the need to go to court. The police had to have sufficient evidence for a realistic chance of a successful prosecution, the young person had to admit the offence and the parents had to consent to the caution. Police cautions for young offenders were replaced by Reprimands and Final Warnings introduced by the Crime and Disorder Act 1998, ss. 65–66. The given rationale accompanying this development was to 'toughen up' cautions which, it was argued, had fallen into disrepute by seemingly being too 'soft'. Press stories had emerged of young people getting four or five cautions and still offending and the idea in future was that it would be a simple three-stage process – a reprimand (first offence) followed by a final warning (second offence) and then, third time, an automatic court appearance. Others believed the old system of cautions to have worked perfectly well (see Pitts, 2003: 6–9).

Under the following regime of Reprimands and Final Warnings, the police still needed sufficient evidence, and the young person still had to admit their wrongdoing, but parental consent was no longer required. The danger from a rights perspective was that the police could persuade children and young people, as first time offenders who were unfamiliar with the procedures, to take this course of action. Those same children might admit to things they had *not* done just to get things over with and go home. They would not know whether or not the police actually did have sufficient evidence. In some instances the admission became the evidence. (For a full exposition of these and other matters see *R* v. *Durham Constabulary and another ex parte R (FC)*, 2005, UKHL 21.) In fact, it is possible to ask the police to delete cautions, along with fingerprints and DNA samples (see below), under the so-called Exceptional Case Procedure but the Home Office notes this right of appeal is 'rarely exercised' (Home Office, 2009: paras 6.20–21).

Regulating behaviour and the case of the Anti-Social Behaviour Order

The ASBO was created by the Crime and Disorder Act 1998 and can be seen as an illustration of the tensions between child rights and the forces at work in the way legislation and practice develop in the area of youth justice. Its stated aim was an attempt to alter the behaviour of particular people who were not necessarily committing crime but were causing public annoyance and distress to people. The ASBO was intended for people of all ages but, in practice most have been made on young people aged 10–18. The ASBO was developed as a civil order made on application to the civil courts rather than the criminal court. The subject of an ASBO has various prohibitions placed on their behaviour and, as long as they are compliant with those conditions, no further action is taken. The stated aims of these prohibitions are to confront the anti-social behaviour in question and would include requirements to desist from particular activities, for example a requirement to stay away from particular areas. If conditions laid down in the ASBO are breached the subject is summoned to the *criminal courts* – rather than the civil courts – where the breach is dealt with as a criminal offence.

The main concern with ASBO breaches related to the apparent fast-tracking of children into the criminal justice system, and even into custody, for behaviour that was not necessarily even criminal. Far from being a regulatory measure to keep them out, it was drawing more and more young people into the system in a 'net widening' exercise. As the ASBO was made in the civil courts the anonymity automatically available in the youth courts did not apply. (For further discussion of this area in relation to rights see Chapter 3.)

The subject of the ASBO might have his or her name publicised in the press or elsewhere regardless of age. This posed the paradox that young people could have their names and photographs in the public domain for anti-social activities that could include non-criminal behaviour – but have anonymity for criminal behaviour that is arguably more serious than anti-social behaviour.

The press published details and photographs under the general rubric that this is all about 'naming and shaming' yobs and thugs. It has been argued that shaming in this kind of context is a form of punishment (Braithwaite, 1989) and ASBOs are – by definition – nothing to do with punishment. Hence its presence in relation to ASBOs is contradictory and problematic. The formal government position was that it was nothing to do with shaming, and that publicity was intrinsic to the success of the ASBO policy because members of the community could see if an individual was breaching their ASBO and could report any breaches to the police. Some local authorities produced leaflets complete with names and photographs of young people and lists of the conditions that had been imposed on them. The provisions of the UN Charter on Children's Rights (s.40) that required youth justice to be closed to the public simply did not apply because ASBO's were *not* made in criminal proceedings. Critics have pointed out the damaging effect this publicity has on young people (see Thomas, T., 2004) but the government seems undeterred. When asked if the Home Office had any intention to commission research into the effect this publicity was having on young people, then Home Office Minister Hazel Blears simply said she was not aware of any intention to do so (House of Commons, 2005, Ev. 111 Q579). This situation is not static, but government has, persistently, shown itself reluctant to act to remove legislation such as ASBOs. When the Blair government gave way to the Brown government, for example, there were hints that the use of ASBOs might have been on the decline. Balls, Secretary of State for Children, Families and Schools at that time, said that he wanted to live in the 'kind of society that puts ASBOs behind us' (quoted in Travis, 2008; see also Ford, 2008), but shortly after this, the Home Secretary Johnson decided to revive their fortunes (Travis, 2009a). The example of the history and development of ASBOs illustrates the ways in which areas of the UNCRC, such as the necessity of prioritising the 'best interests' of children and young people, may not be well served by government actions and aspects of societal negative attitudes towards young people.

Custodial punishments

Custodial punishments are the most severe punishments available to the Youth Court. These settings range from Young Offender Institutes (YOI) and Secure Training Centres (STCs) run by HM Prison Service to Local Authority Secure Children's Homes (LASCHs). The campaign group Barnardo's using Ministry of Justice figures calculate an increased use of custody for 10–14 year olds of 550 per cent between 1996 and 2008 (Barnardo's, 2008: 2). Child imprisonment is both costly and ineffective in reducing crime (Goldson, 2005). One of the more blatant denials of children's rights in custodial settings – including police stations – took place when children and young people were the victims of assaults by staff or other detainees (see, for example, Howard League, 1995). The local child protection procedures that would automatically come into play for any other child similarly assaulted in their own home did not apply. Custody settings were seemingly islands where the welfare-focused Children Act 1989 simply did not apply.

In 2000 the Howard League for Penal Reform tested this anomalous position and the courts agreed with them (*R* v. *Secretary of State*, 2002, EWHC 2497). Local child protection procedures had to be integrated into the prison service wherever children and young people were being held. HM Prison Service had to redraft its Prison Service Order 4950 and every YOI had to appoint a Safeguarding Manager to ensure child protection services had access to children in custody (YJB/NCB, 2008). Further recourse to the courts sought to clarify appropriate restraint techniques that could be used on children in secure settings. The government had always been hesitant about its stance on physical restraint in children's homes or prison establishments for young people. Earlier Department of Health guidance on restraint had openly declared 'we may have gone too far in stressing the rights of children at the expense of upholding the rights and responsibilities of parents and professionals in supervising them' (DoH, 1993).

EXAMPLE 14.2   Secure Training Centre

In 2004, two boys in Secure Training Centres died within six months of each other in separate incidents. Gareth Myatt aged 15 died after being restrained by staff at Rainsbrook STC near Rugby, and Adam Rickwood aged 14 was found hanging in his room shortly after being restrained by staff at Hassockfield STC in County Durham. Staff had used a so-called 'nose distraction' technique on Adam – placing brief upward pressure on the nose to cause pain – that left his nose bleeding for an hour and badly swollen (Travis, 2009). Adam's inquest heard that his restraint had been used in circumstances outside Home Office Rules (Secure Training Centre Rules 1998, SI 472) that restraint should only be used in order to prevent an escape, prevent damage to property or prevent injury to the person restrained or another. The managers of the STCs said this was too limiting and made it impossible to run an STC. The Home Office responded by rewriting the Rules and adding in a new one that allowed restraint for the maintenance of 'good order and discipline' (Secure Training Centre (Amendment) Rules 2007, No. 1709). In their turn they too were ruled against in the courts as being too vague and in breach of Articles 3 and 8 of the European Convention on Human Rights (*R (C)* v. *Secretary of State for Justice*, 2008, EWCA Civ 882).

What does the above scenario say about the rights of young people in secure settings, and how these might be safeguarded?

To what extent might restraint be seen as a form of discipline, and how does this link with children's rights?

How might the government's response in rewriting the restraint rules be seen as legitimating the restraint practices that had gone on previously?

Summary

The UK persists in using its youth justice system to try and resolve what are really social problems. It does this in an interventionist and punitive way that tends to marginalise the rights of children and young people. At present there is no political will to raise the age of criminal responsibility that would in turn require a new way of thinking about children and their (mis)behaviour.

Question 14.1   What have been the key recent developments in UK policy and legislation on criminal justice regarding children and young people?

Review Activity

1   Think about the fact that the age of criminal responsibility in the UK is 10, and that no distinction is made between the ways in which a 10-year-old is treated compared with a much older child. How do you think the differences in maturity and moral development of children of different ages might be played out here, particularly in relation to children's rights?

2   How do you think that the climate of 'popular punitivism' clashes with a rights perspective which might emphasise the need to look at the child behind the crime and to see children as children first and offenders second?

Question 14.2   What are the key aspects of the current criminal justice system in the UK?

Review Activity

1   Think back to your own childhood experiences. Are there things you did which might now be interpreted as 'criminal' or which could have caused 'alarm, harassment or distress' – the basis for the making of an ASBO today?

2   How might you feel if some behaviour from your childhood had led to a criminal record which prevented you as an adult following your chosen career?

〰 **Question 14.3   How might some of the features of the current criminal justice system interconnect with the notion of 'children's rights'?**

Review Activity

1 Thinking about your own professional setting, or a setting in which you have worked in the past, how has the notion of 'child welfare' being paramount been implemented?
2 How does this contrast with how children and young people are treated once they engage in behaviours which the state interprets as troublesome?

Further Reading 📖

Burney, E. (2009) *Making People Behave: Anti-Social Behaviour Politics and Policy*, 2nd edn. Cullompton: Willan.
Examines why anti-social behaviour has become such a focus of political rhetoric and given such a high political profile, and examines the recent historical dimension of anti-social behaviour.

Muncie, J. (2009) *Youth and Crime: A Critical Introduction*, 3rd edn. London: Sage. The latest edition of this comprehensive introduction to youth justice also takes on the historical, feminist and comparative perspective. All key concepts are explained and each chapter has recommendations for further reading; a useful glossary of terms is also included.

Smith, R. (2007) *Youth Justice: Ideas, Policy and Practice*, 2nd edn. Cullompton: Willan.
Good on the historical and political context as well as suggestions for the way forward for youth justice.

Squires, P. and Stephen, D. (2005) *Rougher Justice: Anti-Social Behaviour and Young People*. Cullompton: Willan.
Uses empirical studies to try to look at youth justice from the 'inside' and from the point of view of young people themselves.

Part 3

Reviewing Children's Rights in Practice

15

Reviewing Children's Rights in Practice

Phil Jones and Gary Walker

Chapter Overview

The ways in which child rights, policy and practice with children interact has been examined within a number of different disciplines and areas of professional practice. The first part of the book introduced broad themes, specific rights conventions and legislation and gave guidance on where specific issues were reflected in chapters. The second part contained different accounts and analysis of practice with children, focusing upon particular professions or provision such as play or education, youth work or health promotion. This final chapter is designed to help the reader to reflect across the book, to engage critically with the issues raised and to consider the practical implications of commonalities and differences across areas of provision or professional boundaries. The aim is to foster critical thinking and interdisciplinary awareness about rights in practice. The chapter does so by selecting themes which have emerged as common within areas of the book and then gives excerpts from different chapters and invites the reader to make connections with further areas from other chapters and to reflect on key areas of rights and practice with children. Given the wide variety of rights and rights-related issues which the book has engaged with, the chapter does not seek to be exhaustive. It demonstrates the value of drawing on perspectives from different disciplines and encourages a way of reading and thinking rather than addressing all areas of rights. One of the broad themes often used within different chapters to approach rights has been to see them in terms of participation, provision and protection: the chapter uses this as a basic way of reading across disciplines, though the activities make many suggestions for other kinds of interconnection between children's and practitioners' ideas and experiences. The chapter will return to some of the themes identified in the book as a whole and encourage the reader to consider specific elements from different chapters in order to deepen their understanding of the ways rights relate to practice. The chapter will invite the reader to consider and contrast the ways that practice and child rights are reflected in policy and practice across disciplines. It will identify areas of the book that offer contrasts and contradictions in the way policy, practice and rights relate to each other and will invite the reader to consider what can be learnt from these differences and tensions. Consideration of the different parts of the book will encourage not only broad reflective thinking but also an examination of specific issues pertinent to the reader's profession, area of study or intended practice. The themes touched upon are participation, involvement and action; provision; safeguarding and protection; and social exclusion, equality and diversity.

Participation, involvement and action

A number of chapters considered the relationship between rights and participation. The interaction between values, policy and practice have considered a number of themes: how participation rights for children are reflected in the values and training in areas such as social work or education, ways of working with participation and difference in relation to factors such as age and how social exclusion can affect children's right to participate. The chapters examined participation strategies in a number of ways:

- national levels (see pages 50–2);
- local levels (see pages 180–2); and
- individual service provider levels (see pages 117–20 and 168–73).

They also considered some of the tensions and difficulties in this area. One of the tensions concerned the ways in which service provision can involve a veneer of participation – for example, providing information or consulting children without engaging in any meaningful way with their views and opinions. Another tension concerned the ways in which some children are seen as 'worthy' of participation while others are excluded due to factors such as disability, ethnicity or age. This process is not intentional but occurs because of factors which are discussed in a variety of chapters in relation to different issues and services.

The following extracts reflect a number of these themes.

EXCERPT 15.1   Chapter 13

Examples of this are the concept and practice of 'reach' or 'contact' whereby the profession seeks to build a relationship with a young person; a key aspect of the relationships formed concerns supporting and enabling access to provision which can result in benefit for the young person. Rights-informed approaches to practice can be seen in a variety of areas of youth work, from community action to leisure, from counselling to housing support. The National Youth Agency's *Act By Right* is an example of this approach with its emphasis on participation and empowerment in the creation of five 'stages' relating to 'a journey' to enable young people to develop the knowledge and skills they need to take effective action on issues that concern them ...

They create a structure involving active steps to doing this work. Key factors include:

- developing agreements within the organisation;
- raising staff awareness;
- developing goals with young people, staff and volunteers;
- developing ideas, involving young people into the process, plans, goals and necessary resources;
- looking at areas such as training and support for young people, staff and volunteers;
- work to include groups and individuals to ensure access and inclusion for young people with disabilities and ways to facilitate involvement, review and evaluate progress.

(Adapted from *Youth Participation: Getting Started*, National Council for Voluntary Youth Services at http://www.ncvys.org.uk)

EXCERPT 15.2   Chapter 7

Prompt-based approaches may turn the children into *passive responders* rather than *active agents* who spontaneously express their own needs, exert control over their environments and develop as self-determined individuals. Enhancing a child's spontaneous communication then becomes, not a skill to be taught, but a human right to be celebrated and encouraged, as a vehicle for the child's liberation – and consequently should be a major educational goal ...

(Continued)

(Continued)

In our view, it is essential that children are taught to communicate their needs and wants spontaneously, as the lack of such skills in adulthood can understandably lead to frustration and the development of less appropriate and more challenging behaviours. This, in turn, can lead to restricted lifestyles and opportunities for self-fulfilment and enjoyment with Cederlund *et al.* (2008) reporting increased use of residential care in young adults with severe autism and limited communication. In this way, limited opportunities for children to access their right to freedom of expression may lead to even fewer rights as adults (Emerson, 2001) ...

Why do disabled children have so little access to self-determined behaviour? In the UK, Franklin and Sloper (2009) cite the negative attitudes of adults who do not believe children capable of engaging in decision-making as well as the complexity of service structure and operation which precludes children's participation. A lack of training on how to involve disabled children is another important barrier.

EXCERPT 15.3   Chapter 9

There is clear indication that children and young people's engagement in decision-making processes is only meaningful if it is *real* consultation that potentially gives over some degree of power to them. Perhaps their involvement in decisions concerning teaching and learning issues – found lacking by Whitty and Wisby (2007) – is a manifestation of traditional power relations between practitioners and students. The possible reluctance by professionals for such core decisions about school business to be subject to the uncertainties presented by children and young people's involvement may be indicative of central tensions in rhetoric about school standards, pupil and parental choice and practitioner professionalism (Henricson and Bainham, 2005). As Whitty and Wisby conclude:

> ... policy makers and schools should beware of viewing pupil voice as merely a means of supporting the current policy agenda. Genuine provision for pupil voice requires some power and influence to be passed to pupils, at which point it becomes unpredictable. Where this does not happen, there is the danger that pupil voice, and school councils in particular, could produce a cohort of young people who are cynical about democratic processes. (Whitty and Wisby, 2007: 4)

Activities: Participation, involvement and action

ACTIVITY   15.1

Excerpt 15.1 talks about the relationship between *knowledge, skills* and *action* and sees this as a sequence, useful in thinking about how to engage in enabling young people to develop the use of their participation rights. The authors refer to a 'structure' with stages or steps. Other chapters in the book use such an approach: a sequence of stages in developing participation rights. These include:

- Lowcock and Cross reviewing the idea of a 'ladder' or 'wheel' of participation (see pages 142–3);
- Tan reviewing processes of participation in education (see pages 117–20).

1 Compare these approaches and consider:

(a) the parallels and differences between them;
(b) the different kinds of participation identified or implied in the approaches (the chapters differentiate between participation of children in developing national, local and service policy, for example, or participation in relation to specific areas such as decision-making in health, or daily decisions about what to do);
(c) any particular strengths and weaknesses in the stages, ideas or relationships they propose.

2 Consider your setting and/or your working relationship with young children and see what elements from the different approaches could be gathered together or adapted to involve, or further develop, participation.
3 How might your workplace or setting respond to the issues raised in Excerpt 15.3 relating to:

(a) power, influence and the need to address the dynamics between workers and children?
(b) the importance of decision-making being linked to a real involvement?

Consider the opportunities and tensions that might be encountered in relation to these issues and participation. How might the opportunities be best initiated or developed in relation to increasing participation? How might the tensions be understood and worked with to develop the kinds of participation discussed in the three excerpts?

ACTIVITY 15.2

Excerpt 15.2 engages with a common thread within the book's consideration of participation rights: how social divisions and equality are key issues
to consider in relation to participation. Other chapters raise issues concerning participation and social exclusion. These include:

- Race and Bennett looking at issues concerning race and equity in relation to participation (pages 164–7);
- Walker raising issues concerning marginalisation and contradictory attitudes in relation to young people and participation (pages 34–5).

1 Consider Potter and Whittaker's division between *passive responders* and
  active agents (page 85) and the challenge they speak of in relation to:

  (a) adults working to support and work towards removing barriers to
      communication;
  (b) developing ways of engaging with children that re-frame relation-
      ships to allow children to be seen as capable and as able to make
      decisions rather than in terms of deficits.

How can adult workers encourage relationships to develop with children
that stimulate active engagement in participating?

2 Consider barriers to participation that emphasise adult-orientated ways
  of thinking or acting and how these could be changed. Excerpt 15.3
  raises some of these issues. Look at different areas of your service provision, for example:

  - broad decisions about ways of providing services in areas such as
    policy;
  - everyday ways of relating to children – use Potter and Whittaker's
    chapter.

Think about how differences in areas such as ways of communicating
could be changed. Reflect on the parallel issues and differences between
how adults communicate or make decisions and how children do so.
Examples from this book to assist your thinking about this include children
with autistic spectrum disorders (pages 84–5), young people who are disaf-
fected (pages 170–3), or young children who do not easily use verbal language (pages 103–6).

Provision rights

The related area of provision rights was considered in a number of different
ways. These included the ways in which social divisions within society affect
whether, and how, children can access services, and also looked at innovative ways in which government, local authorities and individual providers
were rethinking policy and practice concerning widening participation and

designing more child-orientated services. The various chapters also looked at issues concerning the development of autonomy, empowerment, control and the idea of the importance of children's perspectives in service design and implementation. Examples of this include

- Wragg on play provision and the design of play spaces (page 76–9);
- Marshall and Thomas on the tensions between adult and young people's views on areas such as community spaces (page 191–2).

EXCERPT 15.4   Chapter 11

'Empowerment' ... is viewed as being centrally concerned with ideas or beliefs about control or 'being in control'. In relation to health this means control over health in terms of both decision-making and health-related behaviour. However, as Tones and Green (2004) argue, empowerment can also be viewed as the way in which health is actually achieved. Issues to do with control clearly sit within a child rights framework when this is viewed as having control over what happens with, and to, you and being able to make a difference in your everyday experience (being listened to, having views acted upon, etc.). This directly relates to, for example, informed choice which is key to the areas of mental health and sexual health. The World Health Organisation revisited its definition of health promotion in 2005 in the Bangkok Charter to read 'the process of enabling people to increase control over their health and its determinants and thereby improve their health' (WHO, 2005). This refers both to the macro level – broader issues of children's rights with regard to health promotion – and the micro level – the day-to-day outworking and experience of health promotion.

EXCERPT 15.5   Chapter 12

Often social workers come into a child's life at a point of crisis, so it is critical that they possess the skills to be able to communicate effectively with children. Children who come into contact with social workers at these critical times in their lives are likely to be those who are least able to articulate their wishes and feelings, and their very need for social work intervention determines that they are vulnerable in a range of ways. The opportunity of social workers to be able to promote a child's right to participate at these critical points can be understood as an uneasy position, where they are trying to balance competing values perspectives. Children have

(Continued)

(Continued)

expressed the following views from their experience of working with social workers:

> Social workers need to understand more from a child's perspective about any situation ... [they need] understanding of a person's feelings and to understand that all children are different ... With children in care, they need to always know they have someone they can turn to and talk to ... You just want people to listen, understand and be there on a regular basis. (GSCC, 2008: 2)

Without having an accurate understanding of a young person's perspective the social worker will not be effective in responding to the needs or promoting the rights of the child.

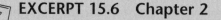

EXCERPT 15.6   Chapter 2

Jeffs considers the tensions between the notion of children's rights and what he calls the 'authoritarian, repressive and standardised school system' (2002: 55). His central argument is that the two are incompatible: children's rights to be consulted on their whole 'learning experience' (ibid.) are undermined by an approach which values uniformity and testing, and which seems to have no place for children as active citizens. His conclusion is that schools, in their current guise, are 'contemptuous of [children's] opinions [and] the concept of democracy ... if we cannot create schools that respect the rights of children and actively foster democracy then we must not flinch from actively supporting alternatives that do' (ibid.: 57).

Activities: Provision rights

ACTIVITY   15.3

Read through Excerpts 15.4 to 15.6. Consider the following:

1 What parallels can you identify between the issues concerning rights and provision raised within the excerpts?
2 What differences can you identify between the issues concerning rights and provision within the excerpts?

ACTIVITY   15.4

Excerpt 15.4 talks about a child within the service they are engaged with 'having control over what happens with, and to, you and being able to make a difference in your everyday experience' and Excerpt 15.4 makes a direct connection between the efficacy of any service for children and a 'young person's perspective'.

1 What do you understand of the importance of a young person's perspective in relation to making a service effective?
2 How do you see these issues relating to your own service or setting?
3 Can you identify any tensions or difficulties in relation to practically connecting the way a service is provided and a 'young person's perspective' of that service in terms of children 'having control over what happens with, and to, you'?

Safeguarding and protection

Developments in awareness and societal attitudes towards children together with their implications for practice and protection rights featured within the book. Walker, for example, showed not only the positive aspects of recent changes in areas such as policy and professional guidelines concerning safeguarding children, but also the complexities and contradictions in relation to protection and the different issues that remain unresolved and which have an impact on children's lives and those working with them. Other areas concerning protection are included in:

- Lowcock and Cross in their discussion of health promotion (pages 140–61);
- Chapter 10 in the consideration of children's own perspectives on their rights (pages 50–2).

The following extracts relate to three aspects of this area.

EXCERPT 15.7   Chapter 5

First, when attempting to work within a general 'safeguarding' approach, either to promote a child's welfare, or to prevent impairment to health or development as defined in section 17 of the Children Act 1989, professionals have no right to impose themselves on the family. All this work is entirely voluntary, and dependent on the agreement, not of the child, but of the parents concerned. Thus

(Continued)

(Continued)

if the parents of a particular child whom professionals feel would benefit from support and services do not share this view, and there is no evidence of 'significant' harm to the child, then the professionals have no option but to withdraw from the family, even if the wishes and feelings of the child are that they (the child) would welcome support. The rights of the child here are 'trumped' by the rights of parents to bring their child up as they wish (so long as they don't abuse them and cause 'significant' harm to them). The child has no independent right to receive support – the law conceptualises them as the 'private property' of the parents, and this 'ownership' of the child cannot be breached unless there is evidence of 'significant' harm.

EXCERPT 15.8   Chapter 5

'Smacking' of children is not unlawful in England, and parents retain the right, under section 58 of the Children Act 2004, to use the defence of 'reasonable chastisement' against any charge of physical abuse amounting to common assault, though not against charges of wounding, causing grievous bodily harm, assault occasioning actual bodily harm or cruelty. Therefore, when, say, a child tells a teacher they have been hit and there are no dramatic injuries, the teacher has to make a decision whether what they have heard and what they know about the child and the circumstances might amount to abuse or 'significant harm'. From a child rights perspective, the child, first, has no right to protection in law from 'reasonable chastisement' (an interesting phenomenon when one considers that the law protects adults from a similar level of violence), and, second, may well experience a further layer of 'harm' by the professional hearing about this physical punishment deciding that the situation does not warrant any further action in light of the similar experiences of many other children similarly unprotected by the law.

EXCERPT 15.9   Chapter 14

In 2004, two boys in Secure Training Centres died within six months of each other in separate incidents. Gareth Myatt aged 15 died after being restrained by staff at Rainsbrook STC near Rugby, and Adam Rickwood aged 14 was found hanging in his room shortly after being restrained by staff at Hassockfield STC in County Durham.

Staff had used a so-called 'nose distraction' technique on Adam – placing brief upward pressure on the nose to cause pain – that left his nose bleeding for an hour and badly swollen (Travis, 2009). Adam's inquest heard that his restraint had been used in circumstances outside Home Office Rules (Secure Training Centre Rules 1998, SI 472) that restraint should only be used in order to prevent an escape, prevent damage to property or prevent injury to the person restrained or another. The managers of the STCs said this was too limiting and made it impossible to run an STC. The Home Office responded by rewriting the Rules and adding in a new one that allowed restraint for the maintenance of 'good order and discipline' (Secure Training Centre (Amendment) Rules 2007, No. 1709). In their turn they too were ruled against in the courts as being too vague and in breach of Articles 3 and 8 of the European Convention on Human Rights (*R (C)* v. *Secretary of State for Justice*, 2008, EWCA Civ 882).

Activities: Safeguarding and protection

ACTIVITY   15.5

Chapter 1 referred to the UK Human Rights Act's statement that children should be protected from abuse, and to the UNCRC's statements which both parallel this commitment to protect and concern the 'best interests' of the child. The latter are presented in Article 3 which states that: 'in all actions concerning children, whether undertaken by public or private social welfare institutions, courts of law, administrative authorities or legislative bodies, the best interests of the child shall be a primary consideration'. Unicef notes that this article and the concept of 'best interests' relates to the legal protection of children and to evidence-based care of children and that the principle requires governments and other agencies involved in provision, legislation, policies and programmes 'to review *any* of their actions for the impact on children' (Unicef, 2009: 9, authors' emphasis).

Consider how these notions of protection, abuse and the best interests of the child relate to the material in Excerpts 15.7, 15.8 and 15.9. How are issues relating to protection and best interests present in each of the excerpts? For example:

1 Are they reflected in a clear commitment to the protection and best interests of children? *Or*
2 Do they seem to act against children being protected and their best interests served? *Or*
3 Do they contain contradictory positions?

ACTIVITY   15.6

What issues do you think they raise for professionals in the kinds of contexts above? Look at each excerpt and try and identify how the relationship between the state, those working with children, their parents/guardians and the children themselves is constructed or seen. Consider the following:

1 How does the professional association for the discipline you are concerned with or the setting you are working within provide guidance on how to handle these opportunities and tensions regarding child rights, protection and 'best interests'?
2 The issues arising from your analysis of Excerpts 15.7, 15.8 and 15.9 and Walker's comment that 'This could mean that, contrary to the notion of basic rights, a child could be left in circumstances which a range of professionals agree is harmful to the child and about which the child has expressed disquiet' (page 61). Do you agree, or disagree, with this comment? What could be changed to be more effective in relation to this area of child rights?

Social exclusion, equality and diversity

The different ways in which rights relate to social exclusion has been considered in a number of chapters:

- from a broad perspective (see pages 35–6, 202–3)
- connections between equality, diversity and in different aspects of exclusion concerning, for example, race (see page 83, 116), sexuality (see pages 18, 146–7) or poverty (see pages 35–7, 65).

The following excerpts look at aspects of this relationship in relation to practice with children.

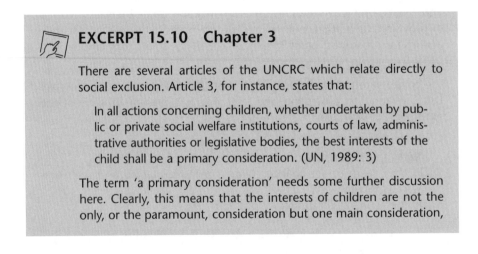

EXCERPT 15.10   Chapter 3

There are several articles of the UNCRC which relate directly to social exclusion. Article 3, for instance, states that:

> In all actions concerning children, whether undertaken by public or private social welfare institutions, courts of law, administrative authorities or legislative bodies, the best interests of the child shall be a primary consideration. (UN, 1989: 3)

The term 'a primary consideration' needs some further discussion here. Clearly, this means that the interests of children are not the only, or the paramount, consideration but one main consideration, possibly to be addressed along with other competing considerations (Freeman, 2002) ...

In taking this harsh line with young children who offend, the UK seems to be reinforcing the social exclusion of this group. Muncie (2004, quoted in Moss, 2008) demonstrates that severe punishment, including the use of secure placements, is ineffective in reducing reoffending rates, with these being between 70 and 80 per cent. As Moss concludes, perhaps the reason why the government persists with harsh punishments in the face of evidence that this clearly does not work is to reinforce to the wider society what is acceptable and unacceptable behaviour, and that this function of the system is perceived to be more important than true support and rehabilitation of children who offend and the upholding of their rights, which could be said truly to be in their best interests.

EXCERPT 15.11   Chapter 8

Viruru's (2001) nursery school study problematises the high status bestowed solely upon the spoken word as the main vehicle of human expression and communication. According to Viruru this is yet another example of Western adult majority culture imposing its cultural norms upon less dominant cultures and communities – and, in particular, children. Viruru asks whose interests are best served when spoken '... language is privileged over other modes of communication' (2001: 31). The ethnographic study, set in India, suggests that children 'engage in complex forms of communication that do not involve language' (2001: 31) and questions the common assumption in dominant Western adult discourses that the spoken word is 'almost overwhelmingly unilingual; however, most of the world's children use and live in multilingual environments' (2001: 31).

EXCERPT 15.12   Chapter 10

In this way both the family's and the individual child's rights to have their first language valued and their bilingualism nurtured were both being promoted. One of the project's main aims was to encourage mothers to talk with their children more, in order to develop home language skills and to boost everyone's confidence:

> Although I can't speak English I do help her look at books and tell the story in my own language and also we talk about the things that are going on in the book and tell the story that

(Continued)

(Continued)

way. At first I was very shy to read to my son in public. I had to be on my own when I read to him where no one was listening and looking. I am more confident now and don't mind reading to him in front of other people.

The outreach workers acted as a bridge between home and school for mothers who felt intimidated because they spoke little or no English and so felt unable to come into school to discuss their children's learning. One grandmother commented that:

... we feel that we are more important. My other grandchildren used to attend this place; however, we were not that comfortable about bringing our children because there was no Punjabi-speaking staff and we didn't feel valued. I now feel I can speak and communicate with the staff and can understand how I can help.

EXCERPT 15.13   Chapter 13

Table 13.1   Extract

Column 1 **Youth work values (DfES, 2002: 6)**	*Column 2* **Connections to a rights agenda**
It seeks to help young people achieve stronger relationships and collective identities – for example, as black people, women, men, disabled people, gay men or lesbians – and through the promotion of inclusivity, particularly for minority ethnic communities	Article 2, UNCRC: Children must be treated without discrimination of any kind, irrespective of race, colour, sex, language, religion or other status Article 30, UNCRC: The right to enjoy their own culture, religion and language Article 23, UNCRC: The right to a full life and to active participation in the community for disabled children

---

Activities: Social exclusion, equality and diversity

ACTIVITY   15.7

Excerpt 15.10 talks about different kinds of tensions in relation to whose rights are being addressed and how these relate to different aspects of social exclusion. Other chapters discuss these tensions:

- around best interests (see pages 37–9);
- conflicts between the state, workers and children over whose rights are being respected or acted on (see pages 38–40);

- how social exclusion in relation to poverty (pages 62–4), race (page 214) and gender (page 18) connects with child rights.

1 Consider Excerpts 15.12, 15.13 and 15.14 and see if you can identify how the tensions identified in Excerpt 15.11 might relate to the issues raised in each excerpt.

2 How might these tensions be present in your workplace or setting?

ACTIVITY   15.8

Excerpts 15.11, 15.12 and 15.13 each talk about how values and ways of working seek to address children and young people's rights and how these ways of working relate to addressing exclusion. Articles from the UNCRC such as 2, 20 and 33 are mentioned in this context. List the ways in which they talk about values and practices and add more of your own in thinking about practices that are important in relation to such UNCRC articles concerning different aspects of rights, exclusion and the role of your setting.

Summary

Alderson has made the following broad comment about rights:

> British adults have gained many new liberties and choices over the past four centuries, and few now expect to be overtly deferential. Relative to adults, children have many fewer rights of the kind which adults take for granted: freedoms of physical and mental integrity, speech, information, association and assembly, thought, conscience and religion … adults construct and reconstruct their power as rights holders in ways denied to young people … (Alderson, 2002b: 26)

This book reflects all of these areas of rights and this chapter has explored the tensions it refers to: between adults, children and the 'holding' of rights. The book has also, however, shown rights as an active, developing arena where children, young people and adults are reconstructing their relationships and their relationships to child rights in new, evolving ways. This chapter has encouraged the reader to examine what commonalities emerge across disciplines in relation to the practical implications of children's rights. It has returned to themes identified in the book as a whole and helped consider specific elements from different chapters in order to deepen understanding of the ways rights relate to practice. It has also made contrasts between the ways that practice and child rights are reflected in policy and practice and offered the opportunity to reflect upon what can be learnt from these differences and tensions. It has shown how comparing experiences can support rights-informed practice with children by enabling the reader to connect specific issues pertinent to their profession, area of study or intended practice with the key themes of participation, provision, safeguarding and protection and of social exclusion, equality and diversity.

Contextual Glossary

The glossary below cites examples of where key terms feature in the book. It is designed to help the reader place terms that are used throughout the book in a context that will help not only in understanding the *meaning* of the term, but in giving a sense of some of the *issues* which are contained within this book's treatment of the term.

Best interests of the child

The United Nations Convention on the Rights of the Child makes clear that '[t]he best interests of children must be the primary concern in making decisions that may affect them. All adults should do what is best for children' (UNCRC, 1989; Article 3). (Chapter 9, page 110; see also pages 37–9.)

Caretaker and liberationist

The former takes the view that, due to their developmental immaturity, children should only be afforded rights of protection and provision but not participation; adults should make decisions on their behalf. Liberationists do not believe that this argument is strong enough to deny children participatory and liberty rights, and argue that children should be allowed and encouraged to exercise every possible right as early as possible (Chapter 3, page 34; see also page 121.)

Child

The United Nations Convention on the Rights of the Child was adopted by the United Nations in 1989. Child, within the UNCRC, is defined as an individual aged 17 or under. (Chapter 1, page 5; see also pages 33–4.)

Childhood as a construction

Moss and Petrie (2002) have summarised this approach as arguing that, though childhood is a biological fact, the way it is understood and lived varies considerably. (Chapter 1, page 12; see also page 73.)

Empowerment

For the purposes of this discussion, empowerment is viewed as being centrally concerned with ideas or beliefs about control or 'being in control' ... To be empowered is to be able to exercise *power from within*. (Chapter 11, page 141; see also pages 180–1.)

European Convention on Human Rights

The European Convention on Human Rights (ECHR) and the UK's Human Rights Act (HRA) 1998, which commit all public organisations to follow the rights in the ECHR. These include early years provision, play work, schools, children's services, health, youth and social services, the police and youth courts. (Chapter 1, page 14; see also page 196.)

Family

The *family* is meant to be supporting the child as an individual while ensuring they develop positive relationships as part of the family and as part of society. However, each family will have a set of beliefs and values that influence their expectations of the child and their relationships. These may not be in keeping with either the principles of the UNCRC or with the expectations of state policies. (Chapter 1, page 8; see also pages 37–9.)

Multi-agency

The re-emphasis of *multi-professional* approaches that involve partnership with parents and their communities has further interwoven institutional, parental and professional responsibilities to children and young people. Such a connection between professionals and parents is clear within the kinds of approaches developed. (Chapter 9, page 112; see also page 58.)

Non-discrimination

Non-discrimination is reflected in Articles such as Article 2 which states that signatories 'shall respect and ensure the rights set forth in the present Convention to each child within their jurisdiction without discrimination of any kind, irrespective of the child's or his or her parent's or legal guardian's race, colour, sex, language, religion, political or other opinion, national, ethnic or social origin, property, disability, birth or other status' (Unicef, 2009: 9). (Chapter 1, page 6; see also page 116.)

Participation

The concept of *participation* is central to any discussion about children and young people's rights (Participation Works, at: http://www.participation-works.org.uk). When examining definitions of participation two main themes are evident: firstly 'being present and taking part'; and secondly recognising that when young people participate what they say and do should be listened to and acted upon. (Chapter 11, page 142; see also pages 43–56.)

Paternalism

The political and philosophical concept of *paternalism* is generally understood to reflect the patriarchal family system whereby the dominant figurehead, or father, makes decisions on behalf of his subordinates – his wife and children. To advocates of paternalism the wise and powerful figurehead acts benevolently towards the poor and disempowered. To its libertarian detractors this practice serves only to further marginalise and oppress the disempowered. (Chapter 6, page 74; see also page 150.)

Poverty

Even under the definition of *poverty* designed to reduce the number of children reflected therein (which excludes housing costs), at least 20 per cent of children live in poverty in England (Child Poverty Action Group, 2008) ... What is apparent, however, is that any notion of child rights which ignores the plight of, or normalises the everyday damaging experience of, large numbers of children living in long-term poverty is deeply flawed both morally and in practical terms. (Chapter 5, page 64; see also pages 19, 35–7.)

Protection

The national guidance on safeguarding children emphasises the need to place 'child *protection*' within a broad approach to raising children in order that they meet the prescribed *Every Child Matters* outcomes. It states that ... 'If they are denied the opportunity and support they need to achieve these outcomes, children are at increased risk not only of an impoverished childhood, but also of disadvantage and social exclusion in adulthood. Abuse and neglect pose particular problems' (DCSF, 2010: 29). What is striking about this is that there is *no* mention of children's rights. (Chapter 5, page 65; see also pages 58, 163–9.)

Safeguarding

The term *safeguarding* first began to emerge in around 2003 ... One key aspect of this was a new emphasis on the idea of prevention: rather than waiting for a family crisis to occur and responding only to acute incidents of serious harm, professionals were now expected to step in early in the affairs of families to prevent any crisis from happening in the first place. (Chapter 5, pages 57–8; see also pages 60–3, 196.)

Self-advocacy

Self-advocacy, where disabled people run organisations and control research and social policy agendas is a major tenet of social model theory and practice (Chapter 7, page 84; see also page 23.)

Social exclusion

Walker and Walker provide a definition of social exclusion which distinguishes it from poverty. According to them, social exclusion is a 'dynamic process of being shut out, fully or partially, from any of the social, economic, political or cultural systems which determine the social integration of a person in society' (Walker and Walker, 1997, quoted in Byrne, 2005: 8). (Chapter 3, pages 35–6; see also page 147.)

Social justice

Miller argues that social justice involves a commitment to ensuring 'each person gets a fair share of the benefits, and carries a fair share of the responsibilities, of living together in a community' (2005: 3). (Chapter 3, page 33; see also page 52).

United Nations Convention on the Rights of the Child

The United Nations Convention on the Rights of the Child was adopted by the United Nations in 1989 ... The rights guaranteed by the Convention are afforded to all children without exception. The UNCRC is defined as an agreement between countries and consists of a number of articles. Specific governments need to ratify such a convention. This means that they agree to obey the articles set out in that convention. (Chapter 1, page 5; see also pages 17–31.)

Youth

The defined age range of 'youth' served varies between different countries. The approach of Richmond, as a representative example (see below) of the UK framework, states that its services are for those between the ages of 11 and 25, with a 'priority age range of 13–19'. (Chapter 13, page 176; see also page 189.)

References

Abery, B. and Zajac, R. (1996) 'Self-determination as a goal for early childhood and elementary education', in D. J. Sands and M. Wehmeyer (eds), *Self-Determination Across the Life Span*. London: Paul Brookes.

Aggleton, P. and Campbell, C. (2000) 'Working with young people – towards an agenda for sexual health', *Sexual and Relationship Therapy*, 15 (3): 283–96.

Aggleton. P. and Homans, H. (1987) *Educating about AIDS. NHS Training Authority*. Bristol: University of Bristol.

Ainscow, M., Conteh, J., Dyson, A. and Gallanaugh, F. (2007) *Children in Primary Education: Demography, Culture, Diversity and Inclusion*. Primary Review Research Survey 5/1. Cambridge: University of Cambridge Faculty of Education. Available at: http://www.primaryreview.org.uk/Downloads/Int_Reps/4.Children_development-learning/Primary_Review_5-1_report_Demography-culture-diversity-inclusion (accessed 26 June 2010).

Alderson, P. (2000) *Young Children's Rights: Exploring Beliefs, Principles and Practice*. London: Jessica Kingsley.

Alderson, P. (2002a) 'Young children's health care rights and consent', in B. Franklin (ed.), *The New Handbook of Children's Rights: Comparative Policy and Practice*. London: Routledge.

Alderson, P. (2002b) 'Students' rights in British schools: trust, autonomy, connection and regulation', in R. Edwards (ed.), *Children, Home and School: Regulation, Autonomy or Connection?* London: Routledge.

Alerby, E. (2004) *Some Reflections on Time as a Phenomenon within School*. Paper for AARE Conference, Melbourne, 27 November–2 December.

Allen, N. (2002) *Making Sense of the Children Act*, 3rd edn. Chichester: John Wiley & Sons.

Anning, A. (2005) *New Forms of Professional Knowledge in Multi-Agency Delivery of Services for Children. End of Award Report*. Swindon: Economic & Social Research Council.

Apple, M. and Beane, J. (eds) (1999) *Democratic Schools: Lessons from the Chalk Face*. Buckingham: Open University Press.

Archard, D. (1993) *Children: Rights and Childhood*. London: Routledge.

Arnstein, S. (1969) 'A ladder of citizen participation', *Journal of the American Institute of Planners*, 35 (4): 216–24.

Asa, A. and Barnlund, D. C. (1998) 'Boundaries of the unconscious, private, and public self in Japanese and Americans: a cross-cultural comparison', *International Journal of Intercultural Relations*, 22 (4): 431–52.

'Assert Yourself'. Available at: http://www.voiceuk.org.uk/publications.htm.

Baker, C. (1996) *Foundations of Bilingual Education and Bilingualism*, 2nd edn. Clevedon: Multilingual Matters.

Baker, C. (2007) *A Parents' and Teachers' Guide to Bilingualism*. Clevedon: Multilingual Matters.

Bandalli, S. (1998) 'Abolition of the presumption of *Doli Incapax* and the criminalisation of children', *Howard Journal of Criminal Justice*, 37 (2): 114–23.

Barkham, P. (2005) 'Liberty challenges child curfew and dispersal orders', *Guardian*, 27 May.

Barnardo's (2008) *Locking Up or Giving Up – is Custody for Children Always the Right Answer?* London: Barnardo's.

Barwell, R. (2004) *Teaching Learners of English as an Additional Language: A Review of Official Language.* Watford: National Association for Language Development in the Curriculum (NALDIC).

BBC News (2007) 'Ministers rule out smacking ban' [Internet]. London: BBC News. Available at: http://news.bbc.co.uk/1/hi/uk_politics/7061603.stm (accessed 2 June 2009).

Beadle, P. (2009) 'Who do you think you are?', *Guardian*, 6 February 6.

Bentley, L. (2008) *SHRC Celebrates 60 Years of the Universal Declaration.* Available at: http://www.scottishhumanrights.com/news/latestnews/article/shrc60 (accessed 15 May 2010).

Biestek, F. P. (1961) *The Casework Relationship.* London: Allen & Unwin.

Bishton, H. (2007) *Children's Voice, Children's Rights: What Children with Special Needs Have to Say About Their Variously Inclusive Schools.* Research Associate Report, National College for School Leadership. Available at: http://www.ncsl.org.uk (accessed 21 February 2009).

Blenkin, G. and Kelly, A. (1996) *A Developmental Curriculum*, 2nd edn. London: Chapman.

Bourne, J. (2001) 'Doing "what comes naturally": how the discourses and routines of teachers' practice constrain opportunities for bilingual support in UK primary schools', *Language and Education*, 15 (4): 250–68.

Boyden, J. and Ennew, J. (1997) 'Children I focus: manual for participation research with children', Stockholm: Radda Barnen; cited in D. McNeish (1999) *From Rhetoric to Reality. Participatory Approaches to Health Promotion with Young People.* London: Health Education Authority.

Bradwell, J., Crawford, D., Crawford, J., Dent, L., Finlinson, K., Gibson, R. and Porter, E. (2008) *Have Your Say.* National Youth Agency. Available at: http://www.nya.org.uk/integrated-youth-support-services/young-researcher-network/yrn-research-reports (accessed 15 May 2010).

Braithwaite, J. (1989) *Crime, Shame and Reintegration.* Cambridge: Cambridge University Press.

Breeze Leeds (2010) *Out of Schools Activities: Positive Activities for Young People.* Available at: http://www.breezeleeds.org (accessed 26 June 2010).

Brereton, A. (2008) 'Sign language use and the appreciation of diversity in hearing classroom', *Early Years*, 28 (3): 311–24.

Broach S. *et al.* (2003) *Autism: Rights in Reality.* London: National Autistic Society.

Broadhead, P. (2001) 'Investigating sociability and cooperation in four and five year olds in reception class settings,' *International Journal of Early Years Education*, 9 (1): 23–5.

Brock, A. (1999) *Into the Enchanted Forest – Language, Drama and Science in the Primary School.* Stoke-on-Trent: Trentham.

Brock, A. and Rankin, C. (2008) *Communication, Language and Literacy in the Early Years.* London: Sage.

Brooker, L. (2002) *Starting School: Young Children Learning Cultures*. Buckingham: Open University Press.

Brooker, L. (2006) 'From home to the home corner: observing children's identity maintenance in early childhood settings', *Children and Society*, 20 (2): 116–27.

Brown, F. (2008) 'Playwork theory and playwork practice in the UK', in F. Brown and C. Taylor (eds), *Foundations of Playwork*. Maidenhead: Open University Press.

Brown, S. and Vaughn, C. (2009) *Play: How it Shapes the Brain, Opens the Imagination and Invigorates the Soul*. London: Penguin Books.

Burke, J. (2008) *Solitary Play by Children with Impairments in Accessible Playgrounds*. Research Conference, School of Education, University of Ballarat. Available at: http://www.aare.edu.au/07pap/bur07606.pdf (accessed 18 June 2010).

Burnett, R. and Roberts, C. (2004) *What Works in Probation and Youth Justice: Developing Evidence-Based Practice*. Cullompton: Willan.

Burney, E. (2009) *Making People Behave: Anti-Social Behaviour Politics and Policy*, 2nd edn. Cullompton: Willan.

Burtney, E., Fullerton, D. and Hosie, A. (2004) 'Policy developments in the United Kingdom', in E. Burtney, and M. Duffy (eds), *Young People and Sexual Health*. Basingstoke: Palgrave.

Byrne, D. (2005) *Social Exclusion*, 2nd edn. Maidenhead: Open University Press.

Camina, M. (2004) *Understanding and Engaging Deprived Communities*, Home Office Online Report 07/04. London: Home Office.

Cannella, G. S. and Viruru, R. (2004) *Childhood and (Post)colonization: Power, Education, and Contemporary Practice*. New York: Routledge.

Carpenter, B., Ashdown, R. and Bovair, K. (eds) (1996) *Enabling Access: Effective Teaching and Learning for Pupils with Learning Disabilities*. London: Fulton.

Case, S. and Haines, K. (2009) *Understanding Youth Offending: Risk Factor Research, Policy and Practice*. Cullompton: Willan.

Cattan, M. and Tilford, S. (2006) *Mental Health Promotion: A Lifespan Approach*. Maidenhead: McGraw-Hill and Open University Press.

Cederlund, M., Hagberg, B., Billstedt, E., Gillberg, I. C. and Gillberg, C. (2008) 'Asperger's Syndrome and autism: a comparative longitudinal follow-up study more than 5 years after original diagnosis', *Journal of Autism and Developmental Disorder*, 38: 72–85.

Charlop, M. H. and Haymes, L. K. (1994) 'Speech and language acquisition and intervention: behavioral approaches', in J. L. Matson (ed.), *Autism in Children and Adults*. Pacific Grove, CA: Brooks/Cole.

Charlton, M. (2008) 'Youth service and provision', in P. Jones, D. Moss, P. Tomlinson and S. Welch (eds), *Childhood: Services and Provision for Children*. Harlow: Pearson.

Chiang, H. M. (2009) 'Naturalistic observations of elicited expressive communication of children with autism', *Autism*, 13: 165–78.

Chiang, H. M. and Carter, M. (2008) 'Spontaneity of communication in individuals with autism', *Journal of Autism and Developmental Disorders*, 38: 693–705.

Child Poverty Action Group (2008) *Child Poverty: the stats. Analysis of the latest poverty statistics*. London: CPAG.

Children and Young People's Unit (2001) *Building a Strategy for Children and Young People Consultation Document*. London: HMSO.

Children and Young People's Unit (2002) *Report on the Consultation for Building a Strategy for Children and Young People (Various)*. London: DfES.

Children in Europe (2008) *Young Children and Their Services: Developing a European Approach* (English version). Available at: http://www.childrenineurope.org (accessed 26 July 2010).

Children in Scotland (2009) *Children's Rights.* Available from: http://www.childreninscotland.org.uk/html/poly_righ.htm (accessed 21 July 2009).

Children in Wales (2009) *Decide and Do: Involving Younger Children in Decisions About Their Care.* Available at: www.childreninwales.org.uk (accessed 21 February 2009).

Children's Rights Alliance for England (2008) *Survey of Children's Rights.* London: CRAE.

Children's Rights Alliance for England (2009) *The Children's Plan One Year On: A Progress Report. Children's Rights Impact Statement.* London: CRAE.

Children's Rights Alliance for England (2010) *Children's Rights Part of UK Law.* Available at: http://www.crae.org.uk/protecting/uk-law.html (accessed 22 April 2010).

Children's Rights Officers Association (2000) *A Training Manual for the Participation of Young People.* London: Children's Rights Officers Association.

Children's Society (1997) *I'll Go First: The Planning and Reviews Toolkit for Use with Children with Disabilities.* London: Children's Society.

Children's Society (2006) *Good Childhood? A Question of Our Times.* London: Children's Society.

Chisholm, L. and Furlong, A. (eds) (1997) *Youth and Citizenship in a European Perspective.* Avebury: Aldershot.

Clark, A. (2008) *An Introduction to How and Why We Listen to Very Young Children,* Listening as a Way of Life series. London: ECU.

Clark, A. and Moss, P. (2001) *Listening to Young Children: The Mosaic Approach.* London: National Children's Bureau for the Joseph Rowntree Foundation and Department for Education and Skills.

Clark, A. and Moss, P. (2005) *Spaces to Play: More Listening to Young Children Using the Mosaic Approach.* London: National Children's Bureau.

Clark, A., Kjørholt, A. T. and Moss, P. (2005) *Beyond Listening: Children's Perspectives on Early Childhood Services.* Bristol: Policy Press.

Clark, A., McQuail, S. and Moss, P. (2003) *Exploring the Field of Listening to and Consulting with Young Children,* Research Report 445. London: Thomas Coram.

CoE (Council of Europe) (1950) *European Convention on Human Rights.* Strasbourg: Council of Europe.

CoE (Council of Europe) (1992) *Recommendation No. R (92) 16, on the European Rules on Community Sanctions and Measures.* Strasbourg: Council of Europe.

CoE (Council of Europe) (2000) *Improving the Implementation of Community Sanctions and Measures.* Strasbourg: Council of Europe.

Cohen, G. A. (1995) *Self-Ownership, Freedom, and Equality.* Cambridge: Cambridge University Press.

Cohen, J. and Emanuel, J. (1998) *Positive Participation: Consulting and Involving Young People in Health-Related Work – A Planning and Training Resource.* London: HEA.

Comptroller and Auditor General (2006) *Tackling Obesity – First Steps.* London: National Audit Office, Health Care Commission and Audit Commission.

Conteh, J. (ed.) (2006a) *Promoting Learning for Bilingual Pupils 3–11: Opening Doors to Success*. London: Sage.

Conteh, J. (2006b) 'Widening the inclusion agenda: policy, practice and language diversity in the curriculum', in R. Webb (ed.), *Changing Teaching and Learning in the Primary School*. Buckingham: Open University Press.

Conteh, J. (2007) 'Opening doors to success in multilingual classrooms: bilingualism, codeswitching and the professional identities of "ethnic minority" primary teachers', *Language and Education*, 21 (6): 457–72.

Conteh, J. (2010) 'Making links across complementary and mainstream classrooms for primary children and their teachers', in P. V. Lytra and Martin (eds), *Sites of Multilingualism: Complementary Schools in Britain Today*. Stoke-on-Trent: Trentham Books, pp. 149–60.

Conteh, J., Beddow, D. and Kumar, R. (2008) 'Investigating pupil talk in multilingual contexts: sociocultural learning, teaching and researching,' *Education 3–13*, 36 (3): 223–35.

Conteh, J., Martin, P. and Robertson, L. H. (2007) 'Multilingual learning stories in schools and communities: issues and debates', in J. Conteh, P. Martin and L. H. Robertson (eds), *Multilingual Learning Stories in Schools and Communities in Britain*. Stoke-On-Trent: Trentham.

Coppard, H. (2004) 'The experimental playground', *Green Places*, 5: 34–6.

Corson, D. (1993) *Language, Minority Education and Gender: Linking Social Justice and Power*. Clevedon: Multilingual Matters/Toronto: Ontario Institute for Studies in Education.

Cosh, J. (2005) 'What are they thinking?', *Children Now*, 9 (15): 20–1.

CPAG (Child Poverty Action Group) (2008) *Child Poverty: The Stats. Analysis of the Latest Poverty Statistics*. London: CPAG.

CRAE (Children's Rights Alliance for England) (2008) *State of Children's Rights in England: Review of UK Government's implementation of the Convention on the Rights of the Child*. Available at: www.crae.org.uk (Accessed 18 February 2011).

Creese, A. and Blackledge, A. (2010) 'Translanguaging in the bilingual classroom: a pedagogy for learning and teaching?', *Modern Language Journal*, 94: 103–15.

Crimmens, D., Factor, F., Jeffs, T., Pitts, J., Pugh, C., Spence, J. and Turner, P. (2004) *The Role of Street-Based Youth Work in Linking Socially Excluded Young People into Education, Training and Work*. York: Joseph Rowntree Foundation.

Croke, R. (ed.) (2006) *Righting the Wrongs: The Reality of Children's Rights in Wales*, Summary Report. Wales: Save the Children.

Cummins, J. (2000) *Language, Power and Pedagogy*. Clevedon: Multilingual Matters.

Cummins, J. (2001) *Negotiating Identities: Education for Empowerment in a Diverse Society*, 2nd edn. Ontario, CA: California Association for Bilingual Education.

Cunningham Anderson, U. and Anderson, S. (2004) *Growing Up with Two Languages: A Practical Guide*, 2nd edn. London: Routledge/Sage.

Dahlberg, G., Moss, P. and Pence, A. (1999) *Beyond Quality in Early Childhood Education and Care: Postmodern Perspectives*. London: Falmer Press.

Daniel, P. and Ivatts, J. (1998) *Children and Social Policy*. London: Macmillan Press.

Davey, C. (2008) *What Do They Know? Investigating the Human Rights Concerns of Children and Young People Living in England*. London: Children's Rights Alliance.

Davidson, S. (1998) 'Spinning the wheel of empowerment', *Planning*, 1262 (April): 14–15.

Davies, B. (1999) *From Voluntaryism to Welfare State. A History of the Youth Service in England. Volume 1: 1939–1979,* and *From Thatcherism to New Labour. A History of the Youth Service in England. Volume 2: 1979–1999.* Leicester: Youth Work Press.

Davies, B. (2005) *Youth Work: A Manifesto for Our Times.* London: National Youth Agency.

Davies, J. and Wright, J. (2008) 'Children's voices: a review of literature pertinent to looked after children's views of mental health services', *Child and Adolescent Mental Health,* 13 (1): 26–31.

Davies, L., Williams, C., Yamashita, H. and Ko Man-Hing, A. (2006) *Inspiring Schools: Case Studies for Change. Taking Up the Challenge of Pupil Participation.* London: Esmée Fairbairn Foundation and Carnegie UK Trust.

DCMS (Department for Culture, Media and Sport) (2004) *Getting Serious About Play: A Review of Children's Play.* London: DCMS.

DCSF (Department for Children, Schools and Families) (2006) *Excellence and Enjoyment: Professional Development Learning and Teaching Materials for Primary Bilingual Children.* Nottingham: DCSF Publications.

DCSF (Department for Children, Schools and Families) (2007) *The Children's Plan: Building Brighter Futures.* London: HMSO.

DCSF (Department for Children, Schools and Families) (2008a) *The Play Strategy.* London: DCSF.

DCSF (Department for Children, Schools and Families) (2008b) *The Early Years Foundation Stage: Setting the Standards for Learning, Development and Care for Children from Birth to Five. Principles into Practice Card 1.2. A Unique Child: Inclusive Practice.* Nottingham: DfES Publications.

DCSF (Department for Children, Schools and Families) (2008c) *21st Century Schools: A World-class Education for Every Child.* London: HMSO.

DCSF (Department for Children, Schools and Families) (2008d) *Every Child a Talker: Guidance for Early Language Lead Practitioners.* National Strategies, DCSF. Available at: http://nationalstrategies.standards.dcsf.gov.uk/node/158181 (accessed June 18 2010).

DCSF (Department for Children, Schools and Families) (2008e) *Statuary Framework for the Early Years Foundation Stage: Setting the Standards for Learning, Development, and Care for Children from Birth to Five.* Nottingham: DCSF.

DCSF (Department for Children, Schools and Families) (2008f) *Practice Guidance for the Early Years Foundation Stage.* Nottingham: DCSF.

DCSF (Department for Children, Schools and Families) (2008g) *The Early Years Foundation Stage and Out of School Provision: Setting the Standards for Learning, Development and Care for Children from Birth to Five – An Introduction for Out of School Providers.* 4 Children. Available at: http://www.4Children.org.uk/eyfs (accessed 16 May 2010).

DCSF (Department for Children, Schools and Families) (2008h) *The Children's Plan: One Year On.* London: HMSO.

DCSF (Department for Children, Schools and Families) (2009a) *The Children's Plan Two Years On: A Progress Report.* Available at: http://www.teachernet.gov.uk/publications.

DCSF (Department for Children, Schools and Families) (2009b) *National Strategies.* London: HMSO.

DCSF (Department for Children, Schools and Families) (2010) *Working Together to Safeguard Children: A Guide to Inter-Agency Working to Safeguard and Promote the Welfare of Children*. Nottingham: DCSF Publications.

de Geest, H. (1999) *The Negative Persona of Silence*. Available at: http://interact. uoregon.edu/mediaLit/wfae/library/articles/de_geest_persona.pdf (accessed 18 June 2010).

DES (Department of Education and Science) (1975) *A Language for Life*, The Bullock Report. London: HMSO.

DES (Department of Education and Science) (1985) *Education for All. Report of the Committee of Inquiry into the Education of Ethnic Minority Groups*, The Swann Report. London: HMSO.

DFES (Department for Education and Skills) (2002) *Transforming Youth Work: Resourcing Excellent Youth Services*. Nottingham: DfES Publications.

DfES (Department for Education and Skills) (2003) *Every Child Matters*. London: DfES.

DfES (Department for Education and Skills) (2005) *Higher Standards, Better Schools for All*. London: HMSO.

DfES (Department for Education and Skills) (2006) *Working Together to Safeguard Children: A Guide to Inter-Agency Working to Safeguard and Promote the Welfare of Children*. Norwich: The Stationery Office.

Dickins, M. (2008) *Listening to Young Disabled Children*, Listening as a Way of Life series. London: ECU.

Dimmock, I. and Magraw, L. (2007) *Silence and Presence: How Adult Attitude Affects the Creativity of Children*. National Teacher Research Panel, DfES Innovation Unit. Available at: http://www.standards.gov.uk/innovation-unit (accessed 18 June 2010).

DoH (Department of Health) (1993) *Guidance on Permissible Forms of Control in Children's Residential Care*. London: Department of Health.

Drury, R. (2007) *Young Bilingual Learners at Home and School – Researching Multilingual Voices*. Stoke-on-Trent: Trentham Books.

Drury, R. and Robertson, L. H. (2008) *Young Bilingual Learners at Home and School*. Available at: www.naldic.org.uk. Accessed August 12 2009.

Edwards, C., Gandini, L. and Forman, G. (eds) (1998) *The Hundred Languages of Children: The Reggio Emilia Approach to Early Childhood Education*. Greenwich: Ablex.

Edwards, V. (2004) *Multilingualism in the English Speaking World*. Oxford: Blackwell.

Emerson, E. (2001) *Challenging Behaviour: Analysis and Intervention in People with Severe Intellectual Disabilities*, 2nd edn. Cambridge: Cambridge University Press.

Evans, K. (1994) 'Leisure patterns of young adults in Britain and the role of the Youth Service', *International Journal of Adolescence and Youth*, 4: 179–94.

Fabian, H. (2002) *Children Starting School*. London: David Fulton.

Fawcett, B., Featherstone, B. and Goddard, J. (2004) *Contemporary Child Care Policy and Practice*. Basingstoke: Palgrave.

Flewitt, R. (2005) 'Is every child's voice heard? Researching the different ways 3-year-old children communicate and make meaning at home and in a pre-school playgroup'. *Early Years: International Journal of Research and Development*, 25 (3): 207–22.

Foley, P., Roche, J. and Tucker, S. (eds) (2001) *Children in Society. Contemporary Theory, Policy and Practice.* Basingstoke: Palgrave in association with the Open University.

Ford, R. (2008) 'Brown ditches Respect agenda on youth crime', *The Times*, 11 January.

Foster, M. (2000) *Children's Rights and Advocacy.* London: CRAE.

Foster, N. (2000) *Decide and Do: Involving Younger Children in Decisions About Their Care.* Available at: http://www.ncac.gov.au (accessed 26 June 2010).

Fox Harding, L. (1997) *Perspectives in Child Care Policy.* London: Longman.

Franklin, A. and Sloper, P. (2009) 'Supporting the participation of disabled children and young people in decision-making', *Children and Society*, 23: 3–15.

Franklin, B. (ed.) (2002) *The New Handbook of Children's Rights: Comparative Policy and Practice.* London: Routledge.

Freeman, M. (2000) 'The future of children's rights', *Children and Society*, 14 (4): 277–93.

Freeman, M. (2002) 'Children's rights ten years after ratification', in B. Franklin (ed.), *The New Handbook of Children's Rights: Comparative Policy and Practice.* London: Routledge.

Frost, N. (2011) *Rethinking Children and Families.* London: Continuum.

Frykberg, S. (1998) *Acoustic Dimensions of Communications 1: Study Guide.* Simon Fraser University.

Funky Dragon (2007) *Our Rights, Our Story.* Available at: http://www.funkydragon.org/en/fe (accessed 21 July 2009).

Garcia, O. (2007) 'Foreword,' in S. Makoni and A. Pennycook (eds), *Disinventing and Reconstituting Languages.* Clevedon: Multilingual Matters.

Garland, D. (2001) *The Culture of Control: Crime and Social Order in Contemporary Society.* Oxford: Oxford University Press.

Gee, J. P. (1996) *Social Linguistics and Literacies.* London: Routledge.

Gee, J. P. (2005) *Introduction to Discourse Analysis*, 2nd edn. London: Routledge; cited in C. Conteh P. Martin and L. H. Robertson (eds) (2007) *Multilingual Learning: Stories from Schools and Communities in Britain.* Stoke-on-Trent: Trentham.

Gibbons, J. (1985) 'The silent period: an examination', *Language Learning*, 35 (2): 255–67.

Gibbons, S., Green, A., Gregg. P. and Machin, S. (2005) 'Is Britain pulling apart? Area disparities in employment, education and crime', in N. Pearce and W. Paxton (eds), *Social Justice: Building a Fairer Britain.* London: ippr (Institute for Public Policy Research)/Politico's.

Gill, T. (2007) *No Fear: Growing Up in a Risk Averse Society.* London: Calouste-Gulbenkian Foundation.

Gillick v. West Norfolk & Wisbech AHA &DHSS (1983) 3 WLR (HL).

Gilligan, R. (2009) 'Promoting positive outcomes for children in need', in J. Horwath (ed.), *The Child's World*, 2nd edn. London: Jessica Kingsley.

Goldson, B. (2005) 'Child Imprisonment: a case for abolition', *Youth Justice*, 5 (2): 77–90.

Gollub, R. and Krapf, P. (2007) *Get Ready For Change.* London: CRAE. Available at: http://www.getreadyforchange.org.uk/your-say/archive/debate_1_whats_going_on_in_your_school/ (accessed 21 February 2010).

Granger, C. (2004) *Silence in Second Language Learning: A Psychoanalytic Reading.* Multilingual Matters.

Green, K. (2006) *Reforming the Child Support Agency* [Internet]. London, Child Poverty Action Group. Available from: http://www.childpoverty.org.uk/info/briefings_policy/CPAG_Child_Support_Agency_letter_%20for_Henshaw_Review.pdf (accessed 12 June 2009).

Gregory, E. (1994) 'Cultural assumptions and early years pedagogy: the effect of home culture on minority children's perceptions of reading in school', *Language, Culture and Curriculum*, 7 (20): 111–24.

Gregory, E. (2008) *Learning to Read in a New Language: Making Sense of Words and Worlds*, 2nd edn. London: Paul Chapman.

Gregory, E., Long, S. and Volk, D. (eds) (2004) *Many Pathways to Literacy: Young Children Learning with Siblings, Grandparents, Peers and Communities.* London: RoutledgeFalmer.

Griesel, D. V., Sawrt-Kruger, J. and Chawla, L. (2002) 'Children in South Africa can make a difference: an assessment of growing up in cities in Johannesburg', *Childhood*, 9 (1): 83–100.

GSCC (General Social Care Council) (2004) *Code of Practice for Social Care Workers and Code of Practice for Employers of Social Care Workers.* London: General Social Care Council. Available at: http://www.gscc.org.uk/NR/rdonlyres/8E693C62-9B17-48E1-A806-3F6F280354FD/0/CodesofPractice.doc (accessed 30 June 2009).

GSCC (General Social Care Council) (2008) *Social Work at Its Best: A Statement of Social Work Roles and Tasks for the 21st Century.* London: General Social Care Council.

Hackney Council (2007) *The Youth Charter.* Available at: http://www.hackney.gov.uk/youth-charter-2007 (accessed 26 June 2010).

Hakarrainen, P. (1999) 'Play and Motivation', in Y. Engestrom, R. Miettinen and R. L. Punamaki (eds), *Perspectives in Activity Theory.* Cambridge: Cambridge University Press.

Hall, K. A., Özerk, K., Zulfiqar, M. and Tan, J. E. C. (2002) 'This is our school: provision, purpose and pedagogy of supplementary schooling in Leeds and Oslo', *British Educational Research Journal*, 28 (3): 399–418.

Halle, J. (1987) 'Teaching Language in the natural environment: an analysis of spontaneity', *Journal of the Association for Persons with Severe Handicaps*, 12: 28–37.

Halsey, K., Murfield, J., Harland, J. L. and Lord, P. (2006) *The Voice of Young People: An Engine for Improvement? Scoping the Evidence.* York: NFER.

Hammerton, J. (2001) *In Defence of the Right to Silence.* Available at: http://www.tardis.ed.ac.uk/~james/politics/Right2Silence (accessed 18 June 2010).

Hart, R. (1992) *Children's Participation: From Tokenism to Citizenship*, Florence: UNICEF International Child Development Centre.

Hart, R. A. (1997) *Children's Participation.* London: Earthscan.

Hear by Right (n.d.) Welcome page [Internet]. Available at: http://hbr.nya.org.uk/ (accessed 24 September 2009).

Heller, M. (1995) 'Language choice, social institutions, and symbolic domination', *Language in Society*, 24: 373–405.

Hempton, G. and Grossmann, J. (2009) *One Square Inch of Silence: One Man's Search for Natural Silence in a Noisy World.* New York: Free Press.

Hendrick, H. (1997) *Children, Childhood and English Society 1880–1990.* Cambridge: Cambridge University Press.

Henricson, C. and Bainham, A. (2005) *The Child and Family Policy Divide: Tensions, Convergence and Rights.* York: Joseph Rowntree Foundation.

Herbert, I. (2005) '"Cheeky" 10 year old is youngest to get ASBO', *The Independent,* 10 February.

Hillman, M., Adams, J. and Whitelegg, J. (1993) *One False Move: A Study of Children's Independent Mobility.* London: Policy Studies Institute.

HM Government (2004) *Every Child Matters: Change for Children.* Nottingham: DfES Publications.

HM Government (2006a) *Making Safeguarding Everyone's Business, The Government's Response to the Second Chief Inspectorates' Report on Arrangements to Safeguard Children.* London: Stationery Office.

HM Government (2006b) *Raising Standards – Improving Outcomes. Statutory Guidance: Early Years Outcome Duty Childcare Act 2006.* London: Stationery Office.

HM Revenue and Customs (2002) *Child Trust Fund.* London: HM Revenue and Customs. Available at: http://www.childtrustfund.gov.uk.

HMSO (1987) *Report of the Inquiry into Child Abuse in Cleveland.* London: HMSO.

Hohmann, U. (in press 2010) 'The importance of equal opportunities in the early years', in R. Parker-Rees and C. Leeson (eds), *Early Childhood Studies,* 3rd edn. Exeter: Learning Matters.

Home Office (1997) *Consultation: Tackling Youth Justice* [Internet]. London: Home Office. Available at: http://www.homeoffice.gov.uk/documents/cons-tackling-youth-justice-0997?view=Html (accessed 12 June 2009).

Home Office (2002) *Breaking the Circle: A Review of the Rehabilitation of Offenders Act 1974,* July. London: TSO.

Home Office (2008) *Police and Criminal Evidence Act 1984 (s.60(1)(a) and s.66) Codes of Practice.* Norwich: TSO.

Home Office (2009) *Keeping the Right People on the DNA Database: Science and Public Protection,* London: Home Office.

Hood, S. (2007) *Reporting on Children's Well-being: The State of London's Children Report.* London: Social Indicators Research.

Hopkins-Burke, R. (2008) *Young People, Crime and Justice.* Cullompton: Willan.

House of Commons (2005) *Anti Social Behaviour: Fifth Report of the Home Affairs Committee Session 2004–5 Volume 3,* HC 80-III, London: TSO.

House of Commons (2008) *Policing in the 21st Century Home Affairs Committee 7th Report 2007–8,* HC 364–II, London: TSO.

House of Commons Health Committee (2003) *The Victoria Climbié Inquiry Report – Sixth Report of Session 2002–3.* London: Stationary Office.

Howard League (1995) *Banged Up, Beaten Up, Cutting Up: Report of the Howard League Commission of Inquiry into Violence in Penal Institutions for Teenagers under 18,* London: Howard League.

Huq, R. (2009) 'A young concept in a new country', *Young,* 17 (4): 443–55.

Hyde, B. (2008) *Children and Spirituality: Searching for Meaning and Connectedness.* London: Jessica Kingsley.

Independent Advocacy Campaign (2002) *Report, Independent Advocacy Campaign*. London: Action for Advocacy. Available at: http://www.actionforadvocacy.org.uk/article (accessed 19 June 2010).

Ipsos Mori (2006) *School Omnibus Survey 2006*. Children's Commissioner Topline Results. Available from: http://www.ipsos-mori.com/.../researcharchive (accessed 21 July 2009).

James, A. and Prout, A. (eds) (1997) *Constructing and Reconstructing Childhood: Contemporary Issues in the Sociological Study of Childhood*. London: Falmer Press.

James, A., Jenks, C., and Prout, A. (1998) *Theorising Childhood*. London: Polity.

Jeffs, T. (2002) 'Schooling, education and children's rights', in B. Franklin (ed.), *The New Handbook of Children's Rights: Comparative Policy and Practice*. London: Routledge.

Jeffs, T. and Smith, M. (eds) (1987) *Youth Work*. London: Macmillan.

Jeffs, T. and Smith, M. (eds) (1990) *Young People, Inequality and Youth Work*. London: Macmillan.

Jones, G. (2006) 'ASBO's put mark of Cain on children', *Daily Telegraph*, 24 April.

Jones, P. (2009) *Rethinking Childhood*. London: Continuum.

Jones, P. and Welch, S. (2010) *Rethinking Children's Rights*. London: Continuum.

Jones, P., Moss, D., Tomlinson, P. and Welch, S. (eds), *Childhood: Services and Provision for Children*. Harlow: Pearson Education.

Jordan, R. and Powell, S. (1997) 'Translating theory into practice', in S. Powell and R. Jordan (eds), *Autism and Learning: A Guide to Good Practice*. London: Fulton.

Joseph Rowntree Foundation (2009) *Ending Child Poverty: Making It Happen*. Submission to the DFSCF consultation, Ending Child Poverty: Making It Happen.

Keen, D. (2009) 'Engagement of children with autism in learning', *Australasian Journal of Special Education*, 33: 130:40.

Kegeles, S. M., Hays, R. B. and Coates, T. J. (1996) 'The Mpowerment project: a community-level HIV prevention intervention for young gay men', *American Journal of Public Health*, 86 (8): 1129–36.

Kehily, M. J. (2007) *Understanding Youth Perspectives, Identities and Practices*. London: Sage.

Kellett, M. (2009) 'Children and young people's voices', in H. Montgomery and M. Kellett (eds), *Children and Young People's Worlds: Developing Frameworks For Integrated Practice*. Bristol: Policy Press.

Kellett, M. (2010) *Rethinking Children and Research*. London: Continuum.

Kingston Youth Service (2005) *Curriculum*. Royal Borough of Kingston Upon Thames.

Kirby, P., Lanyon, C., Cronin, K. and Sinclair, R. (2003) *Building a Culture of Participation: Involving Children and Young People in Policy, Service Planning, Delivery and Evaluation*. London: Department for Education and Skills.

Knight, A., Clark, A., Petrie, P. and Statham, J. (2006) *The Views of Children and Young People with Learning Disabilities about the Support They Receive from Social Services: A Review of Consultations and Methods*. London: Thomas Coram Research Unit.

Laming Report (2003) *The Victoria Climbié Inquiry*. London: Stationery Office.

Laming Report (2009) *The Protection of Children in England: A Progress Report.* London: Stationery Office.

Lancaster, P. and Broadbent, V. (2003) *Listening to Young Children.* Milton Keynes: Open University Press.

Lanyon, C. and Sinclair, R. (2005) *My Turn to Talk.* London: National Children's Bureau.

Laverack, G. (2009) *Public Health: Power, Empowerment and Professional Practice,* 2nd edn. Basingstoke: Palgrave Macmillan.

Layard, R. and Dunn, J. (2009) *A Good Childhood: Searching for Values in a Competitive Age.* London: Penguin Books.

Ledgerwood, I. and Kendra, N. (eds) (1997) *Towards the New Millenium for the Youth Service.* Lyme Regis: Russell House.

Leeds Initiative (2003) *Vision for Leeds II 2003–2018.* Leeds: Leeds Initiative.

Leeds Montessori School and Day Nursery (2009) *Children's Rights Policy.* Available at: http://www.leedsmontessori.co.uk/downloads/policy-pdfs/childrens-rights.pdf (accessed 21 July 2009).

Leeson, C., Willan, J. and Savage, J. (eds) (2010) *Early Childhood Studies,* 3rd edn. Exeter: Learning Matters.

Lewis, M. (2001) *Learning to Listen: Consulting Children and Young People with Disabilities.* London: Save the Children.

Local Futures (2004) *The State of the City Region: An Economic, Social and Environmental Audit of then Leeds City Region.* London: Local Futures Group.

Local Futures (2007) *The State of the Borough: An Economic, Social and Environmental Profile of Kingston-upon-Thames.* London: Local Futures Group.

Lupton, C. and Nixon, P. (1999) *Empowering Practice? A Critical Appraisal of the Family Group Conference Approach.* Bristol: University of Bristol.

Macauley, N. (2003) *Right and Wrong* [Internet]. London: British Association of Social Workers. Available at: http://www.basw.co.uk/Default.aspx?tabid=54&language=en-GB&articleID=109 (accessed 12 June 2009).

McCall, D. (2008) *Selected Case Studies of Youth Involvement in Public Decision-making.* Canadian Association for School Health. Available at: http://www.phac-aspc.gc.ca/dc (accessed 12 August 2010).

McLamon, J. (2008) *Listening as a Way of Life – Supporting Parents and Carers to Listen: A Guide for Practitioners.* London: National Children's Bureau/DCSF.

MacNaughton, G., Smith, K. and Lawrence, H. (2003) *ACT Children's Strategy – Consulting with Children Birth to Eight Years of Age. Hearing Young Children's Voices.* Children's Services Branch, ACT Department of Education, Youth and Family Services.

McNeish, D. (1999) *From Rhetoric to Reality. Participatory Approaches to Health Promotion with Young People.* London: Health Education Authority.

McQueen, D. V., Backett, K. C., Curtice, L. and Currie. C. E. (1992) 'Children, empowerment and health promotion: some new directions in research and practice', *Health Promotion International,* 7 (1): 53–9.

Marshall, K. (2006) 'Children's voices – early years', in *Let's Talk About Listening to Children: Towards a Shared Understanding for Early Years Education in Scotland,* Perspectives series (2). Learning and Teaching Scotland.

Martin, P. W., Bhatt, A., Bhojani, N. and Creese, A. (2006) 'Managing bilingual interaction in a Gujarati complementary school in Leicester', *Language and Education,* 20 (1): 5–22.

Maruna, S. and King, A. (2009) 'Youth crime and punitive public opinion', in M. Barry and F. McNeill (eds), *Youth Offending and Youth Justice*, Research Highlights 52. London: Jessica Kingsley.

Massey, J. M. (2000) 'Be silent!', *Soundscape: The Journal of Acoustic Ecology*, 1 (2): 25–9.

Masten, A. S. and Coatsworth, J. D. (1998) 'The development of competence in favourable and unfavourable environments: lessons from research on successful children', *American Psychologist*, 53 (2): 205–20.

May, H. (2005) 'Whose participation is it anyway? Examining the context of pupil participation in the UK', *British Journal of Special Education*, 32 (1): 29–34.

Mayall, B. (2005) 'Values and assumptions underpinning policy for children and young people in England', *Children's Geographies*, 4 (1): 1–17.

Meire, J. (2007) *Qualitative Research on Children's Play: A Review of Recent Literature*. Belgium: Childhood & Society Research Centre.

Mental Health Foundation (1999) *Bright Futures: Promoting Children and Young People's Mental Health*. London: Mental Health Foundation.

Miller, D. (2005) 'What is Social Justice?' in N. Pearce and W. Paxton (eds), *Social Justice: Building a Fairer Britain*. London: ippr (Institute for Public Policy Research)/Politico's.

Miller, L., Drury, R. and Campbell, R. (2002) *Exploring Early Years Education and Care*. London: David Fulton.

Miller, W. (1993) *Silence in the Contemporary Soundscape*. Simon Frazer University. Available at: http://interact.uoregon.edu/MediaLit/FC/readings/Thesis (accessed 21 February 2009).

Mills, J. (2004) 'Research with children, a contradiction in terms?', *Primary Practice*, 36: 29–34.

Ministry of Justice (2009) *Young People's Guide to the Green Paper on Rights and Responsibilities*. Available at: http://www.justice.gov.uk/ publications/young-persons-guide-rights-responsibilities.htm. (accessed 21 February 2009).

Mithaug, D. E., Mithaug, D. K., Agran, Martin, J. E. and Wehemeyer, M. L. (eds) (2003) *Self-determined Learning Theory: Construction, Verification and Evaluation*. Mahwah, NJ: Erlbaum.

Morris, J. (2001) 'Social exclusion and young disabled people with high levels of support needs', *Critical Social Policy*, 21 (2): 161–183.

Morris, J. (2003) 'Including all children: finding out about the experiences of children with communication and/or cognitive impairments', *Children and Society*, 17 (5): 337–48.

Moss, D. (2008) 'Children who offend', in P. Jones, D. Moss, P. Tomlinson and S. Welch (eds), *Childhood: Services and Provision for Children*. Harlow: Pearson Education.

Moss, P. and Dahlberg, G. (2008) 'Beyond quality in early childhood education and care – languages of evaluation', *New Zealand Journal of Teachers' Work*, 5 (1): 3–12.

Moss, P. and Petrie, P. (2002) *From Children's Services to Children's Spaces: Public Policy, Children and Childhood*. London: RoutledgeFalmer.

Mouffe, C. (1997) *The Return of the Political*. London: Verso.

Mroz, M. (2006) 'Teaching in the Foundation Stage – how current systems support teachers' knowledge and understanding of children's speech and language', *International Journal of Early Years Education*, 14 (1): 45–61.

Muncie, J. (1999) 'Institutionalized intolerance: youth justice and the 1998 Crime and Disorder Act', *Critical Social Policy*, 19 (2): 147–175.

Muncie, J. (2002) 'Children's rights and youth justice', in B. Franklin (ed.), *The New Handbook of Children's Rights: Comparative Policy and Practice*. London: Routledge.

Muncie, J. (2009) *Youth and Crime: A Critical Introduction*. 3rd edn. London: Sage.

NACRO (National Association for the Care and Resettlement of Offenders) (2008) *Some Facts about Children and Young People who Offend*. London: NACRO.

Naidoo, J. and Wills, J. (2009) *Health Promotion: Foundations for Practice*, 3rd edn. London: Balliere Tindall.

National Council for Voluntary Youth Services (n.d.) *Youth Participation: Getting Started*. Available at: http://www.ncvys.org.uk (accessed 26 June 2010).

National Society for the Prevention of Cruelty of Children (NSPCC) (1997) *Turning Points: A Resource Pack for Communicating With Children*. London: NSPCC.

National Society for the Prevention of Cruelty of Children (NSPCC) (2009) *Home Alone: Your Guide to Keeping Your Child Safe*. London: NSPCC.

National Teacher Research Panel (2006) *Silence and Presence: How Adult Attitude Affects the Creativity of Children*. National Teacher Research Panel for the Teacher Research Conference. Available at: http://www.standards.dfes.gov.uk/ntrp. (accessed 21 September 2007).

National Youth Council (2009) *Young Equalism*. London: National Youth Council.

Nelson, F. (1995) 'Bullying: youngsters find their own solutions. Young people are finding their own methods of tackling social and health problems such as bullying and homelessness in a peer education project based in Surrey', *Healthlines*, pp. 8–9.

Nutbrown, C. (ed.) (1996) *Respectful Educators – Capable Learners: Children's Rights and Early Education*. London: Paul Chapman.

Nutbrown, C. and Clough, P. (2006) *Inclusion in the Early Years*: *Cultural Analyses and Enabling Narratives*. London: Sage.

NYA (National Youth Agency) (2004) *Act By Right*. London: National Youth Agency.

NYA (National Youth Agency) (2008) *Buzz Off Campaign* (press release), January.

Nyland, B., Ferris, J. and Dunn, L. (2008) 'Mindful hands, gestures as language: listening to children,' *Early Years,* 28 (1): 73–80.

Office for the Children's Rights Director for England (2009) *Rights 4 Me*. London: Office for the Children's Rights Director for England. Available at: http://www.rights4me.org (accessed 21 February 2009).

Ofsted (2010) *Children on Rights and Responsibilities: A Report of Children's Views by the Children's Rights Director for England*. Manchester: Ofsted.

Oliver, K. G., Collin, P., Burns, J. and Nicholas, J. (2006) 'Building resilience in young people through meaningful participation', *Australian e-Journal for the Advancement of Mental Health*, 5 (1):1–7.

Oliver, M. (1993) *Disability and Dependency: A Creation of Industrial Societies?* London: Sage.

Oliver, M. (1996) *Understanding Disability: From Theory to Practice.* Basingstoke: Macmillan.

Participation Works (2009) *Your Rights to Be Heard.* Available at: http://www.participationworks.org.uk (accessed 22 April 2009).

Participation Works (2010) *Introduction to Children's Rights* [Internet]. Available at: http://www.participationworks.org.uk/topics/rights (accessed 26 June 2010).

Parton, N. (2006) *Safeguarding Childhood.* Basingstoke: Palgrave/Macmillan.

Pasco, G., Gordon, R. K., Howlin, P. and Charman, T. (2008) 'The Classroom Observation Schedule to Measure International Communication (COSMIC): an observational measure of the international communication of children with autism in the unstructured classroom setting', *Journal of Austim and Development Disorders,* 38: 1807–18.

Paxton, W., Pearce, N. and Reed, H. (2005) 'Foundations for a progressive century', in N. Pearce and W. Paxton (eds), *Social Justice: Building a Fairer Britain.* London: ippr (Institute for Public Policy Research)/Politico's.

Pearson, G. (1983) *Hooligan: A History of Respectable Fears.* London: Macmillan.

Pierpoint, H. (2006) 'Reconstructing the Role of the Appropriate Adult in England and Wales', *Criminology and Criminal Justice.* 6 (2): 219–38.

Pitts, J. (2003) *The New Politics of Youth Crime: Discipline or Solidarity.* Lyme Regis: Russell House.

Playwork Principles Scrutiny Group (2005) *Playwork Principles Held in Trust as Honest Brokers for the Profession by the Playwork Principles Scrutiny Group.* Available at: http://www.playwales.org.uk. (accessed 26 June 2010).

Potter, C. A. and Whittaker, C. A. (2001) *Enabling Communication in Children with Autism.* London: Jessica Kingsley.

Powell, S. and Wellard, I. (2008) *Policies and Play: The Impact of National Policies on Children's Opportunities to Play.* London: Play England/National Children's Bureau.

Power, M. and Brock. A. (2006) 'Promoting positive links between home and school', in J. Conteh (ed.), *Promoting Learning for Bilingual Pupils 3–11: Opening Doors to Success.* London: Sage.

Primary National Strategies (2003) *Aiming High: Raising the Achievement of Gypsy Traveller Pupils.* London: DfES.

Prout, A. and James, A. (1997) 'A new paradigm for the sociology of childhood?', in A. James and A. Prout (eds), *Constructing and Reconstructing Childhood: Contemporary Issues in the Sociological Study of Childhood,* 2nd edn. London: Falmer Press.

Qualifications and Curriculum Authority (QCA) (2000) *National Curriculum in Action. Creativity: Find it, Promote it.* Available at: http://www.ncaction.org.uk/creativity/index.htm. Accessed 26 June 2010.

Reed, J. and Robinson, P. (2005) 'From social mobility to equal life chances: maintaining the momentum', in N. Pearce and W. Paxton (eds), *Social Justice: Building a Fairer Britain.* London: ippr (Institute for Public Policy Research)/Politico's.

Riley, C. (2005) *Eye Opening: A Collection of Prose and Poetry,* 2nd edn. Leeds: Gbakhanda.

Rinaldi, C. (2005) *In Dialogue with Reggio Emilia.* London: Routledge.

Robb, M. (2007) *Youth in Context: Frameworks, Settings and Encounters*. London: Sage/Open University.

Roche, J. and Tucker, S. (eds) (1997) *Youth in Society*. London: Sage.

Rogoff, B. (2003) *The Cultural Nature of Human Development*. Oxford: Oxford University Press.

Rowling, L. (2006) 'Adolescence and emerging adulthood (12–17 years and 18–24 years)', in M. Cattan and S. Tilford (eds), *Mental Health Promotion: A Lifespan Approach*. Maidenhead: McGraw-Hill/Open University Press.

Runyan, D. (1998) 'Children who prosper in unfavourable environments: the relationships to social capital', *Paediatrics*, 101 (1): 12–18.

Safford K. (2003) *Teachers and Pupils in the Big Picture: Seeing Real Children in Routinised Assessment*. Watford: National Association for Language Development in the Curriculum (NALDIC).

Salt, T. (2010) *Independent Review of Teacher Supply for Pupils with Severe, Profound and Multiple Learning Difficulties (SLD and PMLD)*. Nottingham: DCSF Publications.

Samuelson, I. (2004) 'How do children tell us about their childhoods?' *Early Childhood Research and Practice*, 6 (1), cited in L. Miller (ed.) (2006) *Extending Personal Professional Development*, Course Reader. Milton Keynes: Open University Press.

Sandbaek, M. and Einarsson, H. (2008) 'Children and young people report to the UN on their rights', *NOVA Report*, 2b/08. Available at: http://www.reassess. no/index. (accessed 21 February 2009).

Sands, D. J. and Wehmeyer, M. L. (eds) (1996) *Self-Determination Across the Life Span: Independence and Choice for People with Disabilities*. Baltimore, MD: Paul H. Brookes.

Sapin, K. (2009) *Essential Skills for Youth Work Practice*. London: Sage.

Save the Children (2005) *Child Rights Programming Handbook*, 2nd edn. Sweden: Save the Children.

Save the Children (2006) *Children's Rights: A Teachers Guide*. London: Save the Children.

Save The Children (2009) *Righting the Wrongs: The Reality of Children's Rights in Wales*. Cardiff: Save the Children.

Savill, R. (2005) 'Playtime stopped after noise complaints', *Daily Telegraph*, 9 August, p. 17.

Saville-Troike, M. (1985) 'The place of silence in an integrated theory of communication', in D. Tannen and M. Saville-Troike (eds), *Perspectives on Silence*. Norwood, NJ: Ablex.

Saville-Troike, M. (1988) 'Private speech: evidence for second language learning strategies during the "silent period"', *Journal of Child Language*, 15: 567–90.

Scottish Executive (2004) *Protecting Children and Young People: Framework for Standards*. Available at: http://www.scotland.gov.uk/publications/2004/03/19102/34603 (accessed 26 June 2010).

Scraton, P. and Haydon, D. (2002) 'Challenging the criminalization of children and young people: securing a rights-based agenda', in J. Muncie, G. Hughes and E. McLaughlin (eds), *Youth Justice: Critical Readings*. London: Sage.

Scriven, A. and Stiddard, L. (2003) 'Empowering Schools: translating health promotion principles into practice', *Health Education*, 103 (2): 110–18.

Shakespeare, T. (2006) *Disability Rights and Wrongs*. Abingdon: Routledge.

Shier, H. (2001) 'Pathways to participation: openings, opportunities and obligations', *Children and Society*, 15 (2): 107–17.

Shogren, K. A., Faggella-Luby, M., Bae, S. J. and Wehmeyer, M. L. (2004) 'The effect of choice-making as an intervention for problem behaviour. A meta-analysis', *Journal of Positive Behavior Interventions*, 6: 228–37.

Silin, J. (2005) 'Who can speak? Silence, voice and pedagogy', *Critical Issues*, cited in N. Yelland (ed.) (2005) *Early Childhood Education*, Milton Keynes: Open University Press.

Sinclair, R. (2004) 'Participation in practice: making it meaningful, effective and sustainable', *Children & Society*, 18: 106–18.

Smith, R. (2007) *Youth Justice: Ideas, Policy and Practice*, 2nd edn. Cullompton: Willan.

Social Exclusion Unit (1999) *Teenage Pregnancy*. London: HMSO.

Social Exclusion Unit (2005) *Transitions: Young Adults with Complex Needs. A Social Exclusion Unit Final Report*. London: Office of the Deputy Prime Minister.

Souhami, A. (2007) *Transforming Youth Justice: Occupational Identity and Cultural Change*. Cullompton: Willan.

Squires, P. and Stephen, D. (2005) *Rougher Justice: Anti-Social Behaviour and Young People*. Cullompton: Willan.

Stone, W. L. and Caro-Martinez, L. M. (1990) 'Naturalistic observations of spontaneous communication in autistic children', *Journal of Autism and Developmental Disorders*, 20: 437–53.

Strange, V., Forrest, S., Oakley, A., and the Ripple Team (2002) 'Peer-led sex education – characteristics of peer educators and their perceptions of the impact on them of participation in peer education programme', *Health Education Research*, 17 (3): 327–37.

Street, B. (2003) 'What's "new" in New Literacy Studies? Critical approaches to literacy in theory and practice', *Current Issues in Comparative Education*, 5 (2): 77–91.

Strozzi, P. (2001) *Daily Life at School: Seeing the Extraordinary in the Ordinary*, in Reggio Children, the President and Fellows of Harvard College and the Municipality.

Sturcke, J. (2009) 'DNA details of 1.1 million children on database', *Guardian* 27 February.

Swain, J. And French, S. (2008) *Disability on Equal Terms: Understanding and Valuing Difference in Health and Social Care*. London: Sage.

Sylva, K., Siraj-Blatchford, I., Taggert, B., Sammons, P., Elliot, K. and Melhuish, E. (2002) *The Effective Provision of Preschool Education (EPPE) Project Summary of Findings*, DfES Research Brief. London: DfES and Institute of Education, University of London.

Tannen, D. (1985) 'Silence: anything but', in D. Tannen and M. Saville-Troike (eds), *Perspectives on Silence*. Norwood, NJ: Ablex.

Taylor, M. J. and Johnson, R. (2002) *School Councils: Their Role in Citizenship and Personal and Social Education*. Slough: NFER.

Teenage Pregnancy Unit (2001) *A Guide to Involving Young People in Teenage Pregnancy Work*. London: Teenage Pregnancy Unit.

Telford and Wrekin Council (2009) Available at: http://www.telford.gov.uk/Education+learning/Support+for+young+people (accessed 21 February 2009).

Thomas, G. and Hocking, G. (2003) *Other People's Children: Why Their Quality of Life is Our Concern*. London: Demos.

Thomas, N. (2004) 'Law Relating to Children', in T. Maynard and N. Thomas (eds), *An Introduction to Early Childhood Studies*. London: Sage.

Thomas, N. And O'Kane, C. (1999) 'Children's participation in reviews and planning meetings when they are "looked after" in middle childhood', *Child and Family Social Work*, 4: 221–30.

Thomas, N., Phillipson J., O'Kane, C. and Davies, E. (1999) *Children and Decision-Making: Tool Box and Training Pack*. Cardiff: Children in Wales.

Thomas, T. (2004) 'Anti-Social Behaviour Orders: Publicity and Young People', *Childright*, 208: 6–7.

Thomas, T. (2008a) 'Children and fingerprinting: sleepwalking into a surveillance society', *Childright*, 245: 22–4.

Thomas, T. (2008b) 'DNA sampling: why are children targeted?', *Childright*, 247: 18–20.

Thompson, N. (2001) *Anti-Discriminatory Practice*, 3rd edn. Basingstoke: Palgrave Macmillan.

Thompson, N. (2005) *Understanding Social Work*, 2nd edn. Basingstoke: Palgrave Macmillan.

Tilford, S. (2006) 'Mental health promotion', in M. Cattan and S. Tilford (eds), *Mental Health Promotion: A Lifespan Approach*. Maidenhead: McGraw-Hill/Open University Press.

Tobin, J., Wu, D. Y. H. and Davidson, D. H. (1989) *Preschool in Three Cultures: Japan, China and the United States*. London: Yale University Press.

Tones, K. and Green, J. (2004) *Health Promotion: Planning and Strategies*. London: Sage.

Travis, A. (2008) 'Asbo's in their death throes as number issued drops by a third', *Guardian*, 9 May.

Travis, A. (2009a) 'Alan Johnson pledges to revive anti-social behaviour orders to tackle intimidation and harassment', *Guardian*, 2 July.

Travis, A. (2009b) 'Fresh inquest ordered into teenager's death in prison', *Guardian*, 23 January.

Trawick, M. (1990) *Notes on Love in a Tamil Family*. Berkeley, CA: University of California Press.

Tregaskis, C. (2002) 'Social model theory: the story so far ...', *Disability and Society*, 17 (4): 457–70.

Treseder, P. (1996) *Empowering Children and Young People*. London: Save the Children.

Treseder, P. (1997) *Empowering Children and Young People: Training Manual. Promoting Involvement in Decision-Making*. London: Children's Rights Office and Save the Children.

UN (United Nations) (1989) *The Convention on the Rights of the Child*. Geneva: United Nations.

UN (United Nations) (1990) *Standard Minimum Rules for Non-custodial Measures (The Tokyo Rules)*. New York: United Nations.

Unicef (1989a) *United Nations Convention on the Rights of the Child*. Available at: http://www.unicef.org (accessed 21 February 2009).

Unicef (1989b) *Summary of the UNCRC Made for Children*. Available at: http://www.unicef.org.uk (accessed 21 February 2009).

Unicef (2008) *Children's Rights and Responsibilities*. Available at: http://www.unicef.org.uk (accessed 30 November 2008).

Unicef (2009) *The State of the World's Children, Special Edition*. New York: United Nations Children's Fund. Available at: http://www.unicef.org.

United Kingdom Government (2007) *The Consolidated 3rd and 4th Report to the United Nations Committee on the Rights of the Child*. London: DCSF.

United Kingdom's Children's Commissioners (2008) *United Kingdom's Children's Commissioners' Report to UN Committee on the Rights of the Child*. Available at: http://www.sccyp.org.uk/UK_Childrens_Commissioners_UN_Report.pdf (accessed 21 July 2009).

United Nations Committee on the Rights of the Child (2008) *Consideration of Reports Submitted by States Parties Under Article 44 of the Convention. Concluding Observations: United Kingdom of Great Britain and Northern Ireland*. Geneva: United Nations.

Viruru, R. (2001) 'Language as colonization: the case of early childhood education', *Contemporary Issues in Early Childhood*, 2 (1): 31–47.

Viruru, R. (2005) 'Postcolonial practices in teacher education', in S. Ryan and S. Grieshaber (eds), *Putting Postmodern Theories into Practice*. Greenwich, CT: Jai Press.

Viruru, R. and Cannella, G. S. (2001) 'Postcolonial ethnography, young children and voice', in S. Grieshaber and G. S. Cannella (eds), *Embracing Identities and Early Childhood Education*. New York: Teachers College Press.

Voce, A. (2008) 'The state of play in England', in F. Brown and C. Taylor (eds), *Foundations of Playwork*. Maidenhead: Open University Press.

Walker, J. (2001) 'A qualitative study of parents' experiences of providing sex education for their children: the implications for health education', *Health Education Journal*, 6 (2): 144–52.

Wallerstein, N. (2006). *What Is The Evidence on Effectiveness of Empowerment to Improve Health?* Copenhagen: WHO Regional Office for Europe.

Walsh, C. (2002) 'Curfews: no more hanging around', *Youth Justice* 2 (2): 70–81.

Ward, L. (1997) *Seen and Heard: Involving Disabled Children and Young People in Research and Development Projects*. York: Joseph Rowntree Foundation.

Warren, J. (2007) *Service User and Carer Participation in Social Work*. Exeter: Learning Matters.

Warwick, I. (2005) 'Evaluating healthy schools: perceptions of impact among school-based respondents', *Health Education Research*, 20 (6): 697–708.

Wehmeyer, M. (2007) *Promoting Self-Determination in Students with Developmental Disabilities*. New York: The Guilford Press.

Wehmeyer, M. and Schwartz, M. (1998) 'The relationship between self-determination and quality of life for adults with mental retardation', *Education and Training in Mental Retardation and Developmental Disabilities*, 33 (1): 3–12.

Wehmeyer, M. L., Agran, M. and Hughes, C. (2000) 'A national survey of teachers' promotion of self-determination and student-directed learning,' *Journal of Special Education*, 34: 58–68.

Welch, S. (2008) 'Childhood: rights and realities', in P. Jones, D. Moss, P. Tomlinson and S. Welch (eds), *Childhood: Services and Provision for Children*. Harlow: Pearson Education.

Wetherby, A. M., Cain, D. H., Yonclas, D. G. and Walker, V. G. (1988) 'Analysis of intentional communication of normal children from the prelinguistic to the multiword stage', *Journal of Speech and Hearing Research*, 31: 240–52.

Whalley, M. (2008) *Involving Parents in their Children's Learning*, 2nd edn. London: Sage.

Wheal, A. and Sinclair, R. (1995) *It's Your Meeting. A Guide to Help Young People Get the Most from Their Reviews*. London: National Children's Bureau.

Wheeler, R. (2006) 'Gillick or Frazer? A plea for consistency over competence in children', *British Medical Journal*, 332: 807.

Whittaker, C. A. (2009) The Psycho-Medical construction of severe autism: some reflections on its economic and emotional costs. Todai Forum 2009 in UK. Disability and Economy: Creating a Society for All. Manchester Metropolitan.

Whittaker, C. A. and Potter, C. A. (1999) 'Inclusive schools need an inclusive national curriculum', in J. Swain and S. French (eds), *Therapy and Learning Difficulties: Advocacy, Participation and Partnership*. London: Butterworth-Heinemann.

Whitty, G. and Wisby, E. (2007) *Real Decision-making? School Councils in Action*, DCSF Research Briefing. London: DCSF.

WHO (World Health Organisation) (1986) *The Ottawa Charter for Health Promotion*. Geneva: WHO.

WHO (World Health Organisation) (2005) *The Bangkok Charter for Health Promotion in a Globalized World*. Geneva: WHO.

Williamson, H. (1997a) 'Youth work and citizenship', in J. Bynner and J. Wood (eds), *Work with Young People: Theory and Policy for Practice*. London: Sage.

Williamson, H. (1997b) 'Status ZerO youth and the "underclass": some considerations', in R. MacDonald (ed.), *Youth, the "Underclass" and Social Exclusion*. London: Routledge.

Willow, C. (2006) *Convention on the Rights of the Child: Activity Book*. London: CRAE.

Winn, M. (1996) 'Sexual health promotion', *Venereology*, 9 (1): 68–73 cited in H. Lee (2007) 'Why sexual health promotion misses its audience', *Journal of Health Organization and Management*, 21 (2): 205–19.

Wood, J. and Hine, J. (2009) *Work with Young People: Theory and Policy for Practice*. London: Sage.

Wright, P., Turner, C., Clay, D. and Mills, H. (2006) *The Participation of Children and Young People in Developing Social Care*, Practice Participation Guide 6. Available at: http://www.scie.org.uk/publications/practiceguides/practiceguide06//files/pg06.pdf (accessed 26 June 2010).

YJB (Youth Justice Board) (2006) *Managing the Behaviour of Children and Young People in the Secure Estate: Code of Practice*. London: YJB.

YJB/NCB (Youth Justice Board/National Children's Bureau) (2008) *A Review of Safeguarding in the Secure Estate.* London: YJB.

YMCA (2006) *Young People and Children 'Are Being Criminalised' Says YMCA England* (press release) 24 April.

YouGov – Barnardo's (2008) *Breaking the Cycle. Believe in Children.* Ilford: Barnardo's.

Young Equals (2009) *Online Survey: September–December 2009. The Unequal Equality Bill: Evidence of Unfair Age Discrimination Against Children and Young People.* Available at: http://www.byc.org.uk/.../resources_pbcr_parliamentary_evidence_the_unequal_equality_bill (accessed 26 June 2010).

Young Minds (2009) *Children and Young People's Voices Conference,* March 2009, PowerPoint presentation. Available at: http://www.earlydetection.csip.org.uk/silo/files/vik-presentation.ppt (accessed 26 June 2010).

Youth Rights UK 'Manifesto'. Available at: http://www.youth-rights-uk.org/manifesto.shtml (accessed 21 July 2009).

YouthLink Scotland (2007) *Being Young in Scotland Survey.* Available at: http://www.youngscotlandinmind.org.uk/resources (accessed 21 July 2009).

Index